2/02

SO-ALD-913

940.54013
Delaney, John.
The Blitzkrieg campaigns :
Germany´s ´Lightning War´
strategy in action
London : Caxton Editions,

Discarded by
Santa Maria Library

GAYLORD MG

5/02

THE
BLITZKRIEG
CAMPAIGNS

THE BLITZKRIEG CAMPAIGNS

Germany's 'Lightning War' Strategy in Action

John Delaney

CAXTON EDITIONS

This edition published in 2000 by
Caxton Editions
20 Bloomsbury Street
London WC1B 3QA
an imprint of the Caxton Publishing Group

© John Delaney, 1996

All rights reserved. No part of this book may be reproduced or transmitted
in any form or by any means electronic or mechanical including photocopying,
recording or any information storage and retrieval system without permission in
writing from the Publisher.

British Library Cataloguing-in-Publication data:
A catalogue record for this book is available from the British Library

ISBN: 1 84067 233 1

Edited and designed by DAG Publications Limited
Cover design by Open Door Limited

Printed and bound in Singapore by Star Standard

Frontispiece:
A burning red Army KV-1 on the steppe. September 1941. Note that the vehicle has been hit
in the rear, the only sure way of being able to knock out the new Soviet tanks in a gun duel.

Contents

Introduction

The term blitzkrieg (lightning war) has been part of the English language now for over 50 years. The campaigns of 1939-1941 which very nearly brought total victory for the Third Reich heralded in a new age in warfare. The completeness and speed of these German successes forced all the other participants in the Second World War to re-examine their strategies for the fighting of modern war. Indeed, Allied preconceptions about the primacy of the defensive were a major contributory factor to the catastrophic defeats of this period. However, in most peoples' minds this early success is associated with the supremacy of the German panzer division over anything with which the Allies could oppose them.

I have tried in this book to describe these stunning victories and how they were achieved, by careful German planning, initiative and luck. I have contrasted this with the Allies' inefficient, ineffective and incompetent responses. Before describing these campaigns in detail I have first attempted to explain the underlying foundation of the strategy that so very nearly brought Hitler complete victory.

Surprisingly perhaps, many of these ideas first surfaced during the First World War, a conflict popularly conceived as being one of battlefield deadlock and stagnancy in military thought. Also, the early advocates of mechanised warfare, whose theories were taken up and expanded by the Germans, were in fact their opponents between 1914 and 1918. To their ideas the Germans wedded the practical experience of infiltration and shock tactics, gained from their successful 1918 offensives.

While the Allies sat back in the post-war years reflecting on past glories, the Germans, stung both by defeat and the harsh terms of the Versailles peace treaty, experimented with these new ideas, eventually coming up with a blitzkrieg theory that has become the basis for much of today's military strategy.

After showing how this theory developed I have attempted to describe how Hitler put these ideas into practice. I have concentrated on the three early blitzkrieg campaigns of the war; Fall Weiss (Case White), the attack on Poland in 1939; Fall Gelb (Case Yellow), the battle for France in 1940 and Operation Barbarossa, the invasion of Russia in 1941, because they show the German strategy at its high watermark. After 1941, the Germans, unable to compete with the Allies in the war of industrial production that the conflict had become, were doomed to eventual defeat. By failing to knock out the Soviet Union in 1941 and foolishly declaring war on the United States in the same year, Hitler in effect signed his own death warrant and that of the Third Reich.

Before the end of that year industrial might had yet to exert a decisive influence and Hitler's forces, often inferior in numbers and quality of equipment, managed to inflict massive battlefield defeats on Poland, France, Britain and Russia. It is the objective of this book to show how all this came about.

Acknowledgements

I would like to thank all the staff of the Imperial War Museum Photograph Archive for their kind help and assistance, and the Delaney and Edmondson families for their support during the months it took to prepare this volume.

I would like to thank my partner Helen most of all. Without her patience, understanding and the long hours she put in proof-reading and re-typing my original manuscript this book would never have seen the light of day.

All the numbered photographs appearing in the book are available on application from the Imperial War Museum Photograph Archive.

John Delaney

CHAPTER ONE

The Origins of Blitzkrieg

Blitzkrieg as a theory of fighting war developed during the First World War. When the conflict broke out in August 1914 all sides believed that the war would be a short one. The Germans thought that their Schlieffen Plan would enable them to knock France out of the war in six weeks, allowing troop transfers to the Eastern Front where they would defeat Russia. The Allies were likewise optimistic. The French Plan XVII envisaged an attack on the German centre followed by a march into Germany. Berlin would be reached in six weeks. The Russians too felt that the German capital was an attainable objective; the war would undoubtedly be over by Christmas.

However, the demise of the Schlieffen Plan, the failure to completely outflank the Allied land armies and encircle Paris led to stalemate. The bloodbath of the Battle of the Frontiers, with 300,000 French casualties in the first few days of the war, put paid to any thoughts the French may have had of marching on Berlin. The Russian Army, cumbersome and incompetently led, tasted an equally bitter defeat at Tannenberg.

By the end of the year the war on both fronts had lapsed into deadlock. Mobility had disappeared from the battlefield. Troops looked out at each other across no-man's-land from two trench lines running from the North Sea to the Swiss frontier and the Baltic to the Carpathian Mountains.

Why had this come about? In the years before the outbreak of war, military theory had emphasised offensive action as being the only sure way to achieve victory in modern European war. Strategists harked back to the days of Napoleon when armies marched across the European landscape, each attempting to outmanoeuvre the other, bring superior forces to bear and achieve a decisive battlefield victory. Generals of both sides viewed future conflict in these outdated terms, although the American Civil War, the Russo-Turkish War, the Boer War and the Russo-Japanese War had all pointed toward increasing firepower and decreasing movement on the field of battle.

Between 1915 and 1917 it was increasingly believed that the trench deadlock that had ensued could be broken by a sufficient superiority in firepower at the point of attack (the German Schwerpunkt). Major assaults were preceded by intense artillery bombardments, often days, even weeks in length. This it was hoped would destroy the enemy defensive line, leaving the attacking infantry to consolidate the captured position. Cavalry would then be released through the rupture in the defences, restoring mobility to the battlefield.

Alas it was not to be. Both the Germans and the Allies soon found that the effects of these bombardments could be countered by digging deeper and fortifying more. Trench lines became more permanent than ever. The ground between the opposing armies would inevitably be torn up by the artillery fire, turning into a quagmire after the slightest amount of rain. Getting to grips with the enemy, once difficult because of their machine guns, barbed wire and artillery, became near impossible because of the terrain that had to be crossed.

Generals on both sides, led to believe that the war would be one of manoeuvre, were unable to change their preconceptions and come up with new ideas on how the bloody deadlock could be broken. More and more artillery was used in the vain hope that there would come a time when the enemy would crack.

By 1917 it was at last becoming clear to more enlightened officers on both sides that another approach was necessary if movement was to be restored and victory achieved. The British and French, quite independently of one another, came up with a technological solution to the problem, the tank. The Germans found an answer by reshaping their battlefield tactics allowing a much more flexible approach to war fighting. In the postwar years the Wehrmacht, combining the best elements of both these answers, came up with blitzkrieg, a strategy that so very nearly led to the defeat of the Allies.

The invention of the tank cannot be attributed to any one man or agency. In Britain, the Admiralty, which had been involved with Royal Naval Air Service armoured car operations in the opening stages of the war, soon began to show interest in the concept of landships for use on the battlefield. At

the same time the Army began to show interest in the idea through a group of officers, including Colonel Maurice Hankey, Secretary to the Committee for Imperial Defence, and Colonel Ernest Swinton, official government war correspondent on the Western Front. In February 1915 a Landships Committee was formed. The first prototype vehicle, *Little Willie*, was produced in June. The French were at this time also experimenting with fully tracked vehicles, although their tank design expertise lagged some way behind that of the British. The Schneider armaments firm spent the first half of 1915 exploring the possibilities of a tracked armoured car.

By 1916 the British had developed a vehicle they thought capable of traversing the difficult terrain of no-man's-land and smashing through the German barbed wire defences. Field Marshal Earl Haig, impressed with a paper on the tank's potential written by Swinton, asked for some to be made available for his summer Somme offensive. However, in spite of being promised 75 for the attack, only 60, with barely trained crews were ready by the end of August.

British tanks first saw action on 15 September near the town of Flers. Although successful they did not create the gaping hole in the German line necessary for the restoration of mobility, only 49 tanks being used in the attack. They did cause widespread panic and certainly contributed to the overall success of the operation but they did not appear to be the wonder weapon some had hoped for. It was obvious to those involved in the development of tank theory that not enough vehicles had been used.

Major (later Major-General) J. F. C. Fuller, Chief of Staff to Colonel H. J. (later General Sir Hugh) Elles, commander of the fledgling Tank Corps, identified the need to concentrate a much larger force of tanks for use against the enemy line to secure the necessary breakthrough. He initially advocated a series of combined tank and infantry raids of approximately 200 tanks and one or two infantry divisions. These raids would break into the German line and cause as much mayhem as possible. Fuller hoped that a succession of these attacks might lower German morale enough for a later major offensive to succeed.

General Sir Julian Byng (commanding Third Army), having read Fuller's reports, took up his idea of massed tank attacks against the enemy line and proposed an assault for late 1917 against the Germans in the Cambrai area. The rolling chalklands in this sector provided good tank country, having been less churned up by artillery fire than many other areas of the front. Unfortunately for Fuller, Byng decided to upgrade the attack into a major attempt to break through the German lines. Instead of a series of raids, yet another hammer blow was to be made on the Hindenburg line in an attempt to bring about a decisive victory.

The battle of Cambrai opened on 20 November 1917. Taking part were 376 Mark IV gun tanks, 32 grapnel tanks for wire clearing and eighteen resupply tanks, Brigadier General Elles leading the assault in person in his own Mark IV. The first day of the battle was overwhelmingly successful, troops advancing into the German positions by up to five miles along a seven-mile front. Unfortunately this is where the

Infantrymen practise assaulting enemy positions in conjunction with a Mk IV tank prior to the battle of Cambrai. (IWM.CO.3337)

attack began to fail. A cavalry corps of four divisions was supposed to pass through the breach created by the infantry and tanks, and secure the town of Cambrai and the crossings over the river Sensée. This would provide a jumping-off point for a further British attack to the north-west to roll up the German line. Unfortunately the cavalry commander was of the old school and failed to appreciate the need to position his troops well forward to enable them to react quickly, his headquarters being several miles to the rear. By the time the advance had been organised, German troops were already plugging the gap. The tank crews, exhausted after twelve hours of continuous combat, without replenishment for their vehicles, and tank losses increasing due to poor mechanical reliability, were in no position to exploit the situation themselves.

It was for many of these reasons that the Germans initially felt that the tank was not a war-winning weapon and decided to concentrate on other avenues of approach to overcome the trench deadlock. They reasoned that the tanks' poor reliability (early British Mark IVs needed a complete overhaul after only 70 miles) and their lack of range limited them to an infantry support role. They did not see them as an independent arm of decision. An anti-tank rifle and anti-armour 'K' rounds were quickly developed capable of penetrating the steel plate of early British tanks, further undermining German enthusiasm for the vehicle. However, they seemed to ignore the tank's potential for mechanical improvement and up-armouring that were bound to come with practical battlefield experience.

By the time the British unleashed a major tank offensive on them in 1917 the Germans had already put much time and effort into breaking the battlefield stalemate by other means. In 1915 they had begun to experiment with a new type of infantry formation, the sturmtruppen or storm trooper unit.

The first unit, Sturmabteilung Calsow, was formed in May of that year. It consisted of two combat engineer companies supported by a 77mm artillery battery. In August the unit was enlarged, adding a machine gun platoon, trench mortar troop and flamethrower troop. These early experiments were so successful that the unit was quickly turned into a training cadre to help form other sturmtruppen units in preparation for the Verdun offensive. The troops performed so well in this battle that a permanent training camp was established and over the next eighteen months a storm trooper battalion was created for each German army.

Storm trooper units differed from the standard infantry of the line both in the way they were organised and equipped. Individual storm troopers always carried at least one satchel of grenades and had a high proportion of machine guns per unit compared to normal infantry formations. They were also plentifully equipped with flamethrowers and trench mortars, all useful in close-range trench fighting. In support each unit had its own 77mm artillery battery, ready to bring heavier fire on strongpoints too difficult for the infantry to overcome. In addition ,training and leadership differed widely from that in the regular infantry. Emphasis was placed upon individual initiative at all levels, junior officers and NCOs being given much more responsibility than normal. Discipline and officer-man relations were also much more relaxed and informal than in other units of the German Army. Men were taught the value of constant offensive action and imbued with a sense of eliteness.

Allied to these new storm units was the development of a new style of artillery bombardment that helped rather than hindered the penetration of Allied defences. Developed by Colonel Georg Bruchmüller, the bombardment relied on mathematical range-finding, rather than registering targets with actual shells, so as not to give away the potential axis of attack. He also emphasised short severe bombardments rather than lengthy artillery shoots. Bruchmüller realised that the role of artillery was not so much to physically destroy the enemy's forces but rather to cause dislocation and confusion, lowering the Allies' ability to respond effectively.

Bruchmüller's artillery bombardments concentrated first on enemy gun positions, disrupting their ability to provide counter-fire that could break up the attack. Bombardments were precisely timed so that the maximum concentration of fire could be brought to bear against the break-in point (schwerpunkt) on the enemy line. The shoot itself could be altered by the use of flare signals from the advancing infantry formations, thus overcoming the problem of keeping the enemy positions in a suppressed state until the attackers were upon their trenchline.

The Germans chose to test these new tactics first on the Eastern and Ital-

German storm troopers move forward during an exercise at their Sedan training ground, May 1917. Note the grenade satchels carried by each man. (IWM.Q.48453)

ian Fronts rather than against Allied forces in France. In the summer of 1917 the German Eighth Army commanded by General Oscar von Hutier found itself facing the Russian Twelfth Army across the river Dvina in Latvia. At the mouth of the river stood the port of Riga, second most important in the Tsarist empire. Its capture would be a major blow to the Russians. Opposite the city on the south bank of the river they had managed to form a substantial bridgehead, from which offensives could be launched against the Germans when the time was right. General Klembovsky, the Russian commander, placed his best troops in this area, surmising that if the Germans were to attack it would be against this dangerous point in the line. Troops of lower quality were assigned to guard the river bank further inland. The Dvina was a wide river and this Klembovsky felt would further influence the Germans to attack the bridgehead. Von Hutier decided, however, to use the indirect approach and capture the port by crossing the river to the south-east of the city and sweep round behind it. This tactic would later become the centre-piece of blitzkrieg strategy.

Up to this point it had been thought that victory would best be achieved by bringing the main force of the enemy's army to contact and destroying it on the battlefield. Von Hutier realised that it could be more easily gained by outmanoeuvring his opponent and making his position untenable. If he could get into the rear of the defending Russians lines of communication would be cut, supply centres captured and enemy headquarters overrun. This would induce panic amongst the troops at the front and paralysis in the enemy's ability to respond effectively.

To get across the formidable river barrier that faced him von Hutier realised that he would have to rely heavily on surprise. Because of this he kept his bombardment (under the control of Colonel Bruchmüller) short, only five hours of preliminary artillery preparation taking place. Bruchmüller was also careful to make sure that firing took place along the entire length of the line so as not to give away the schwerpunkt. To facilitate the breakthrough a high ratio of gas shells (diethyl sulphide) were used to incapacitate and further disrupt the Russian defence. German aircraft schlacht-staffeln (battle flights) were also used to strafe defences and rear areas, spreading panic and confusion, making it difficult for messengers to move around with ease.

The attack began on 1 September and was a tremendous success, over 9,000 Russians being captured for minimal German losses. Troops of the Eighth Army swept round the city, forcing the Russians to evacuate Riga with scarcely a shot fired.

Encouraged by the success of this new tactic, the Germans decided on a further assault on the Isonzo Front in Italy, beginning on 24 October 1917. General von Below's Fourteenth Austro-German Army breached the Italian lines near Caporetto after a six-hour bombardment, using the same type of artillery preparation and mix of gas shells. The results were even better than at Riga. The Italians' line ruptured almost immediately and a cohesive defence was only restored on the line of the river Piave, some 80 miles to the rear of the original position. The Italians lost over 300,000 casualties and some 2,500 guns in the retreat.

The Germans used the same tactics during the Cambrai counter-offensive which began on 30 November 1917. Some 20 divisions attacked the British salient, using the same short preparatory bombardment to achieve surprise and infiltration tactics to break into the defenders' positions. After the first 48 hours the defence had been thrown into complete confusion. By 7 December the British had been pushed back some three miles.

The successes of Riga and Caporetto led the Germans to refine their tactics further during the winter of 1917/18. The attack would now consist of four phases. First a short artillery bombardment would concentrate on neutralising (not destroying) the enemy front and support lines. Special units of sturmtruppen would then move forward under the cover of a creeping barrage. They would infiltrate the defensive lines, bypassing centres of resistance, and make for headquarters and artillery positions to the rear. Behind them would follow 'battle units' consisting of infantry armed with a heavy complement of machine guns and mortars. Accompanying them would be combat engineers with flamethrowers and forward artillery observation officers. Their job was to invest the strongpoints missed by the lead sturmtruppen. The observation officers were given authority to change artillery fire plans on their own initiative, thus adding to the flexibility of the attackers. Finally, conventional infantry would follow behind to mop up any remaining pockets of resistance. The three waves would advance in bounds, an echelon moving forward when the one to its rear caught up with it. All members of the lead units were imbued with the necessity to keep pushing forward, further into the Allied rear.

General Erich von Ludendorff felt that with Russia now out of the war, a decisive blow on the Western Front using these new tactics might well bring victory. Von Hutier, von Below and Bruchmüller were all transferred to France to begin preparations for this new 1918 offensive. Ludendorff reasoned that France would not stay in the war if Britain's armies, now the most formidable Allied force on the Western Front, were defeated. The spring offensive was therefore delivered

German storm troopers assault enemy positions during the opening phases of the spring offensive, March/April 1918. (IWM.Q.55483)

against Byng's Third and Gough's Fifth British Armies. By aiming to knock the British out of the war

Ludendorff had made a major mistake that was later to become apparent. All other blitzkrieg operations to date had been delivered against the weakest point of the enemy's line. A main tenet of the strategy, the notion that areas of tough resistance should be avoided, was ignored. If the offensive's schwerpunkt had been on the French sector of the front, the breakthrough might have been total.

As it was the German Spring Offensive (Operation Michael) which opened on 21 March 1918 caught the British completely unprepared. British forces were very stretched both by having to take over an extra 25 miles of front from French troops, who had to be taken out of the line, and by the fact that most British battalions were seri-

ously weak, many being at 50 percent strength. Lloyd George, fearful of Haig beginning another disastrous Ypres offensive, had placed an embargo on all further troop reinforcements.

The Germans opened their offensive with 67 divisions of the Seventeenth, Second and Eighteenth Armies against 33 weakened British ones from the Fifth and Eighth British Armies. The Germans had carefully hoarded 4,010 field and 2,588 heavy/medium guns along the attack front, against 1,710 and 976 British pieces respectively. Total artillery domination of the battlefield was quickly achieved.

By the end of the first day along a front of 40 miles the Germans had penetrated deep into the British defence line and in some cases completely through it. Gough's army was thrown back in complete confusion. French reinforcements rushed north found themselves caught up in the retreat. For the next two days the advance continued in this sector at a rapid pace. Further north Byng's troops fared a little

better; facing a smaller number of German divisions, their retreat was not quite as precipitous.

On 23 March Ludendorff made his second fatal mistake. Instead of reinforcing the success of von Hutier's Eighteenth Army against the retiring Gough, he ordered a dispersion of effort by the three armies in different directions. After several days of fighting without respite, the lead German sturmtruppen were exhausted and when on the 28th they reached the vicinity of Albert the advance ground to a halt.

Further French reinforcements had played a part in this stalling of the attack but the lack of rotation of front-line units for the Germans played a major role, not enough trained sturmtruppen being available to relieve the lead elements of the advance. Troops now coming across major Allied stores in the rear areas were turning to looting and pillaging and drunkenness became rife. At this stage of the war the Royal Navy blockade of Germany had bitten deep. Men coming across unaccustomed luxuries such as new boots and plentiful food and drink quickly fell out to award themselves the fruits of victory.

On the same day that Operation Michael came to an end, Ludendorff gave orders for another attack to be mounted, beginning on 9 April. This offensive, codenamed Operation Georgette, was to take place further to the north in the area of the river Lys. Although Ludendorff managed to mount the offensive with 26 divisions, only twelve were sturm divisions as compared with 47 used during Operation Michael. Nevertheless the attack initially met with considerable success. Of the six British divisions defending this sector, only one, the 55th West Lancashire Territorial, was up to strength. Some units in the area, such as the 1st Portuguese Division, were in such a low state of morale that they broke and ran almost as soon as the first shots were fired.

Using the same type of artillery preparation and infiltration tactics, the Germans managed to punch a hole six miles deep and ten miles wide in the British line. During the next three days the Germans managed to continue to push forward but, as before, the assault gradually ran out of steam. By the 12th, the ground fog which had been aiding the German advance lifted and RAF planes were able to strafe the advancing troops with some effect. By the end of the month the offensive had come to a halt. The British had learned some lessons from their earlier defeats and had adopted a less rigid, more flexible stance, allowing withdrawals to be made in better order. The Germans still suffered with problems of lack of rotation for front-line units and lax discipline. Again after several days of combat, troops began to become distracted by stores and supply dumps.

Another noteworthy event of this offensive was that it saw in its closing stage the first tank versus tank engagement. German engineers had begun to experiment with a competitor to the British and French vehicles soon after they appeared on the battlefield in late 1916. The design settled on, which became known as the A7V after the initials of the government department responsible for tank development, was a monster of a machine with no less than eighteen crew members. Armed with 57mm guns, the vehicle potentially challenged the dominance of the Allied tank. Unfortunately it turned out to have a very poor cross-country performance. This, allied to the fact that only twenty were ever built, limited their effectiveness on the battlefield. The number of vehicles produced was in part due to the lack of raw materials prevalent in Germany during the later stages of the war. But it was also the case that the Germans envisaged the vehicles being integrated into the sturmtruppen units as a form of mobile infantry support gun. There was no thought of creating an independent German tank corps as the British had done. So tanks were to be an adjunct to the tactics of the storm troopers, not a replacement for them. The first two sturmpanzerkampfwagen

Two German A7V tanks (Wotan and Hagen) move into action against British troops, June 1918. (IWM.Q.37344)

A captured British Mk IV tank (Beutepanzer-kampfwagen) is turned against its former owners during Operation Michael, March 1918. Note the storm troopers accompanying the tank, one of whom carries a man-pack flame-thrower. (IWM.Q.45348)

abteilungen (tank companies) were formed in the autumn of 1917.

This is not to say that the Germans ignored the new concept of mobility through mechanisation. In 1916 Rumania had entered the war on the side of the Allied powers. Late in the year the Germans were to carry out the first of what in the next war would become known as panzergrenadier operations.

German troops had managed to capture the strategically important Vulkan Pass but were unable to press on into the Rumanian interior because of the determined resistance of an infantry division at the Iron Gate, a Danube gorge that formed an extensive natural defensive position. Through the gorge ran the main north-south railway line. This was needed by the Germans to move supplies, as roads in the area could not support the traffic necessary to keep an army in the field. Behind the gorge lay the fortified town of Turnu Severin. It was decided to attempt to capture it by *coup de main*. The *ad hoc* force detailed to take the town consisted of an infantry battalion, three machine-gun platoons, a signals section and a troop of dragoons, some 500 men in total; all of whom, except for the dragoons, rode in lorries. The force set

off at dawn on 20 November. That evening Captain Picht, the battlegroup commander, and his men stormed the town from the east, the least expected direction, and held it for 36 hours against repeated Rumanian counter-attacks. Resistance at the Iron Gate soon crumbled and the German advance into the Rumanian interior was able to begin. This operation shows that the benefits of motorisation were not lost on the Germans and that the strategy of the indirect approach by motorised units was being practised several years before theorists such as J. F. C. Fuller advocated them in written form.

The Cambrai counter-offensive brought the Germans a bonus in that they managed to capture a significant number of British Mark IV tanks. These were called Beutepanzerkampf-wagen (booty tanks) and were formed into a further six five-tank Abteilungen. Nine tanks were used in the initial phases of Operation Michael although they were ineffective, six of them quickly breaking down. Indeed, no British reports of the battle mention enemy tanks being used.

The Germans did not use their tanks again until a month later. On 24 April,

near the village of Villers-Bretonneux, British and German tanks met for the first time. The Germans had managed to gather a force of fourteen A7Vs to lead an attack by four sturm divisions. The assault began as planned with the German troops quickly overrunning the village. At this point, however, three British tanks arrived on the scene, two Mark IV 'females' armed only with machine guns and a Mark IV 'male' armed with a six-pounder gun. The females were quickly forced to retire due to their inability to affect the oncoming vehicles but the male gamely opened up with its main armament. One A7V was knocked out and two other forced to retire by the Mark IV's intense fire. This left the German infantry in the area without any tank protection. Seven British Whippet light tanks now arrived on the scene and thoroughly machine-gunned the unprotected infantry. The German troops turned and fled, leaving behind some 400 casualties.

After the strategic failure of his first two offensives Ludendorff realised that he should have been attacking the weak link in the Allied camp, not its strongest. The third German offensive opening on 27 May was therefore directed against French forces in the Chemin des Dames area. Marshal Foch had stated that the only way to defeat these determined German attacks was to fight tenaciously for every inch of ground. This would have had disastrous consequences for the defenders had it been adhered to, rigidity in defence playing straight into the German hands. However, General Pétain, after studying the previous offensives and captured German leaflets, decided that what was needed was a flexible defence in depth. As a consequence the Germans obtained the biggest first-day advance of all their offensives so far, over twelve miles. Pétain, however, kept his head and instead of committing his reserves piecemeal held them well back. Once again the German offensive began to slow, with exhaustion and looting setting in. Ludendorff now found himself with a very exposed salient to defend. His next assault was intended to widen this gap. However, Pétain was ready and now committed his reserves, stopping the German attack dead in its tracks.

By now the effectiveness of the entire German Army on the Western Front was deteriorating rapidly. Lack of supplies, exhaustion and ill discipline had rendered it incapable of any more major offensives. Ludendorff, however, was willing to give it one more try. The final German thrust of the war was launched on 15 July on either side of the city of Rheims. The French commander to the east of the city, General Gouraud, was a follower of Pétain and adopted a flexible in-depth defence. The German attack in this area was halted relatively quickly. To the west of the city the Germans met with much more success, managing to cross the river Marne without too much difficulty. However, on the second day of the offensive they ran into Pétain's reserve forces and the advance began to slow. Two days later the French put in a fierce counter-attack led by tanks and the German advance was halted.

Already commanders were learning that flexible defences in depth helped defeat these new blitzkrieg tactics. German forces were by now well past their best. The numbers of sturmtruppen available had never been quite enough to allow a major offensive to succeed. The Allies would have to wait for another 22 years before feeling the effectiveness of a German blitzkrieg by well-trained fresh troops with high morale and high-quality mechanised support.

While the Germans were busy reintroducing mobility to the battlefield via new artillery and infantry tactics,

A storm trooper company pose for the camera before going into action against French positions on the Marne, July 1918. (IWM.Q.55371)

A tank attack in progress, viewed from the receiving end! British Mk V tanks, supporting an attack by the American V Corps, trundle across no-man's-land under artillery fire, October 1918. (IWM.Q.45352)

the British persisted in tank development as a potential way to unlock the battlefield stalemate.

Colonel J. F. C. Fuller, still Chief of Staff at British Tank Corps headquarters, developed a strategy that was to became known as 'Plan 1919'. His new thesis was that the primary objective of an armoured attack should be the disorganisation of the enemy rather than its physical destruction. Emphasis was particularly laid on the need to attack corps and army headquarters, deep behind enemy lines. This, Fuller felt, would paralyse the defenders, who would be unable to react to the break-in attack being mounted elsewhere along the main enemy defence line. As well as organisational paralysis, Fuller felt that an attack of this type would spread panic through the ranks of an enemy, perhaps leading to a precipitate withdrawal. The plan, which was to become central to blitzkrieg theory in the interwar years, foresaw an attack of three stages.

First a force of medium tanks supported by aircraft would break through the enemy line and head for rear area headquarters. They would bypass all centres of resistance, concentrating on passing through the defence line to the enemy rear. This would incapacitate the enemy and reduce his ability to repel the next force to attack the main line of defence, which Fuller called 'the breaking force'. This would consist of heavy tanks, infantry and artillery. Their role would be to open and secure a breach in the enemy defences. Following them would be 'the pursuit force' consisting of light tanks, cavalry and motorised infantry. These would pass through the gap into the rear areas of the enemy and chase back the now-retreating troops for a distance of up to 150 miles, which Fuller felt would be enough to secure a strategic victory.

Fuller felt that a force of 5,000 tanks would be needed if any attack was to bring a total victory on the Western Front. Even though this would put enormous strain on Allied production capacity, Foch agreed to the plan in principle for the next year should the war drag on.

Unfortunately Fuller was never given the chance to prove his theory.

The German Army had shot its bolt. The last desperate offensives of 1918 had totally exhausted them. The strain placed on the German war economy by the naval blockade and the resumption of Allied offensive action against the dispirited German line forced an armistice.

So by the end of the war all the essential elements of blitzkrieg were tried and tested. The Germans had perfected the art of infiltration by infantry and shock action through artillery fire and the British had developed the tank and put forward a new theory of armoured warfare. Both sides had used air power in a ground attack role, albeit in a rather limited form. Most important, however, was that both sides had come to realise that victory could be won not only by the physical destruction of enemy forces but by the dislocation and paralysis of their command structure. The strategy of the indirect approach had been proven in combat.

CHAPTER TWO

The Interwar Years

The terms of the Treaty of Versailles which formally ended the war in Europe sought to ensure that Germany could never again wage a war of aggression. The German Army (now called the Reichsheer) was limited to a maximum size of 100,000 men, conscription was banned and the military term of service raised to a minimum of twelve years. There were also severe restrictions on the types of weapons that the new Reichsheer could possess. No artillery above 105mm calibre was allowed, and there was a limitation on the number of small arms (rifles and machine guns) that the army could possess. Article 171 of the treaty outlawed the manufacture or purchase of gas, along with the importation and construction of tanks and armoured cars. The Reichsheer was allowed to possess a few unarmed armoured carriers for internal security operations. Article 198 banned the German armed forces from having an air force or even possessing any planes at all. Germany was thus left without any of the means to practise or train for blitzkrieg warfare.

Throughout most of the interwar period Britain was the world leader in the field of mechanisation and the development of progressive theories for the future use of tanks in battle.

Immediately after the end of the First World War J. F. C. Fuller had begun to write a book detailing the important role the tank had played in achieving victory over Germany. When published in 1920, *Tanks in the Great War* not only detailed the history of the Tank Corps on the Western Front but also put forward Fuller's own views as to what the future shape of Britain's armoured forces should be. With his promotion to lecturer at the British Army Staff College, Camberley in 1922, he was able to press his views further, building on his 'Plan 1919' and advocating an all-tank army (with the possible inclusion of some fully mechanised infantry) in his lectures and in books such as *The Reformation of War*. His theories, although appearing somewhat naive and rather muddled in places, gave cause for thought amongst many of his contemporaries and helped ensure that throughout the interwar period the debate over mechanisation was at the forefront of British military thinking. By 1929 and his last major contribution to the armour debate, a book based on his earlier lectures on field service regulations, entitled *Lectures on FSR III*, he had become firmly wedded to the idea of the all-tank army. He envisaged it being made up of two main components, the tank force, which provided the heavily armed and armoured vehicles necessary to break through the enemy defences, and an anti-tank force of mobile guns which would protect the flanks of the advancing tank force.

These ideas stimulated argument inside the British Army and led to the rise in prominence of several other armoured warfare theorists.

Chief amongst these was Captain Basil Liddell Hart, who in 1920 was tasked to revise the then current Brit-

A column of Reichsheer Kfz 13 armoured cars on exercise. This vehicle, the only armoured combat vehicle allowed under the Versailles Treaty, was either unarmed (Kfz 14) or fitted with a pedestal-mounted MG 13 machine gun (Kfz 13). Either way it was a poor substitute for the type of vehicle needed to effectively carry out blitzkrieg operations. (IWM.HU.15899)

ish Infantry Training Manual and chose as his starting point the German storm trooper tactics of 1918. He was then asked to write an entry for the *Encyclopedia Britannica* describing how infantry were still 'Queen of the Battlefield'. He then realised that he could not come up with a satisfactory argument to bolster this thesis. It was at this point that he became interested in the idea of using all-arms mechanised formations to achieve victory on the battlefield. Because of Liddell Hart's infantry background his theories tended to advocate a more balanced approach to the future of the British Army and its mechanisation than did Fuller's. In his books, *Paris, or the Future of War*, *The Remaking of Modern Armies* and *The Strategy of the Indirect Approach*, he developed his theory of the 'Expanding Torrent'. His idea was similar in some ways to Fuller's plans for using tanks to get into the enemy rear but Liddell Hart placed much more value on the psychological effect such a breakthrough would have. He also felt that there was a distinct role the infantry

could play on the modern battlefield but only if it were fully mechanised. Tanks were not to be regarded as an additional infantry support weapon or a replacement for the horsed cavalry but a new and separate arm of decision on the battlefield. Deep attacks into enemy rear areas, bypassing centres of resistance and destroying enemy headquarters and centres of communication, would restore mobility to the battlefield, ensure a rapid and decisive victory and confirm a central role for the tank in future wars.

Other supporters of the mechanisation process included Brigadier Giffard le Q. Martel and Brigadier Charles Broad. Martel, like Fuller, was a strong advocate of the all-tank army. Up until 1927 and his command of the Experimental Armoured Force Engineer Company, he saw no role for infantry on the future battlefield. After these experiences he revised his opinion and in his 1931 book *In the Wake of the Tank* he argued for mechanised infantry to accompany tank units, to take and hold difficult ground.

Above left: A formal portrait photograph of Colonel J. F. C. Fuller taken after the war's end when he was the leading advocate of the total mechanisation of the British Army. (IWM.Q.71653)

Above right: Brigadier Giffard le Q. Martel talks to a Soviet officer during his visit to Minsk in September 1936. Martel and General Archibald Wavell (far left) visited the Soviet Union to see at first hand Tukhachevsky's new mechanised formations in the field. Deeply impressed, he returned to England and advocated the immediate raising of British armoured divisions. (IWM.HU.50225)

Charles Broad, who commanded the highly successful wireless equipped tank brigade in the 1931 British Army manoeuvres, advocated all-arms mechanised formations and emphasised army/air force cooperation. In his book *Mechanised and Armoured Formations 1920 (Provisional)* he also pointed to the crucial role that modern communications would have to play in the control of fully mechanised formations.

Through the influence of these men the British Royal Tank Corps was able to survive the contraction of the British Army that took place at the end of the First World War and the severe cut-

backs forced by the economic depression of the early 1930s.

Indeed, up until 1934 it seemed that the British Army would be the world's first to have permanent armoured divisions. In 1927 the first ever totally mechanised formation, The Experimental Armoured Force, was created and took part in exercises on Salisbury Plain. Consisting of a battalion of armoured cars and machine-gun carriers, a tank battalion, a mechanised machine-gun battalion, mechanised artillery and a mechanised engineer company, it showed the way forward for the modern mechanised all-arms formation.

Following on from the success of the Experimental Armoured Force came the first, albeit only temporary, Army Tank Brigade which was formed in 1931. The stunning success of this unit in that year's summer exercises led directly to the creation of the 1st Tank Brigade, commanded by Brigadier Percy Hobart, in 1934. The 1931 manoeuvres had been so successful because of Broad's insistence that the vehicles of the Tank Brigade were all equipped with radios. He also introduced the notion of the specially equipped command tank, fitted with several radios, to enable commanding officers to control the brigade via different nets, when in action.

Left, top: The Experimental Armoured Force drawn up for inspection on Salisbury Plain, 1927. The force, the first in the world to combine tanks with mechanised infantry, mobile artillery and engineers in a single formation, was watched closely by advocates of mechanisation in Germany, such as Lutz and Guderian. (IWM.HU.41015)

Left, centre: Brigadier Charles Broad in his specially built wireless command tank during an exercise of the 1st Brigade, Royal Tank Corps, Salisbury Plain, 1931. Standing on the side of the vehicle is Brigadier George Lindsay, another pioneer of British armoured warfare. (IWM.HU.41017)

Left, bottom: A Light Tank Mk II leads a column of British armour on exercise, 1932. Note that three of the four tanks visible carry radio aerials, indicating that Charles Broad's innovations in communications were followed through. (IWM.HU.31225)

Reichspresident Field Marshal Paul von Hindenburg and General Hans von Seeckt, Commander in Chief of the Reichswehr (right with monocle), visit the Tannenberg Memorial, the memorial to the German victory of 1914. (IWM.Q.71364)

The 1st Tank Brigade, although successfully used in conjunction with a motorised infantry brigade and an armoured car battalion in the 1934 manoeuvres, was the last major experiment with a mobile all-arms formation until 1939 and the creation, far too late, of the first two British armoured divisions.

Unfortunately for the advocates of mechanisation, traditionalists inside the British Army contrived to fix the results of the 1934 manoeuvres to make it appear that British infantry had proved superior to tank units during the exercises. Because of this and the appointment of General Montgomery-Massingberd, an arch conservative, as CIGS (Chief of the Imperial General Staff) the British armoured force fell into decline and was ill-prepared to meet the demands placed on it on the outbreak of the Second World War.

The significance of the British theorists' ideas were not lost on the Germans. Heinz Guderian was later to state that 'it was principally the books and articles of the Englishmen, Fuller, Liddell Hart and Martel, that excited my interest and gave me food for thought. I learned from them the concentration of armour, as employed in the battle of Cambrai. Further, it was Liddell Hart who emphasised the use of armoured forces for long-range strokes, operations against the opposing army's communications, and also proposed a type of armoured division combining panzer and panzer-infantry units.'

The German Army found itself hamstrung after the First World War's end by the terms of the Versailles Treaty. A new force to replace the old Imperial German Army, the Reichsheer, consisting of 100,000 long-service professional soldiers, came into being in March 1920. The new commander of this force was General Hans von Seeckt. A supporter of the concept of the professional, rather than the conscript army, he was faced with the tremendous task of ensuring that this small force was capable of providing Germany with an adequate defence.

He rapidly came to the conclusion that the Reichsheer was not capable of fighting a protracted conflict in defence of her borders. To counter this problem he favoured the extensive motorisation of the army, thus making up in mobility what he lacked in numbers. Von Seeckt had spent most of the First World War on the Eastern Front where trench lines had been less rigid. He therefore looked more favourably upon the ideas of the proponents of mechanisation, such as Guderian. As early as 1921 units of motorised infan-

A German artillery battery on the move during winter exercises in 1937. This shows the extent to which field artillery was still heavily reliant on horse-power in the Third Reich. The vast majority of German field and heavy artillery was horse-drawn throughout the entire Second World War. (IWM.HU.20722)

try were exercising in the Harz Mountains.

Lack of manpower also forced von Seeckt into rethinking the basic structure of the Reichsheer. From this the concept of the Führerarmee developed. Every soldier in the new Reichsheer was trained a level or two above his current rank. Privates were trained in the duties of non-commissioned officers, non-commissioned officers to be junior officers and officers to fill the higher levels of command. Thus the Reichsheer became a cadre army; in time of war it would rapidly expand, filling in at its base with raw recruits. This suited Hitler perfectly, for when he came to power in 1933 the basis of the Wehrmacht was already in place.

The army was to consist of 18 cavalry and 21 infantry regiments, divided between three cavalry and seven infantry divisions. Every company, battery and squadron upheld the traditions of a particular regiment of the German Imperial Army in preparation for its future expansion.

The army, restricted to such a small size, could also afford to be selective, only recruiting the very best troops. The interwar Reichsheer was made up of highly competent officers and men, all in peak physical condition.

Von Seeckt was of the opinion that the First World War had been lost due to the German inability to interfere with the French mobilisation process. If in any future conflict German troops could penetrate into the enemy's rear areas quickly then that enemy might well be overcome before mobilisation could occur. Thus von Seeckt was further interested in mechanisation and the blitzkrieg process.

The Allied Control Commission, the organisation based in Germany until 1928 to oversee the implementation of the Versailles Treaty, had little knowledge of the clandestine activities of the Reichsheer, designed to enable them to modernise and mechanise the

Tank crews who will form the first panzer divisions receive basic driver training at the Kraftfahrlehkommando (Motorisation Instructional Command) at Zossen, summer 1934. (IWM.KID.4103)

army in secret. Of particular importance to the development of the German mechanised arm was the Rapallo Agreement of 1922 under which tank research was carried out at a secret training ground at Kazan in Russia, the first German Reichsheer trainees being sent there in 1924. Within four years German tank designers had despatched nine prototype vehicles to Kazan for testing. They had been developed under the guise of agricultural tractors and were built in Germany and Russia, with some parts being developed in Sweden. The two types of vehicle tested were named the Leichter (Light) and Gross (Heavy) Traktors and mounted 37mm and 75mm guns respectively.

To deceive the Control Commission further, the units tasked with the development of the Reichsheer's mechanisation and motorisation policies operated under the cover of the Truppenamt (Transport Troops Directorate). Ostensibly this organisation existed to provide logistical back-up to the infantry and cavalry. It was split into two branches, the Fahrtruppe (horse drawn transport) and Kraftfahrtruppe (motorised transport).

In reality the Fahrtruppe provided a cover behind which the Reichsheer prepared to break the Versailles Treaty.

German artillery relied heavily on horse-drawn transport up until the end of the Second World War and so it was vital that artillerymen were well trained in all equine matters. When the expansion of the German Army came in 1935, these 'transport troops' provided men for the new artillery regiments, whilst the gaps in the Fahrtruppe were filled with recruits familiar with horses straight from civilian life.

The Kraftfahrtruppe provided the perfect cover for the training of tank crews, so that when the first three panzer divisions were formed in 1935 the seven existing Kraftfahrtruppe battalions provided a ready-trained cadre. Experiments in the mechanisation of the Reichsheer had begun in 1922 when the Inspector of Transport Troops, General Eric von Tschischwitz, was tasked with devising methods of utilising mechanised transport to overcome the problems of defending Germany's long frontiers and her lack of troops. Much of the work for this project was delegated to his subordinate, Captain Heinz Guderian.

Born in 1888 at Kulm in Prussia, Guderian had served between 1914 and 1917 as an officer in a signals battalion and towards the end of the war had become a staff officer, being on the staff of XVIII Reserve Corps during the German summer offensive of 1918. He thus appreciated the importance of radio communications and fully understood the blitzkrieg principles used in Germany's final attacks of the war. Detailed to investigate the possibilities of enhancing the Reichsheer's capability through increased mobility, Guderian read widely on the subject, taking particular note of the works of the British theorists of the time. As he later stated, 'deeply impressed by these ideas I tried to develop them in a sense practicable for our own army.' Rapidly becoming the leading German expert on mechanisation, he regularly began to contribute articles to the prestigious German military journal *Militär Wochenblatt*. This forward-thinking publication had by the mid-1920s begun to carry a supplement called *Der Kampfwagen* (the tank) which became a forum for the mostly pro-armour sentiments of the German Army. Guderian quickly came to be regarded as the number one expert on the subject of tanks.

The impetus towards the mechanisation of the Reichsheer increased in 1926 when Major General A. von Vollard-Bocklberg began regular train-

A column of dummy tanks during the 1929 Reichsheer manoeuvres. (IWM.Q.71388)

Left: German infantry and dummy tanks practise combined arms cooperation during a 1931 winter exercise. (IWM.NYP.68044)

Below: An anti-tank gun is towed by a multi-axle vehicle (this was against the conditions of the Versailles Treaty) during the 1932 Reichsheer manoeuvres. The two men in the rear of the lorry with white cap bands are exercise umpires. (IWM.Q.71395)

tanks made out of civilian cars with cardboard tank hulls superimposed over their bodies. In 1931 Guderian was given the chance to try out some of his theories on troops of his own when he was given command of the 3rd (Prussian) Motorised Battalion, which consisted of several companies of motorised infantry, an armoured car company, a motorcycle company, an anti-tank company and several dummy tanks.

On successful completion of a year's duty with the unit he returned to the Transport Troops Directorate as its second in command under his old friend Major General Oswald Lutz, another pro-armour officer. Indeed, Guderian never faced the kind of virulent opposition that his British contemporaries did. Most German officers were well

ing of Kraftfahrtruppe officers in theories of armoured warfare, based mainly on British Army pamphlets such as the *Provisional Instructions of Armoured Vehicles, 1927*, which had been used to instruct officers of the British Experimental Armoured Force. In 1928 Guderian, now a major, began to give his own lectures on armoured warfare. In these he expanded upon the British theorists' arguments, adding his own ideas. He advocated fully mechanising a proportion of the army's units, creating balanced all-arms formations as opposed to the tank heavy formations proposed by many British theorists.

In 1929 the concept of the panzer division was tried out for the first time with an imaginary division taking to the field, complete with mock-up

aware of the need to motorise and mechanise as fast as possible and Guderian seemed to be the man most capable of turning theory into practical armoured formations and operations in the field. His supporters included the War Minister, General von Blomburg, the Army's Commander in Chief (from 1934), General Freiherr von Fritsch, and Chief of the Reichswehr Ministerial Office, General Walther von Reichenau.

Guderian's most influential admirer was of course Adolf Hitler, who was

also an advocate of mechanisation. His ideas on the future shape of the German Army dovetailed with Guderian's. As early as 1934, when he accompanied Guderian to the trials of some prototype tanks (later to become PsKpfw Is) at Kummersdorf proving ground, he was heard to remark, 'That's what I want – that's what I am going to have.'

The first major attempt at replicating the all-arms mechanisation theories of Guderian took place during the Reichswehr Autumn Manoeuvres of

1932. Here for the first time battalions of motorised infantry exercised in conjunction with the manoeuvres of dummy tanks, and multi-axled vehicles were used for towing mobile artillery pieces (in direct contravention of Versailles Treaty stipulations).

Above: A German signals platoon with its messenger dogs during the 1932 Reichsheer manoeuvres. (IWM.Q.71397)

Below: An early experiment in artillery mechanisation. A tractor pulls a German field gun during the 1932 Reichsheer manoeuvres. (IWM.Q.71396)

Left, top: A camouflaged machine-gun position during the 1932 Reichsheer manoeuvres. (IWM.Q.71399)

Left, centre: A company of PzKpfw I Ausf B tanks parades for the Führer in front of the Brandenburg Gate, Berlin, 1935. (IWM.MH.8876)

Left, bottom: Panzer crews of the 3rd Panzer Division receive instruction on armoured tactics in the woods near Berlin, 1935. (IWM.NYP.68055)

With the accession to power of Adolf Hitler in 1933, defiance of treaty articles became much more blatant. In 1931 the Reichsheer possessed only three secretly developed tanks. In 1934 Krupps of Essen produced more than 100 PzKpfw Is for the now expanding German Army. At the same time the first operational tank battalion was established, although Hitler still felt it wise to deny its existence, calling it the 'Motor Transport Training Unit'. Later in that same year the Kraftfahrtruppe shed its guise, was reorganised and renamed the Motorised Troops Command. General Lutz remained at the helm with Guderian as his chief of staff.

On 16 March 1935, Adolf Hitler formally repudiated the restrictive clauses of the Treaty of Versailles, stating that in future Germany would rearm as she thought fit. Conscription was reintroduced and the expansion of the armed forces in line with the Führerarmee principle began. The Wehrmacht, as the German Armed Forces were from now on to be known, expanded rapidly, new recruits slipping comfortably into preprepared divisional cadres. The objective of the expansion, as Hitler himself made clear, was to be able to fight a full-scale defensive war by 1939 and an offensive one by 1943.

At that year's Nuremberg Nazi Party rally Hitler proclaimed for the first time the German Army's new philosophy of war. In answer to the question, when would the Third Reich go to war, he answered, 'I shouldn't negotiate for months beforehand and make lengthy preparations, but – as I have always done throughout my life – I should suddenly, like a flash of lightning in the night, hurl myself upon the enemy.' Thus for the first time the term blitz (lightning) was associated with the German Army's new form of mobile mechanised warfare.

In October 1935 the first panzer corps, commanded by Lutz, was formed. It consisted of three panzer divisions, the 1st, based at Weimar, under the command of Major General Freiherr von Weichs, the 2nd, at Würzburg, under the command of Colonel Heinz Guderian, and the 3rd, at Berlin, under the command of Major General Fessman. It is a measure of the regard for the qualities of Guderian as an armoured warfare tactician that he was given his command when only a colonel. Guderian's meteoric rise through the ranks mirrored the rapid expansion of the German panzer force (the 4th and 5th Panzer Divisions formed in 1938 and another, the 10th, in April 1939). To befit his position as divisional commander he was promoted major general in August 1936. In February 1938 he became a lieutenant general when given command of XVI Panzer Corps in Berlin and in November 1938 he was made General der Panzertruppen.

The panzer divisions, balanced all-arms formations according to the operational principles laid out by Guderian, each consisted of a panzer brigade, a motorised infantry brigade and a motorised artillery regiment plus signals, engineer and anti-tank battalions (an anti-aircraft battalion was added later). Each panzer brigade consisted of two regiments, each of two battalions of tanks. Each panzer battalion was made up of one heavy and three light companies, a theoretical total of 562 tanks per panzer division. Unfortunately they were never to reach this establish-ment figure. Tank production just could not keep up with demand. Generally the units had to make do with two light companies (PzKpfw I, II and IIIs) and a severely depleted heavy company (PzKpfw IVs).

The shortage of vehicles for the new divisions was compounded by the fact that the infantry and cavalry both demanded tank units as adjuncts to their own formations. Vital resources for the panzer divisions were diverted into two independent tank brigades (the 4th and the 6th) and an independent tank regiment, for direct support of infantry operations. The cavalry organised their own leichter (light) divisions, units intended to carry out the traditional functions of the cavalry but in a mechanised form. Each division (four were in existence by 1939) consisted of one panzer and four motorised rifle battalions, plus motorised reconnaissance and artillery elements.

Not only was the Wehrmacht drastically short in numbers of vehicles for its new units but it was also forced to use many vehicles in the field originally intended for training use only. The PzKpfw I, with a crew of two, very thin armour and twin machine guns as its armament, was intended primarily as a training vehicle, yet in the campaigns of 1939 and 1940 it had to be used as a

PzKpfw I Ausf A tanks cross a river during a prewar exercise. (IWM.HU.2690)

battle tank. Likewise the PzKpfw II, armed with a 20mm cannon and developed as a reconnaissance vehicle, had also to take on this role. The tanks intended to form the mainstay of the panzer divisions striking force, the PzKpfw III, armed with a 37mm gun, and the PzKpfw IV, armed with a 75mm howitzer, were never produced in big enough numbers, making up less than 25 percent of Germany's indigenous tank force on the outbreak of hostilities in 1939. Without the addition of several hundred Czech PzKpfw 35(t) and PzKpfw 38(t) tanks to the Wehrmacht armoury on the annexation of the country in 1938, it is doubtful whether Germany would have been in any position to wage war against Poland a year later.

An opportunity soon arose for the panzer to prove itself on the field of battle. The Spanish Civil War of 1936–9 soon polarised into a conflict between the right-wing forces of fascism and left wing republicanism. Both the Italian and German governments actively supported General Franco's nationalist insurgents, supplying them with arms and sending significant contingents of their own troops. Likewise the Russians despatched men and equipment to support the republican forces.

The tank did not come out of the conflict with an enhanced reputation as a war-winning weapon. No decisive victories were achieved through the use of mechanised forces and the war was perceived as having been won by infantry formations slogging it out in the traditional manner, which indeed it was.

General Pavlov, the senior Soviet commander in the conflict, advised that tanks should in future be limited to infantry support operations. Colonel Wilhelm Ritter von Thoma, the German adviser to the nationalist forces, quickly realised that their lack of success stemmed not from inherent weaknesses in German theories of armoured warfare but in the design of the PzKpfw I itself and the inability to put blitzkrieg principles effectively into practice. Von Thoma was so disap-

Left: PzKpfw II Ausf A tanks practice manoeuvring through heavily forested terrain in the Eifel Mountains. (IWM.KID.I596)

Below left: PzKpfw Is of the German Kondor Legion advance on Guadalla, 1937. The Spanish Civil War taught Colonel Wilhelm Ritter von Thoma, the commander of the Legion, that the PzKpfw I was just not good enough to compete on the contemporary battlefield. (IWM.HU.34723)

Right: Republican T-26 tanks and soldiers retreat from Brunete in July 1937, after their defeat by Nationalist forces. (IWM.HU.33034)

pointed with the performance of his German tanks that he offered a 500 peseta reward for every Russian T-26 (which was armed with a 45mm gun) captured intact, eventually equipping four of his twelve tank companies with them.

The Spanish countryside, mountainous and with few decent roads, did not lend itself to mechanised warfare. Restricted avenues of attack funnelled tank units and made the use of the strategy of the indirect approach difficult.

There were tank victories in the war but they were all short-lived. In October 1936 a republican force containing BT and T-26 tanks defeated nationalist units defending the town of Esquivas. The tanks pursued the retreating enemy several miles beyond the town but were then forced to retire when counter-attacked by fresh nationalist units. Some weeks later nationalist tanks attacked republican positions near Madrid, where their PzKpfw Is were decimated by well-sited anti-tank guns.

Opponents of the tank argued that these defeats proved that mechanised forces could not hold their own against infantry formations adequately supplied with anti-tank weapons. In March 1937 the Italian Black Flames 'Mechanised' Division began an assault on Guadalajara and initially met with success, advancing twenty miles in five days. However, the attack was then stopped in its tracks by a republican counter-attack led by T-26 tanks,

which pushed the Italians back 25 miles beyond their start line, before they themselves were forced to withdraw by nationalist forces.

Von Thoma correctly identified that the reason for the poor performance of armour in the Spanish Civil War lay in the way that tanks were used and in the inferior quality of vehicles available. They tended to be fielded in independent formations, operating without infantry support. This was in direct opposition to the teachings of theorists such as Guderian, who recognised that tanks needed mechanised infantry to enable them to hold any ground gained. The one nationalist all-arms formation that did see combat, the Italian Black Flames Division, suffered from a lamentable lack of quality equipment. Although called a mechanised division it was in reality a motorised unit. The infantry rode not in armoured carriers but in lorries, thus being vulnerable to artillery and small arms fire. In addition the divisional armour consisted of mechanically unreliable machine-gun-armed tankettes and armoured cars, incapable of defeating enemy tanks and easily knocked out by the smallest calibre anti-tank weapons.

While most observers came to the conclusion that the Spanish Civil War

substantiated the claim that infantry were still the decisive force on the modern battlefield, the Germans, learning from the mishandling of armour during the conflict, adapted their techniques to improve even further the offensive power of their panzer formations. Perhaps the most important lesson learnt by the Germans was the importance of air power in deciding the outcome of the land battle.

Since 1918 a debate had raged in military circles as to the future role of air power. The most influential schools of thought in Britain and France argued that the example of the zeppelin and bomber raids in the First World War pointed to the use of aircraft in a strategic role, against the war-making capacity and civilian populations of enemy countries. They felt that a large bomber offensive in itself would be enough to bring victory. This theory, first advocated by Italian General Giulio Douhet in his book *Command of the Air*, published in 1921, seemed to be reinforced by the experience of the Spanish Civil War, when German aircraft had resorted to indiscriminate area bombing in an attempt to weaken the resolve of republican forces. The Luftwaffe itself decided that although terror bombing had a role in future warfare, particularly with its ability to

choke roads in the enemy rear with refugees, the main thrust of air strategy should be directed towards supporting the ground offensive. The Red Army, learning from its combat experience in Spain, also recommended that Russian planes be used in the main for close battlefield support.

Where the Luftwaffe scored over its Soviet counterpart was in the quality of its aircraft and aircrew. The Reichswehr had not been allowed an air force under the terms of the Versailles Treaty. This, however, had not stopped the advocates of air power. The Luftsportverbund, a sporting club set up to teach the German people the joys of gliding, secretly gave future Luftwaffe aircrew basic training. By 1926 the organisation had over 30,000 members. In the same year the Allied Control Commission gave permission for the German government to set up a state airline and Lufthansa was born. Army officers were seconded to the airline to gain flight training and civilian staff clandestinely trained for military duties. When the Versailles Treaty was abrogated in 1935, some 20,000 qualified military aircrew were immediately available for the new Luftwaffe.

Under the Rapallo Agreement German pilots trained at Lipetsk in Russia and German designers were able to test new aircraft away from the scrutiny of the Allied Control Commission. The Soviets benefited from observing these activities, learning new manufacturing and design techniques.

Luftwaffe officers were trained to use the same levels of individual initiative as were army officers. Orders were often given verbally and pilots themselves decided how battlefield objectives could best be achieved. Aircrew were expected to operate flexibly at all times.

By the time war broke out in 1939 the Luftwaffe had developed a highly sophisticated system of ground-to-air communication. Forward air controllers at the forefront of the advance in their own armoured vehicles would request air strikes against enemy strong points and troop concentrations. The request would be made to Air Corps Command who would prioritise them and vector in available bomber aircraft. When the planes neared the battle zone they would be talked into the target by the forward air controller. This enabled last-minute variations in targets to

be made. This flexibility allowed German aircraft to be used as a form of flying artillery, able to keep up with the fastest-moving elements of the mechanised attack.

In addition to battlefield support missions, German bombers also interdicted enemy movement by bombing lines of communication, assembly areas, airfields and headquarters. The objective was to isolate the battlefield, preventing reinforcements from filling any holes in the defensive line and enabling the panzer divisions to keep the battlefront fluid and press their advantage in mobility.

Not only did Germany begin the Second World War with much better close-support tactics than did the Allies, they also had a marked superiority in quality of ground-attack aircraft. The famous German Ju-87 Stuka dive bomber was developed in 1937 after Colonel General Ernst Udet, head of the Luftwaffe Development Section, had witnessed a demonstration of dive bombing techniques by United States Army Air Force Curtiss F8.c Helldivers. Deeply impressed, he purchased two, which were used as the basis for the aircraft's design. The Stuka, an ab-

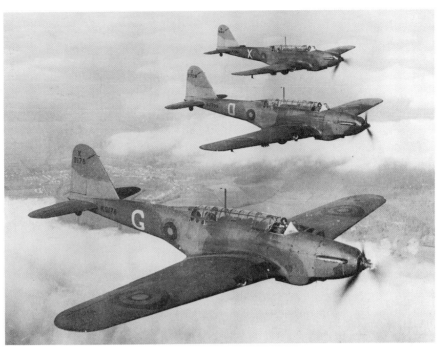

Above left: Three Ju-87 Stukas in formation wearing prewar markings. The Stuka was to become the most feared aircraft of the early blitzkrieg campaigns. (IWM.HU.54422)

Above centre: Feldmarschall Ehrhard Milch, Deputy Head of the Luftwaffe, inspects Handley Page Heyfords of Nos 99 and 149 Squadrons RAF at Mildenhall, whilst on a courtesy visit to Britain in October 1937. Milch, along with Ernst Udet, did much to prepare the Luftwaffe for the war to come, turning it into a highly efficient force with up-to-date equipment, unlike the RAF, which began the war with some atrocious aircraft and an incoherent strategy. (IWM.HU.58770)

Above right: Three Fairey Battle light bombers of No. 266 Squadron RAF in formation over RAF Harwell in October 1937. The squadron later fought in France in support of the BEF and took catastrophic losses. (IWM.HU.59532)

breviation of Sturzkampfflugzeug (diving combat aircraft), could carry one 1,102lb and four 110lb bombs and deliver them against enemy targets with a remarkable degree of accuracy. The British and French air forces had nothing like it, the Armée de l'Air refusing to undertake the development of a dive bomber because of 'prohibitive' costs.

On the outbreak of war the RAF did possess a low-level bomber that was earmarked for use against enemy troop formations and local defences, the Fairy Battle. This aircraft was to prove woefully inadequate when first used in 1940. Basically a stretched fighter, with an additional crewman, the Battle was underpowered and unmanoeuvrable, too slow to fend off German fighters; and because the aircraft approached their targets on straight low-level bombing runs, they were extremely vulnerable to anti-aircraft fire. After terrible losses in the first weeks of the campaign, when it was not uncommon for Fairy Battle squadrons to take over 50 percent casualties in any one attack, the aircraft was withdrawn from front-line service.

However, apart from a lead in dive bomber technology, the Germans were in no better position as regards the quality of their equipment when compared to the arsenals of Britain, France and Russia. Only against Poland did the Wehrmacht have a considerable technological edge. The German panzers used from 1939-41 were undergunned and underarmoured when compared with the likes of the British Matilda, the French Char B and the Russian KV-1. When a Soviet delegation visited Germany in the mid-1930s and were shown tank production facilities, they refused to believe their hosts when they were shown the PzKpfw IV and were told it was the most powerful tank in the German armoury.

Only in fire control equipment, and in inter-tank radio communication did the Germans have a significant advantage. Neither was it the total number of armoured vehicles in the Wehrmacht that gave the Germans their advantage in blitzkrieg warfare. On mobilisation in August 1939 it was found that panzer battalions had barely enough vehicles to equip three of their four tank companies. Consequently the fourth company were left behind at their depots. Both in the invasion of France in 1940 and of Russia in 1941, the Wehrmacht possessed fewer mechanised combat vehicles than did its opponents. The German advantage lay not in what equipment they possessed but in the way they used it on the battlefield.

Since the formation of the first panzer divisions in 1935 twice-yearly Wehrmacht manoeuvres had been held to refine the new formations and define their battlefield role. The insistence by Guderian that all German tanks be fitted with radios helped considerably in the forging of this new

weapon and was to give the units a significant advantage over their enemy equivalents. In the autumn manoeuvres of 1937, at which Hitler and Mussolini were present, the Wehrmacht's three panzer divisions were used in co-ordinated fashion for the first time. The divisions, allocated to 'Blue Army' under the command of General von Rundstedt, successfully outflanked the opposing 'Red Army', creating havoc in their rear areas. The Führer, suitably impressed with the display, ordered the continuing expansion of the panzer arm.

By January 1939 the Wehrmacht had at its disposal five panzer divisions and four motorised divisions. Earlier experiments in mechanisation had tended to suggest that the light divisions, with their single tank battalion, were not 'heavy' enough to constitute a breakthrough force, nor were they particularly effective when used in a traditional cavalry role. For the Polish campaign each division was strengthened by the addition of either one or two extra panzer battalions from the hitherto independent panzer brigades. Even these reinforcements were not enough to significantly improve the light divisions' battlefield performance and before the invasion of France in 1940 they were converted into panzer divisions, the 1st, 2nd, 3rd and 4th Light Divisions becoming the 6th, 7th, 8th and 9th Panzer Divisions respectively.

The infantry divisions to which the independent brigades would have been

Left, top: Adolf Hitler shows off the Wehrmacht to his visiting guest Benito Mussolini during the autumn manoeuvres of 1937. These exercises saw the army's three panzer divisions operate together in a coordinated fashion for the first time. (IWM.HU.3902)

Left, centre: A horse artillery battery changes position during the Wehrmacht autumn exercise of 1936. (IWM.HU.54958)

Left, bottom: A well-camouflaged platoon of infantry lies in wait in a cabbage field during the Wehrmacht autumn exercises of 1936. (IWM.HU.54959)

assigned in time of war, to provide much needed support, were thus left without any tanks at all.

It had been hoped that new Sturm-artillerie batteries would be ready to fill this gap but due to production difficulties they were not to see action until 1940. These units, under the control of the Artillery, not the Panzer Corps, were made up of turretless assault guns based on the PzKpfw III chassis. Nicknamed the StuG, an abbreviation of their full title Sturmgeschutz III, they were armed with the same 75mm howitzer as was carried by the PzKpfw IV and when used in France provided much-needed fire support. However, for the Polish campaign infantry divisions had to make do with their own integral infantry guns which had to be manhandled into forward positions.

All the effort put into developing the panzer arm into an offensive weapon *par excellence* during the late 1930s did not mean that the Wehrmacht overlooked the possibility of having to fight a defensive battle. However, here the German high command did not concur with Allied theorists, proponents of static defence such as the French Minister of War André Maginot.

General Wilhelm Ritter von Leeb, the architect of German defensive strategy, in his 1938 book *Die Abwehr,* was of the opinion that 'Operative defence must meet the threat of offence by using the same weapons and the

Right, top: A platoon of PzKpfw I tanks moves forward during the Wehrmacht autumn manoeuvres of 1936. It is interesting to note that the tanks appear to be armed only with a single machine gun, indicating that these may be prototype vehicles. (IWM.HU.54960)

Right, centre: A field gun prepares to fire during Wehrmacht exercises along the river Werra during 1936. (IWM.HU.54951)

Right, bottom: The commander of an infantry section keeps a sharp look-out for the 'enemy' during Wehrmacht exercises along the river Werra in 1936. (IWM.HU.54950)

same means. The stronger and more mobile are its land and air formations the better it can face a mobile enemy utilising the element of surprise.' So for both the offensive and defensive, mobility was the primary factor in German strategy.

The concepts of the bold advance and the envelopment of the enemy, both encapsulated in blitzkrieg theory, were not new to the German Army. Since the 1860s the emerging Germany faced the constant danger of a war on two fronts. Thus a mobile army and a quick victory (to enable German forces to switch fronts and face each set of opponents on at least equal terms) were vital components of military strategy. The German Vernicht-ungsgedanke (annihilation concept) and Kesselschlacht (cauldron battle) both had their roots in the wars of German unification.

In 1866 the Austro-Hungarian Empire was defeated in just six weeks through the aggressive use of mobility and the rapid concentration of force at the battle of Königgratz. Four years later the French field army was trapped against the German frontier at Sedan and forced to surrender in another classic enveloping movement. The Schlieffen Plan of 1914 once again sought a quick decisive victory through the outflanking of the French Army. Although the plan failed and the war turned into a long battle of attrition, the intention to encircle and annihilate was clear.

The blitzkrieg used these established techniques but in a different way. The German Army, instead of attempting to outflank the enemy and envelop him, destroying his forces on the field of battle, sought to use the weight and velocity of the panzer divisions to break through the enemy line and head for objectives deep in the enemy rear. Instead of aiming to physically destroy the enemy force, blitzkrieg sought to destroy the enemy's ability and will to

fight, through the paralysis of his command and control systems.

The decisive weapons in this new style of warfare were of course the massed tanks of the panzer divisions. Attacking in a wedge (kiel) formation no more than 5,000 yards wide and deployed in two waves (treffen) or wings (flügeln), the speed and weight of their attack took them through the enemy's defended zone. They then accelerated towards their strategic objectives, deep in the enemy's rear.

The rest of the division's units would follow the panzerkeil through the gap they had created. Motorcycle and armoured car reconnaissance units would then quickly motor ahead to locate the route of least resistance for the formation to take. The motor rifle battalions would follow closely behind the tanks, ready to deal with isolated pockets of resistance along the divisional centre line and to hold selected areas of ground. Motorised artillery would follow ready to give fire sup-

Right, top: A group of infantrymen rest after becoming 'casualties' during a Wehrmacht winter exercise in 1937. Each soldier wears a coloured band round his helmet (either red or blue) indicating which 'side' he is on. The officer with the white band round his cap is an exercise umpire. (IWM.HU.20721)

Right, centre: An artillery battery disembarks from its train transport during an exercise in West Thuringia, 1937. (IWM.HU.54962)

Right, bottom: Men of the 15th Infantry Division on the banks of the river Werra during the Wehrmacht autumn exercises of 1937. (IWM.HU.54967)

Far right, top: An anti-tank battery from a motorised infantry division crosses a bridge built by the 9th Infantry Division during Wehrmacht exercises near Kreuzburg, 1937. (IWM.HU.54965)

Far right, centre: A group of SS infantrymen exercise on the army training ground at Königsbruck, near Dresden, autumn 1937. (IWM.HU.8521)

Far right, bottom: Men of the SS Signals Battalion on a line-laying exercise in 1938. The SS as well as the army fully realised the vital role that efficient communications would play in any future war and Heinrich Himmler ensured they were given the best equipment available. The SS Signals Battalion took part in the invasion of Poland as part of Panzerverband Kempf. (IWM.HU.8361)

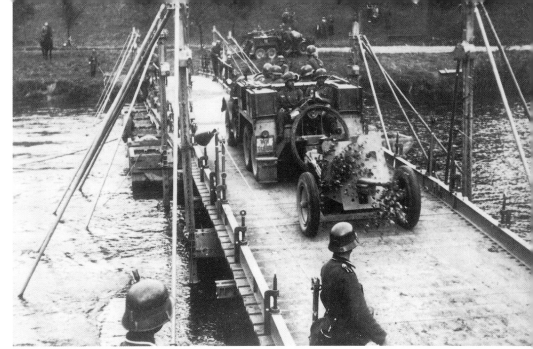

port to the advancing armour or infantry units. Anti-tank guns would be deployed to provide flank screens for the divisional advance as protection against enemy tank counter-attack.

The divisional commander would be located well forward, just behind the lead rank of the panzerkeil in his armoured command vehicle. This had the advantage of enabling him to view the attack as it developed, making real-time battlefield decisions. Revisions to already issued orders could be quickly transmitted via the various radio nets operated by the formation, enhancing the flexibility and mobility of the panzer division yet further. The axis of attack of an entire division could be changed in a matter of minutes; for the Allies this sort of manoeuvre would have taken hours to complete.

This reliance on verbal, as opposed to written, orders and the use of the individual initiative of the battlefield commander (down to a very junior level) was known in the Wehrmacht as Auftragstaktik and made the panzer division a very formidable formation indeed. An officer would be given a battlefield objective and when this was achieved, by whatever means the commander on the spot thought best, another would be issued verbally by his

superior. These 'saddle orders' meant that the panzer division could stay on the move, never having to wait for written directions from higher command.

The first to be on the receiving end of this audacious new strategy was the Polish Army in September 1939. Brave but badly equipped and with an out-of-date military doctrine, they were defeated in the briefest of campaigns. As Britain, France and Russia were to find out, blitzkrieg warfare was equally successful against the leading European powers. It was only the over-confi-

Above and below: Pak 35/36 anti-tank guns on exercise in the summer of 1939. The 37mm gun, which became known as 'the Wehrmacht's door knocker' during Operation Barbarossa, due to its inability to knock out the newer types of Soviet tank, played a vital role in shoring up the flanks of the panzer divisions as they smashed through the enemy lines. Polish, British, French and Russian tank crews were all to fall into the trap of driving head-on into anti-tank gun screens in the early blitzkrieg operations. Not too many survived to try such foolish tactics again. (IWM.STT.62/MH.13403)

dence of Hitler in the military capabilities of the Wehrmacht and the timely arrival of the United States into the war that averted the unthinkable, a Nazi-dominated Europe

CHAPTER THREE

The Attack on Poland, 1939

The Polish Army and Its Defensive Strategy

The Polish Army that faced the might of the Wehrmacht in September 1939 was born out of the struggle for independence that began in 1918. The war had seen Polish troops fighting against the forces of Imperial Germany and Bolshevik Russia. Poland's independence was finally guaranteed after two years of bloody conflict, when in 1920 General Josef Pilsudski's forces defeated Tukhachevsky's Bolsheviks at the gates of Warsaw itself. As a result, the interwar Polish Army closely reflected the organisational and tactical pattern adopted during this period.

Well-led Polish cavalry had been instrumental in throwing back the Red Army and so they understandably held an important position in the armed forces' order of battle. Although armoured cars, aircraft and machine guns had all been used in the conflict, not enough of them had been present on the battlefield to significantly affect the war's outcome. Thus the Polish generals of the interwar years were confident that an army based on the traditional infantry division, supported by fast-moving cavalry brigades, would perform well on the battlefield.

The generals were not so naive as to believe that the Polish Army would be able to defeat a rearmed Germany by themselves if a new war broke out. Poland was a very poor country with little in the way of heavy industry. To equip the Polish Army with one German-style panzer division would have

cost more than the entire annual defence budget. Instead it was hoped that the Polish Army could hold out for a long enough period to enable Britain and France to organise and launch major offensives against Germany's western border which would then relieve pressure on the eastern front.

Pilsudski, who headed the Polish military government from 1926 until his death in 1935, moulded the army into an efficient but outdated warfighting machine. Efforts were made in the interwar years to modernise tactics; for example, mounted charges were discouraged for attacks on foot and the lance was relegated to training and parade use from 1934 onwards, but not enough was done to ensure that the Polish Army could operate effectively on the modern battlefield. In 1936 members of the 'Colonel's Regime' that had succeeded Pilsudski's dictatorship, alarmed at the rapid growth of the Wehrmacht, at last ordered a commission to examine the condition of the armed forces and the role they would have to play in any future conflict. The commission recommended the mechanisation of four cavalry brigades, a rapid expansion of the field artillery and the tank force, and priority effort to build up the numbers of anti-tank and anti-aircraft guns in use. Due to the limited defence budget the modernisation programme was to be phased in and was not due for completion until 1942.

By 1939 one mechanised cavalry brigade was fully formed (the 10th or

'Black Brigade', so-called because of the black leather trenchcoats worn by the unit) and another was being raised. A further three independent battalions of light tanks had been formed and the Polish Army had adopted and added to its inventory the Bofors 37mm anti-tank gun, a very potent weapon against the relatively thinly armoured German panzers. In addition the Polish infantry had been issued with a home-produced anti-tank rifle which was to add further to their defensive capability.

Unfortunately, however, these improvements were too little, too late; and the Polish Army of 1939 was quickly defeated by an enemy superior in all respects except for the bravery of the individual soldier.

The backbone of the Polish Army in 1939 was its 30 active infantry divisions. These were numbered from 1 to 55, 30 of which were active at any one time, the other fifteen being held in cadre status ready for mobilisation in time of war (the 21st and 22nd Divisions were active units designated Mountain Divisions and allocated to the defence of the Carpathians in southern Poland). An active infantry division was made up of three infantry regiments, each of three battalions, an artillery regiment of two battalions of French or Polish 75mm field guns and one battalion of 100mm howitzers (these 100mm guns, mostly of Czech origin were being replaced by Polish-manufactured 105mm and 155mm pieces when the war began), a reconnaissance battalion, an anti-aircraft

company and a signals company. In addition to these divisions there were several independent infantry brigades (at least three of which were designated Mountain Brigades) each of one or two regiments.

Each infantry battalion consisted of three rifle companies, one heavy weapons company, an anti-tank company, a cannon platoon, a signals platoon and an engineer platoon. Each rifle company contained nine light machine guns (these were in fact automatic rifles similar to the United States Army's BAR) and three 46mm mortars. The heavy weapons company had twelve heavy machine guns and two French 81mm mortars. The anti-tank company possessed nine Bofors 37mm anti-tank guns and the cannon platoon two ancient Russian 75mm field guns for infantry support. The total paper strength of an infantry regiment was 1,450 officers and men. All transport and artillery in an infantry division was horse-drawn.

Supporting the infantry in their operations were eleven cavalry brigades, considered to be the elite of the army. Each brigade consisted of three or four cavalry regiments, a reconnaissance squadron of thirteen TK/TKS tankettes and eight W2.29/W2.34 armoured cars, a battery of 75mm pack artillery, a signals squadron and an engineer squadron. Each regiment had three or four rifle squadrons, a machine-gun squadron of twelve machine guns and an anti-tank troop of four Bofors 37mm guns. The total strength of a regiment was somewhere between 720 and 875 sabres depending on the number of squadrons in the formation.

The modern mechanised and motorised cutting edge of the Polish Army was formed by the 10th Mechanised

Cavalry Brigade and two independent motorised infantry brigades. The 10th Mechanised Cavalry Brigade consisted of two battalions of 7-TP tanks (an upgraded Polish version of the British Vickers six-ton tank) one battalion of French-built Renault R-35 light tanks, two scout tankette companies (one TK and one TKS), an independent Vickers light tank company and three companies of obsolescent French Renault FT-17 light tanks of First World War vintage. Each 7-TP battalion contained 49 tanks, the R-35 battalion 45 tanks. The Vickers light tank company and

each FT-17 company consisted of seventeen armoured vehicles, whilst each scout company had thirteen tankettes. Each motorised infantry brigade consisted of two lorried infantry regiments plus two TK/TKS tankette companies and at least one of them appears to have had a Vickers light tank company attached.

In addition there were eleven independent tankette companies attached to various infantry divisions and three independent tankette companies attached to higher-level formations. The partially formed mechanised cavalry

Left: A Polish infantry regiment on the march.

Right: A regiment of Polish Lancers on exercise in July 1939. For the actual invasion troopers took to the field without their lances, carrying only a sabre and carbine. (IWM.HU.40880)

Left: Two TKS tankettes captured by German forces during the opening stages of the invasion of Poland. These vehicles formed the bulk of Poland's armoured forces at the outbreak of hostilities and were no match even for the Wehrmacht's lightest of tanks. (IWM.MH.I8246)

brigade was titled the Warsaw Mechanised Brigade and took part in the defence of the capital. It consisted of one 7-TP light tank and two TKS tankette companies, of seventeen and thirteen vehicles per company respectively.

The Polish defence budget only allowed for a maximum of 280,000 men under arms in peacetime. In 1939 the Polish Army consisted of some 204,600 conscripts, 16,000 regular officers and 30,000 regular non-commissioned officers. Because of these manpower restrictions even the active infantry divisions were below strength. It was hoped, however, that there would be sufficient notice of a German attack to allow reservists to bring these units up to their full establishment. These would hold the line until reinforced by the fifteen reserve divisions, which would have to be virtually created from scratch, only small cadres for these units being in existence in peacetime.

The third and final line of defence would be provided by the National Guard, made up of reservists who had not been allocated places in the reserve divisions, large numbers of men who had been surplus to draft requirements and those not subject to conscription (men under 21 or over 52 years of age). There were eleven brigades altogether, one of which was a naval brigade assigned to help in the defence of Gdynia.

As it was, the German blitzkrieg was so swift that many of the National Guard brigades were unformed even by the end of the war and most of the reserve divisions were defeated before they were able to take the field at full strength. Even the active divisions found themselves fighting with reduced numbers as the speed of the panzer divisions and the air superiority of the Luftwaffe prevented many of those called up from ever joining their units.

The Polish Air Force was organised not as a separate arm of service but as a

A Polish PZL P-37 Los (Elk) bomber on an airstrip during the invasion. The Elk was the most modern aircraft in the Polish armoury; 61 were in service in September 1939 and put up a good showing in the campaign. Behind it can be seen a line of PZL P-IIs, the most numerous fighter in the Polish Air Force and no match for German Me-I09 and Me-II0 aircraft. (IWM.HU.4044)

A Polish horse artillery battery on the move in central Poland, 4 September 1939.

branch of the army. In total there were some 935 aircraft in service at the outbreak of the war. However, only 450 of these were allocated to bomber and fighter squadrons, the rest being given over to reconnaissance or liaison roles. Of these only 159 bombers and 154 fighters were fit for front-line service on 1 September 1939. Most of them were aircraft of the PS P-11 type, that is, high-wing monoplanes with non-retractable under-carriages. They proved to be no match for the German Me-109s and Me-110s, which quickly gained air supremacy over most of Poland.

The Polish Navy contributed an infantry division for the defence of Gdynia and the Hela peninsula in northern Poland. This was made up of two regular naval infantry battalions, a further two battalions of reservists, a National Guard brigade and several *ad hoc* units of naval personnel hastily assigned infantry duties. This formation performed remarkably well, denying German forces the use of the Polish ports for the majority of the campaign.

During peacetime the Polish Army was not formally organised at anything higher than divisional level. On general mobilisation the three permanent headquarters staffs in existence at Torun, Wilna and Lwow would become the basis for any army commands that might arise, depending upon which strategic plan was adopted.

When the Polish Army finally began to mobilise in the last days of August, it was organised into six armies and a seventh 'group' consisting of a varying number of infantry divisions, cavalry brigades and independent units. These formations were strung out in a horseshoe shape covering German approach routes into Poland from the north, west and south. Each formation took its name from the area to which it was assigned.

The Narew Group, under the command of Brigadier General C. Mlot-Fijalkowski, consisted of two infantry divisions and two cavalry brigades protecting north-east Poland and Polish Lithuania from German attacks from East Prussia.

To its west the Modlin Army of two infantry divisions and two cavalry brigades commanded by Brigadier General E. Przedzymirski-Krukowicz sought to defend the direct route from East Prussia south to Warsaw, via the towns of Mlawa and Modlin.

On its left the Pomorze (Pomeranian) Army of five infantry divisions and a cavalry brigade, commanded by Major General W. Bortnowski, was stationed in the Pomeranian corridor. In a position to be potentially attacked from two sides, it was fully realised that the army could do nothing more than put up a token resistance. It was then immediately to retire south-eastwards where it would reinforce the Modlin Army defending the road to Warsaw and cover the northern flank of the Poznan Army as it fell back towards the Vistula.

The Poznan Army of four infantry divisions and two cavalry brigades, commanded by Major General T.

Kutrzeba, lay to the south of the Pomeranian corridor, north and south of the city of Poznan, on both sides of the Warta river. It was positioned both to defend the city itself and the vital Berlin to Warsaw railway line running through it.

Further to the south-east lay the Lodz Army of Major General J. Rommel. Made up of five infantry divisions and two cavalry brigades, it, along with the Krakow Army, defended the most likely route of attack across the central Polish plain towards Warsaw.

The Krakow Army, commanded by Brigadier General A. Szylling, was positioned to the left of the Lodz Army and contained seven infantry divisions, two of which were mountain divisions, one cavalry brigade and the 10th Mechanised Brigade. The largest of the Polish armies, it had the triple role of defending the industrial centre of Krakow, the plains to the north and west of the city and the mountains to its south-west.

The smallest army, the Karpaty (Carpathian) Army, commanded by Major General K. Fabrycy, consisted of only the 1st, 2nd and 3rd Independent Mountain Brigades. It defended the mountain passes from Slovakia into southern Poland. Two infantry divisions from the general reserve were earmarked to join this army as soon as hostilities broke out.

The remainder of the active infantry divisions and independent infantry brigades, along with a cavalry brigade and the partially formed mechanised brigade, were assigned to the general reserve. This was stationed in two zones immediately to the north-east and north-west of Warsaw and in the city itself.

The fifteen reserve divisions were raised all over the country, generally grouped around centres of population. For example, two reserve divisions were raised in the south-eastern city of Lwow. Many of these units had little time to organise before their recruiting areas were overrun and the divisional cadres dispersed or captured.

The Polish Plan of Campaign

At a strategic level the Polish Army faced a tremendous problem in organising a viable defence of the 1,750-mile common frontier with Nazi Germany and her Slovak ally. The border surrounded Poland on three sides, making the planning doubly difficult.

The Poles, faced with the choice of either opting for a forward defence or abandoning most of outlying Poland and taking up a stronger central stance with much shorter interior lines of communication, opted for the seemingly weaker strategy.

Plan 'Z' (Zachod = West in Polish), the strategy for defending Poland against a German invasion, was finalised in March 1939. By concentrating opposite the expected German lines of advance, the Polish Army planned to stage a fighting withdrawal towards the capital using the numerous rivers of central Poland as natural defence lines. It was hoped that using these tactics Poland could stay in the war for as long as six months before being overcome by weight of numbers. This strategy, acknowledged by the Polish High Command to be a weak one, played straight into German hands. The German panzer forces, having pierced the first line of defence, were able to roam the interior at will, encircling the much slower-moving Polish infantry divisions.

In addition the Poles assumed that the ideological rift between Hitler and Stalin was so wide as to preclude any effective cooperation between them in the occupation of their homeland. Unfortunately the Nazi–Soviet non-aggression pact, signed on 23 August, contained just such a provision. In a secret protocol to the treaty the two leaders decided that should Germany invade Poland, Russian troops would attack from the east and the country be divided between the two dictators along the line of the river Bug.

With only limited military resources, the Polish Army was forced to concentrate virtually all of its troops against the German invasion and when the Red Army attacked on 17 September an already dire military situation became a hopeless one.

To be fair to the Polish High Command, it had little option but to adopt a forward strategy. The outlying regions of Poland, particularly those in the east and the Pomeranian corridor, were where large numbers of Poles of German ethnicity lived. Abandoning these areas to the Nazis without a fight would have undermined Poland's claim to the region. In addition most of Poland's heavy industry and raw materials came from the border areas, particularly around Krakow in the south-west of the country. So for both economic and political reasons Poland was forced to adopt this less than perfect strategy.

There were no major natural defence lines in these border areas with the exception of the Carpathian mountains in the south of the country. The rivers running through central Poland, such as the Vistula and the Bzura, were obstacles of a sort, although throughout the summer months water levels were low and they were fordable at many different places. To bolster these natural defences the Polish Army sought to build pre-prepared earthworks and concrete bunkers along projected invasion routes. On 1 September fortifications existed along the Narew river north-east of Warsaw; in the vicinity of Mlawa along the direct route from East Prussia to the capital; at the base of the Pomeranian Corridor along the Vistula; at the towns of Bydgoszcz (Bromberg) and Torun (Thorn); west of Lodz along the Warta river; about the towns of Katowice and Czestochowa to the west and north-west of Krakow; and in the mountains to the south of the city along the Slovakian border. In the main these fortifications consisted of earthen entrenchments, barbed wire obstacles and tank traps. Only in a few areas such as the defences around Mlawa were they of a more solid concrete construction with pillboxes and gun emplacements. On the whole these defences were little more than a minor nuisance for the Wehrmacht, who were able in most cases to use the superior mobility of their motorised and panzer forces to outflank the positions. The Polish Army placed most of its hopes on a rapid intervention

Polish infantry at gas mask drill, near Warsaw, 1 September 1939.

against Germany's western frontier by the French, who promised to launch a major offensive within two weeks of their declaration of war.

The High Command, with some justification, felt that man for man the Polish soldier was every bit as good as his German counterpart and that the campaign would drag on for much longer than the Wehrmacht had planned for.

The Polish soldier was brave, patriotic and well trained, non-commissioned and junior commissioned officers having to undergo regular refresher courses in all aspects of military training. Where it all came unstuck was that they were well trained to fight the wrong sort of war. There was no higher command staff training and virtually all the higher level commanders

had obtained their staff experience in the old German, Austro-Hungarian or Russian imperial armies. Pilsudski had always emphasised the use of initiative at all levels in the fledgling Polish Army. In this manner it had been able to defeat a much larger but much more rigid Bolshevik force. As a result of these successes very little was done in the interwar years to modernise the higher command echelons of the Polish Army. The war of independence of 1918–20 had seemingly proved to them that the old ways were still the best.

Polish intelligence was remarkably accurate (the Poles had cracked the early version of Enigma as early as 1933) and although information declined somewhat after 1938 they were still able to gauge to within ten or so divisions the total number of units ar-

rayed against them, correctly assessing that this would include five panzer divisions and guessing their intended avenues of attack.

Nevertheless, the Germans, through speed of manoeuvre and air superiority, were able to unravel the Polish plans within two or three days of the opening of the campaign. Brave and determined the Poles may have been but without the technology to compete with the blitzkrieg they were doomed to a rapid and disastrous defeat.

Virtually all of the Polish Army's transport and artillery was horse-drawn. The cavalry were seen as the elite, able to recruit the best officers and non-commissioned officers. Modern weapons of war, such as the tank and aircraft, were sadly neglected, with emphasis firmly being placed on the foot soldier as the backbone of the armed forces. The 1936 commission, alarmed at the rapid growth of the German Army, sought to remedy these deficiencies but it was all too little, too late. Perhaps the Polish Army's most damning fault was its woeful lack of modern signalling equipment.

The Wehrmacht and Its Plan of Campaign

Fall Weiss (Case White), the German strategy for the invasion of Poland, first began to take shape immediately following the issuing of the annual armed forces directive of 3 April 1939. In it the Führer had decreed that a plan of attack be prepared in case he decided to settle the dispute with Poland by force.

The German High Command planning staff headed by Field Marshal Walther von Brauchitsch adopted a classic Vernichtungsgedanke strategy. The Polish field armies would be encircled in a vast pincer movement, linking up east of Warsaw, and then annihilated in a traditional Kesselschlacht (cauldron) battle. The pincers themselves would be made up of two army

groups, Army Group North, commanded by Generaloberst Fedor von Bock, advancing into Poland from German Pomerania and East Prussia, and Army Group South, commanded by Generaloberst Gerd von Rundstedt, advancing from German Silesia and Slovakia.

After inspection and approval of the strategy by Adolf Hitler on 26/27 April the headquarters staffs of von Bock and von Rundstedt were set up to formulate lower-level planning. In this they were ably assisted by their Chiefs of Staff, Hans von Salmuth (Army Group North) and Erich von Manstein (Army

Field Marshal Walther von Brauchitsch (right), Commander in Chief of the German Army, and General Franz Halder, Chief of the General Staff, discuss the plan to invade Poland. (IWM.MH.13141)

Group South). After consultation with the commanders, the plan was finally completed at the end of May. The Luftwaffe and German Navy were consulted and asked to prepare plans to support the ground offensive. These were finalised and coordinated with the Army's plan by 20 July.

Army Group North was to consist of two armies, the Third, based in East Prussia and commanded by General Georg von Küchler; and the Fourth, based in German Pomerania and commanded by General Gunther von Kluge. The Third Army was given the primary task of driving south along the most direct route from the Reich to the Polish capital.

Its I Corps, consisting of the 11th and 61st Infantry Divisions, along with the divisional armoured Kampfgruppe Panzerverband Kempf (named after its commander), would lead the assault. They had the difficult task of forcing a passage through the Polish defence at Mlawa and opening the road to Modlin and Warsaw. Following behind I Corps was the 127th Infantry Division, initially allocated to Army Reserve. On their immediate left lay Corps Wodrig, another *ad hoc* formation consisting of the 1st and 12th Infantry Divisions. They were also to push south to Warsaw covering the flank of I Corps and fending off any interference to the main thrust from the Polish Narew Group to the north-east. It was envisaged that as the army got nearer to the city it would be joined by elements of the Fourth Army attacking eastwards from the base of the Pomeranian corridor. To assist them, XXI Corps of the Third Army, consisting of the 21st and 228th Infantry Divisions, was to attack from south-west East Prussia along the eastern bank of the Vistula river, which formed the main defensive obstacle at the base of the Pomeranian corridor. By seizing river crossings at important towns such as Grudziadz (Graudenz), XXI Corps would be assisting the advance of Fourth Army from the west and perhaps forcing a precipitate withdrawal from the Pomeranian corridor itself.

The final corps of Third Army was really a corps in name only. An *ad hoc* formation, Corps Brand (named after its commander) consisted of numerous frontier guard units organised into a brigade-sized kampfgruppe named Brigade Loetzen and a German cavalry brigade.

The PzKpfw III Ausf D command tank of General Kempf, the commander of Panzerverband Kempf, during the invasion. This armoured formation supported Third Army's attack from East Prussia. Note the dummy main armament and the frame aerial mounted around the engine deck. (IWM.HU.8074)

Its task was to hold the frontier between the left flank of Corps Wodrig and the frontier with Lithuania. As a precaution in case the Narew Group attempted a cross-border assault, the 206th Infantry Division of Third Army Reserve was positioned to its immediate rear. In the event that Polish forces displayed no aggressive intent, the infantry division was to be reassigned and the cavalry brigade was to push south into Poland, acting as a screen for the left flank of Corps Wodrig.

Two other independent units operating in the Third Army area were assigned strategic roles for the invasion. A regiment of assault engineers named Kampfgruppe Medem was to advance westwards from East Prussia towards Danzig and seize the vital river crossing at Tczew (Dirschau). At the same time Brigade Kampfgruppe Eberhard was to seize control of the city itself. This unit was pre-positioned in the Baltic port, which was an internationally guaranteed free city garrisoned by both Polish and German soldiers. The small garrison, complemented by armed police and an SS Heimwehr battalion, formed the kampfgruppe. The SS unit was made up of a cadre of Nazi Party officials and SS soldiers, brought up to strength with loyal Danzig citizens armed with modern infantry weapons and even a few 37mm anti-tank guns and Austrian-built armoured cars.

The Fourth Army assembled in German Pomerania to the west of the Polish corridor (the stretch of land between the Baltic coast and central Poland). Three of its five corps, II, III and XIX Panzer, were earmarked for an assault across the base of the corridor; they would then turn south-east towards Warsaw, linking up with elements of the Third Army along the way. The cutting edge of the attacking force was XIX Panzer Corps, commanded by General Heinz Guderian. Consisting of the 2nd and 20th Motorised Divisions and the 3rd Panzer Division (just before the beginning of the campaign this unit was bolstered by the addition of the Panzer Lehr training/demonstration battalion), it formed the northernmost corps of Fourth Army. In the centre was II Corps, made up of the 3rd and 32nd Infantry Divisions and on its right was III Corps, consist-

The driver of a staff car belonging to an infantry battalion leans over to chat to the driver of a SdKfz 221 armoured car; they are no doubt debating how long the traffic hold-up will continue. In the opening phase of the offensive into Poland jams such as this were not uncommon, as units waited their turn to press on into the Polish interior. (IWM.HU.39997)

ing of the 50th Infantry Division and an *ad hoc* infantry kampfgruppe, Brigade Netze.

Two German frontier guard commands, normally responsible for border protection, were converted into corps headquarters for the campaign and attached to the Fourth Army. The 1st Frontier Command, responsible for the German border from the Baltic to the northern flank of XIX Panzer Corps, had the 207th Infantry Division under its command along with numerous frontier guard units. The division was to strike eastwards across the northern end of the Polish corridor to Danzig, bottling up the Polish Navy in the port of Gdynia and opening a land corridor from Pomerania to East Prussia.

The 2nd Frontier Command positioned to the south of III Corps had the 208th Infantry Division under its command. Its role was to protect the right flank of the Fourth Army as it advanced into north-central Poland.

The Fourth Army Reserve, consisting of the 23rd, 73rd and 218th Infan-

try Divisions, plus the newly raised 10th Panzer Division, was positioned to the rear of XIX Panzer Corps, ready to exploit any breakthrough or overcome any stubborn pockets of resistance left by the advancing army.

Army Group South consisted of three armies, the Eighth, Tenth and Fourteenth. The Eighth Army under the command of General Johannes Blaskowitz was positioned on the Silesian–Polish border to the north-east of Breslau. Its northernmost formation was X Corps consisting of the 24th, 30th and 183rd Infantry Divisions. Its task was to protect the flank of the main body of Eighth Army as it pushed north-east towards Lodz.

On the immediate right of X Corps lay XIII Corps. This formation, consisting of the 10th and 17th Infantry Divisions plus the SS Motorised Regiment 'Leibstandarte Adolf Hitler', was to attack north-east towards Lodz, widening the breach created by the motorised and panzer divisions of Tenth Army and forming the northern infantry flank guard for the mechanised assault. Following behind XIII Corps were the 213th and 221st Infantry Divisions of Eighth Army Reserve. As the armoured thrust of Tenth Army pushed on into central Poland, infantry divisions of X Corps, XIII Corps and the reserve would be deployed to the flank to ensure that Polish divisions of the Poznan and Lodz Armies could not sever the lines of communication of the advancing motorised and panzer formations.

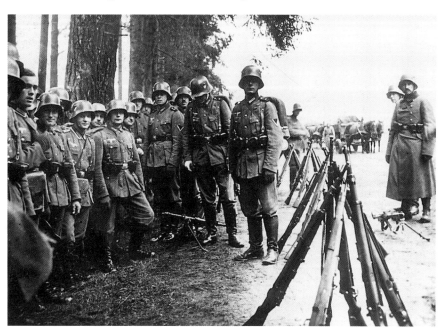

Men of the 19th Infantry Division wait to move across the border into Poland, 1 September 1939. (IWM.HU.42971)

To the south-east of the Eighth Army lay Tenth Army, commanded by General Walther von Reichenau. This formation contained the highest ratio of motorised and panzer units of all the German field armies. It was to be used to smash a hole through the Polish defences and then push on north-eastwards through central Poland to Warsaw. Its cutting edge was provided by XIV and XV Motorised and XVI Panzer Corps.

The northernmost corps of Tenth Army, XI Corps, was, however, an all-infantry formation consisting of the 18th and 19th Infantry Divisions. It assembled on the Polish border almost due east of Breslau. Like XIII Corps of Eighth Army, its role was to widen the breach created by the mechanised units and overcome any stubborn centres of resistance that might be left in the wake of the advance.

On the right flank of XI Corps sat XVI Panzer Corps, commanded by General Erich Hoepner. This powerful formation, consisting of the 1st and 4th Panzer Divisions and the 14th and 31st Infantry Divisions, formed the vanguard of the main thrust into southern Poland. The panzer units were to smash through the Polish defences and then push on with all speed towards Warsaw. The two infantry divisions would follow in their wake, establishing a secure breach in the line and mopping up centres of resistance that might hamper the advance of the following units, and possibly sever lines of communication with the leading panzer divisions.

Immediately to the rear of XVI Panzer Corps was XIV Motorised Corps, consisting of the 13th and 29th Motorised Divisions, advancing as quickly as possible behind the leading panzers, giving them support and relieving them when fatigue or casualties reduced their combat effectiveness.

Positioned on the right flank of XVI Panzer Corps, IV Corps, consisting of the 4th and 46th Infantry Divisions, had the task of advancing north-east into Poland and taking the strategic town of Czestochowa. This would protect the southern flank of the advancing mechanised forces of the Tenth Army and secure the northern flank of XV Motorised Corps to their south. Positioned behind IV Corps was the 62nd Infantry Division of the Tenth Army Reserve. This could either move north to support the breakthrough of XVI Panzer Corps or east to assist the advance of IV Corps.

To the immediate south of IV Corps lay XV Motorised Corps, consisting of the 2nd and 3rd Light Divisions. These were to advance to the south of the main mechanised thrust, taking a slightly more indirect route towards the Polish capital, via the town of Radom. In this way it was hoped that a significant portion of the defending Polish field army would be bypassed and pocketed between XVI Panzer and XV Motorised Corps.

Positioned directly behind XV Motorised Corps was VII Corps, consisting of the 27th and 68th Infantry Divisions. This formation was initially held as the Army Group South reserve ready to move to the support of any sector of the front. If the initial assault went as planned, the corps was to advance behind XV Motorised Corps and support its advance on Radom.

The Fourteenth Army, commanded by General Wilhelm List, consisted of three corps and was the southernmost army in the German order of battle. Its northernmost corps, the VIII, assembled in southern Silesia, on the east bank of the river Oder, immediately south of XV Motorised Corps of the Tenth Army. The corps was made up of the 8th and 28th Infantry Divisions plus the 5th Panzer Division and the SS Motorised Regiment 'Germania'. Its task was to attack eastwards to the north of the Vistula and then swing to the east of Krakow, linking up with units of the Fourteenth Army advancing from south of the city.

XVII Corps assembled on the short-stretch of Moravian-Polish frontier, except for the 7th Infantry Division

General Catlos, Commander in Chief of the three Slovak infantry divisions that took part in the invasion of Poland, decorates some of his men towards the end of the campaign. Although of strictly limited military use to the Wehrmacht, the Slovaks were useful from a propaganda viewpoint. Their participation enabled Goebbels to declare that the invasion was a joint effort against the Polish aggressor. (IWM.HU.40006)

which was positioned in the extreme north-west of Slovakia at the entrance to the strategically important Jablunka Pass. It was to push north-east through the Carpathian Mountains towards Krakow. It was hoped that this attack would tie down a large proportion of the Krakow Army in the south-west corner of Poland, making the envelopment around Krakow all the more effective.

The southern component of this pincer movement was XXII Panzer Corps, consisting of the 2nd Panzer and 4th Light Divisions, positioned along the Slovak–Polish border, south of Krakow. Although initially these armoured units came under the control of XVII (Mountain) Corps, XXII Panzer Corps headquarters becoming active when the Carpathians had been breached.

The 3rd Mountain Division was to force a passage through the Carpathians for the mechanised units who would then advance northwards to link

up with elements of VIII Corps, encircling Krakow. They would then push on with all speed north-east into the Polish interior.

The other two divisions that made up XVIII Corps, the 1st and 2nd Mountain, would become active several days after the opening of the assault further east along the Slovakian–Polish frontier. They would be joined by three Slovakian infantry divisions operating under direct Wehrmacht control. Their objective was to tie down as many elements as possible of the Karpaty (Carpathian) Army in the border area, leaving them potentially outflanked by the fast-moving XXII Panzer Corps.

As can be seen by the deployment plans of the German Army, the vast majority of Wehrmacht units were still unmechanised and unmotorised, the most numerous mode of transport by far being the horse. Men of the infantry divisions had nothing to rely on but their own two feet to get them and

A PzKpfw I Ausf A motors down a Polish street. This photograph was most probably taken when the invasion was well underway, as the panzer's crew have painted over the white crosses the vehicle began the campaign with. An easy aiming point for Polish anti-tank gunners, the panzer crews either painted over the crosses completely or painted out sections of them to make them less conspicuous. (IWM.MH.I8272)

much of their equipment from A to B. Only the cutting edge of the assault formations were made up of armoured units and even these fell well below establishment strength.

The 1939 panzer division was supposed to contain a total of 562 armoured fighting vehicles, yet the most that could be mustered in any one formation was 328. The PzKpfw III, designed to be the backbone of the panzer force, was at the outbreak of war the least numerous tank in the German arsenal.

The vast majority of the machines making up the striking force of the panzer divisions were PzKpfw Is and IIs intended primarily for training and light reconnaissance work. The total of indigenous tanks in the German Army at 1 September 1939 was 2,977 vehicles, of which 1,445 were PzKpfw Is, 1,223 were PzKpfw Is, 98 were PzKpfw IIIs and 211 were PzKpfw IVs.

These were distributed amongst the armoured formations according to the roles they were expected to play in Fall Weiss. So the 2nd, 4th, 5th and 10th Panzer Divisions each had a total of 328 tanks, each panzer battalion consisting of 6 PzKpfw IVs, 5 PzKpfw IIIs, 33 PzKpfw IIs and 34 PzKpfw Is. The 3rd Panzer Division was made up in the same way but had the advantage of operating with the Panzer Lehr training/demonstration battalion armed with PzKpfw I and II tanks. This unit, although technically not part of the 3rd Panzer Division, fought alongside them and gave an added punch to Guderian's XIX Panzer Corps.

The 1st Panzer Division, spearhead of the main thrust of Tenth Army, itself the most important attacking element of Fall Weiss, possessed a total of 324 tanks, less than the other panzer divisions. However, the armoured balance making up the formation was weighted towards the much more effective PzKpfw IIIs and IVs. Each panzer battalion consisted of 16 PzKpfw IVs, 28 PzKpfw IIIs, 18 PzKpfw IIs and 17 PzKpfw Is. Panzerverband Kempf, the *ad hoc* armoured division allocated to Third Army in East Prussia, possessed little in the way of medium tanks and was woefully below strength, only consisting of Panzer Regiment 7 and the 1st Battalion of Panzer Regiment 10. The tanks, however, were well supported by the SS Motorised Infantry Regiment 'Deutschland', the SS Motorised Artillery Regiment and the SS Signals Battalion.

It was fully realised before the beginning of the campaign that the four light divisions were not heavy enough to perform adequately on the battlefield as blitzkrieg formations. Plans were already in hand to convert them into panzer divisions but as a stop-gap measure the light divisions took the field with their original single panzer battalions, augmented by units previously earmarked for independent use with the infantry divisions, and three newly raised battalions, armed with Czech tanks taken into service after the country's occupation the previous year. Indeed, without these extra tanks and the added manufacturing capability of the Czechoslovak armaments industry, it is doubtful whether Germany would have been able to embark on the road to war at all.

The 2nd and 4th Light Divisions were assigned no extra Czech vehicles and even with an additional panzer battalion barely managed to begin the campaign with 100 tanks each. Of these the majority were PzKpfw IIs, with the remainder being PzKpfw Is and a tiny number of PzKpfw IVs for infantry support. The 3rd Light Division fared a little better, being assigned an extra battalion of 59 Czech PzKpfw 38(t) tanks. Armed with a 37mm gun, they were markedly superior to the PzKpfw II with its 20mm cannon. The 1st Light Division, spearhead of XIV Motorised Corps, was assigned an additional two battalions of Czech-built PzKpfw 35(t) tanks, 112 vehicles in total. These were also armed with 37mm guns and when added to the division's integral panzer battalion (again made up largely of PzKpfw IIs) they provided the corps with the best armoured punch of any of the light divisions.

Vital to the success of Fall Weiss was the gaining and maintaining of air superiority over the battlefield by the Luftwaffe. Two Luftflottes (air-fleets) were assigned to the campaign. The 1st, commanded by General der Flieger Albrecht Kesselring, was to operate in the area of Army Group North, and the 4th, commanded by General der Flieger Alexander Loehr, in the area of Army Group South. The combined total of the air fleets amounted to some 1,300 combat aircraft, including Messerschmitt Me-109 and Me-110 fighters, Ju-87 Stuka and Henschel HS-123 ground attack aircraft, and Heinkel He-111 medium bombers. This was a mighty force when compared to the much smaller Polish Air Force armed with much older aircraft.

A PzKpfw I armoured command tank (Panzerbefehlswagen) of the 7th Panzer Regiment, Panzerverband Kempf, races across country near the Polish town of Siedlce, 11 September 1939. (IWM.HU.8073)

Three Henschel Hs-123 ground attack aircraft in formation over Poland. (IWM.HU.2722)

without orders, outmanoeuvred on all sides and with no overall conception of what was happening in the campaign strategically, would lead to paralysis and a severe drop in morale. Units could be easily surrounded and forced into capitulation for relatively few losses, the essence of blitzkrieg.

With the dislocation of the Polish Army's command structure and the disruption of its lines of supply, the Luftwaffe could turn its attention to battlefield support. Squadrons of Ju-87 Stukas and Henschel HS-123 ground attack aircraft would operate as flying artillery, their speed and manoeuvrability enabling them to keep up with the fastest-moving armoured spearheads. The German panzer formations all contained their own forward observers, situated in the van of the attack in specially modified armoured vehicles. They were able to call up ground attack aircraft whenever enemy defences blocked the path of the advancing panzers. However, until the Luftwaffe had completed its primary missions of gaining air superiority and interdicting enemy reinforcements and supplies, the advancing German armies had to rely on their own integral artillery to overcome any stubborn Polish resistance. It must be remembered that the prime objective of blitzkrieg was to avoid combat whenever possible and seek to infiltrate through enemy positions, always following the line of least resistance.

Thus Luftwaffe battlefield support only became necessary when no other attack option existed. Ground attack aircraft were certainly used in large numbers to facilitate river crossings and the capture of vital road and rail junctions, but these tended to be the occasions when a particular piece of ground had to be taken by the advancing German Army. Only 36 HS-123 aircraft

The Luftwaffe planned to open the campaign with a surprise assault on Polish airfields, destroying their air force on the ground and gaining immediate air superiority. Once this was accomplished, priority would be given to interdiction missions against Polish

lines of communication, troop assembly areas and munitions dumps. By operating in this manner it was hoped that enemy front-line divisions, starved of reinforcements and vital supplies, would crack more easily. The severing of communication between front-line units and rear areas would also have the effect of isolating them from their higher command. The psychological disruption of the Polish forces, left

Men of the 76th Infantry Regiment inspect the unit's first trophy of the campaign, a Bofors 37mm anti-tank gun, captured at 6.00am on 1 September. (IWM.MH.18223)

were assigned to the battlefield support role in the initial stages of the campaign. For the opening of the offensive pre-positioned artillery batteries provided all the fire support needed to enable the advancing panzer formations to break in to the Polish defences.

The Fall of Poland

The campaign opened at 4.34am on 1 September 1939 with an attack by Ju-87 Stukas on the Polish units defending the strategic road bridge at Tczew on the Vistula. The crossing was of vital importance to the Germans who wanted to open a land route between East Prussia and Pomerania, via Danzig, as soon as possible.

Six minutes later the German battle-cruiser *Schleswig-Holstein*, ostensibly on a courtesy visit to Danzig, opened

fire on the Polish barracks in the Westerplatte fortress, adjacent to the harbour.

At the same time thousands of artillery pieces began their bombardments of defensive positions within Poland itself, and infantry formations and panzer units crossed the frontier in the face of sporadic resistance from the Polish Frontier Guard and Police.

The Polish High Command was caught by surprise. Although tension between the countries had been very high for some time, full mobilisation had only been ordered on 30 August. Consequently, many of the units facing the initial onslaught were well below strength, still awaiting reinforcements of reservists.

Adolf Hitler announced the opening of hostilities to the assembled Reichstag in the Berlin Opera House at 10.00am. By this time units of all five German Armies had established

firm footholds in Polish territory. Direct Luftwaffe support for the ground offensive in this opening phase was very limited, due both to a lack of dedicated battlefield support aircraft and the fact that very heavy mist lay over most of northern Poland, preventing operations in support of Army Group North. In many areas this did not clear until nearly midday. The Luftwaffe primary targets, the main Polish airfields in the centre of the country, were not so lucky and wave after wave of German aircraft ceaselessly pounded them. So much so that by the end of the second day of the campaign, Hermann Göring, head of the Luftwaffe, felt able to announce to Hitler that the Polish Air Force had been totally destroyed and air supremacy obtained.

This was a gross miscalculation, as was to become apparent in the days to follow. In fact the Polish Air Force, suspecting a surprise attack, had several days earlier dispersed all of their combat aircraft to emergency airstrips which were not attacked at all by the Luftwaffe. As a consequence, the initial German air attacks only managed to reduce to rubble abandoned airfields and destroy already grounded aircraft.

Not all went well for the Germany Army either. Kampfgruppe Medem failed in its surprise attack on the Tczew bridge. The elite assault engineers that made up the unit were unable to crack the stubborn Polish defenders who, alerted by the Luftwaffe attack on them, managed to place and detonate charges which dropped the bridge into the river.

Brigade Eberhard, the other independent Kampfgruppe nominally under the command of Third Army, achieved its objective much more easily. After a few hours of sporadic fighting, the worst of which centred around a pitched battle for control of the main post office, Danzig was in German hands. The remnants of the Polish garrison retreated into the Westerplatte

Fall Weiss, the German invasion of Poland, 1–14 September 1939.

fortress where they were to hold out until the end of the campaign.

The Third Army offensive from East Prussia initially met with little resistance. This stiffened as the day progressed and by mid-afternoon I Corps' drive south had come to a halt north of Mlawa, the offensive held by the Polish 20th Infantry Division and the Novogrodska Cavalry Brigade.

Corps Wodrig's advance to the east of I Corps met with a little more success but by the end of the day they were heavily engaged by the Polish 8th Infantry Division and Mazowska Cavalry Brigade and were still short of the twenty-five-mile advance expected of them. XXI Corps pushed south-west with more ease, encountering limited resistance from elements of the Polish 4th and 16th Infantry Divisions. By the end of the day they were within artillery range of the town of Grudziadz and its vital bridge across the Vistula.

Fourth Army found its advance into the Pomeranian Corridor less difficult than it might have been. The elements of the Pomorze Army stationed in this area had begun an immediate withdrawal to the base of the corridor on commencement of hostilities. The reserve infantry units being raised in the north and the naval infantry battalions retired to Gdynia and the Hela Peninsula where they began to prepare for a long siege.

Nevertheless, the Pomorska Cavalry Brigade detailed to cover the retreat of the rest of the army performed exceptionally well, the 2nd Motorised Divi-

Right, upper: An ADGZ armoured car of the Danzig SS Heimwehr Battalion during the battle for the Danzig Post Office, 1 September 1939. Fourteen of these ex-Austrian vehicles were used by SS forces in the battle for Danzig, and were later to see plenty of action as anti-partisan patrol vehicles behind the lines in Russia. (IWM.GER.1210)

Right, lower: A group of SS infantrymen from the Motorised Regiment 'Deutschland' pose for the camera in a shell-hole created by the first Polish artillery round fired at them in anger, 1 September 1939. (IWM.HU.8045)

Right, upper: An anti-tank gun team rest next to their Pak 36 guarding a regimental headquarters near Rittel, 2 September 1939. (IWM.MH.18227)

Right, lower: A patrol of the 76th Infantry Regiment threads its way through the Tucheler Forest (on the Fourth Army front) in a captured truck, 3 September 1939. (IWM.MH.18229)

sion of Guderian's XIX Panzer Corps even requesting to withdraw in the face of extreme cavalry pressure! It was from the actions of this gallant cavalry brigade, facing the combined might of the 2nd and 20th Motorised Divisions and the 3rd Panzer Division, that the myth of Polish cavalry charging German tanks grew. The specific incident that led to this claim occurred on the first day of the campaign when the 18th Lancers, part of the Pomorska Brigade, caught a German infantry battalion resting in a large clearing in the centre of a forest in the Pomeranian Corridor. The cavalry, able to launch a surprise sabre charge from close range, virtually wiped out the surprised infantry. Unfortunately for the Poles, as the unit reformed to retire back into the woods, a squadron of German armoured cars appeared from the opposite side of the clearing and began raking the still mounted cavalry with machine-gun fire. The lancers took horrendous casualties, losing their commanding officer, and in the confusion galloped for the nearest cover which took some of them through the formation of armoured cars, hence the claim by their crews that they had in fact been charged by Polish cavalry. Despite the stiff rearguard action put up by the Pomorska Cavalry Brigade, all three corps of Fourth Army were able to advance steadily throughout the first day of the campaign.

On 2 September the first major cracks began to appear in the Polish defences facing the advancing Army Group North. XXI Corps pressed on towards Grudziadz, meeting continually stiffer resistance from the Polish 4th and 16th Infantry Divisions who tried desperately to keep open the line of retreat for the Pomorze Army from the Pomeranian Corridor. Continued shelling of the river crossing made the task even more difficult.

The Pomorze Army had originally intended to make its first major stand behind the line of the river Brda in the centre of the corridor. But with the fast-moving mechanised forces of XIX Panzer Corps already overtaking and destroying the most westerly elements of the Polish 9th Infantry Division, and the main escape route to the east across the Vistula being threatened by the advance of XXI Corps, the phased withdrawal rapidly turned into a hurried retreat, as units attempted to reach the comparative safety of north-eastern Poland.

Another lesson was learnt by Guderian on that same day, namely the danger of advancing too far too fast and leaving the support of the infantry divisions far behind. The 3rd Panzer Division, moving as fast as possible, managed to secure a crossing of the Brda early on 2 September. The formation then pushed on eastwards without waiting for supporting infantry units to catch up. Polish troops, outpaced by the panzer division, then severed their lines of communication, forming a defence line along the river bank. The panzer division, cut off, ran out of fuel and ground to a halt. Luckily the Poles, disorganised through their retreat, were unable to capitalise on the situation and after several hours of hard fighting a route was reopened across the Brda and the panzers were resupplied.

Things initially had not gone too well for I Corps and Corps Wodrig driving south from East Prussia. The Polish 20th Infantry Division and Novogrodska Cavalry Brigade fell back into the concrete emplacements and field defences of Mlawa, and I Corps made no further headway at all, a large number armoured vehicles being lost in vain attempts to batter a way through the defences. Corps Wodrig had more success. By early afternoon units had penetrated the lighter defences to the east of the town and began to push south. Showing the inherent flexibility present in the German command structure, Panzerverband Kempf was immediately detached from I Corps and placed under the command of Corps Wodrig. By early evening the division had shifted its axis of attack and was pressing south round the Mlawa citadel.

Corps Brand, the other *ad hoc* formation in Third Army, had very little to do in the opening phase of the campaign, only having to fend off a half-hearted sortie into East Prussia by the Podlaska Cavalry Brigade of the Narew Group. As a consequence, on the second day of the invasion, the 206th Infantry Division was moved south and placed in the army group reserve while the 1st Cavalry Brigade advanced into Poland, acting as a screening force for the left flank of the now rapidly advancing Corps Wodrig.

By the end of the second day Kampfgruppe Medem had managed to capture Tczew but had been forced to look further south along the Vistula for an intact river bridge.

On 3 September the Polish defences in the north began to collapse and the first significant numbers of prisoners were captured. Corps Wodrig, now with Panzerwerband Kempf at its head, advanced rapidly south, then west, threatening an encirclement of Mlawa itself. This pressure, along with a continued assault on the defences from the 11th and 61st Infantry Divisions, was enough to force an abandonment of the fortifications, and Polish units retreated south-west of the town. Nevertheless, the advance of Corps Wodrig had been too rapid for many of the defenders and some 10,000 men were bottled up in Mlawa and forced to surrender.

The 21st and 228th Infantry Divisions of XXI Corps spent 3 September preparing for a full-scale set-piece attack upon the defenders of Grudziadz. This never materialised as the Poles were forced to withdraw hurriedly southwards by the rapidly approaching XIX Panzer Corps.

The breakthrough by Guderian's formation had by the third day of the

Left, upper: A group of Polish prisoners, including a nurse, captured on 3 September. (IWM.HU.42936)

Left, lower: An SdKfz 6 half-track of the 3rd Panzer Division crosses the Vistula near Gniew, 3 September 1939. (IWM.HU.32127)

campaign turned the Pomorze Army retreat into a rout. By the end of the day units of the 3rd Panzer Division were across the Vistula and had linked up with XXI Corps infantry units. The 2nd and 20th Motorised Divisions, following in the wake of 3rd Panzer, had turned and trapped most of the fleeing infantry units of the Pomorze Army on the west bank of the Vistula between themselves and the advancing infantry divisions of II Corps. Meanwhile the 50th Infantry Division and Kampfgruppe Netze of III Corps had forged eastwards towards Bydgoszcz and the junction of the Brda and Vistula rivers, ensuring that Polish units could not retreat south and link up with the Poznan Army By the end of the third day of the campaign some 15,000 prisoners had been taken by the Fourth Army and the 9th, 15th and 27th Polish Infantry Divisions effectively destroyed. A route across the Pomeranian Corridor had been opened, a pontoon bridge having been completed across the Vistula at Gniew, and the 10th Panzer Division (formerly of the Fourth Army general reserve) was in the process of moving across the corridor to join Third Army in its push south to the Polish capital.

The morning of 1 September was clear and bright for Army Group South and the initial stages of the invasion for the Eighth, Tenth and Fourteenth Armies went according to plan. Coordinated resistance was only encountered sporadically and these defences were bypassed by the panzer units and left for the following infantry formations to mop up. By mid-afternoon lead el-

ements of Tenth Army had penetrated some fifteen miles into Poland.

In accordance with a pre-set plan, the Polish defenders from the Lodz and Krakow Armies retreated covered by a cavalry screen. Their intention was to form a defence line behind the three main river barriers of central Poland, the Prosna, the Warta and the Pilica. To get to Warsaw the Eighth Army would have to cross both the Prosna and Warta rivers, XI Corps of Tenth Army would have to force a passage of just the Warta, whilst XVI Panzer and XV Motorised Corps could avoid all these obstacles

by swinging north-east between the Warta and Pilica rivers. This axis of advance had not been overlooked by the Poles and any thrust in this direction would have to break through the strong Polish fortifications in the region of Czestochowa.

At the end of the first day's operations the Eighth Army reported contact with the 25th Infantry Division of the Poznan Army, retreating north-east towards Kalisz, and the 10th Infantry Division of the Lodz Army falling back on the Prosna river. Further south XVI Panzer Corps of Tenth Army reported

Right, upper: The surviving members of the 15th Polish Infantry Division wrapped in greatcoats and blankets after their surrender to elements of the advancing Fourth Army, 3 September 1939. The 2,000 prisoners were concentrated on a hill near the village of Andrzejeva. (IWM.MH.18249)

Right, lower: Field guns of No. 3 Battery, 20th Artillery Regiment, fire on Polish positions. (IWM.MH.18245)

contact with rearguards of the 28th and 30th Infantry Divisions and the Wolynska Cavalry Brigade, also withdrawing to the east. XV Motorised Corps also ran into elements of the Krakowska Cavalry Brigade and the 7th Infantry Division, covering the retreat of the Krakow Army to its first line of defence.

The advance of the Fourteenth Army also progressed well after some initial heavy fighting. A particularly violent action being fought by elements of VIII Corps against the Polish 21st Mountain Division holding the strategically important Jablunka Pass. Further to the west the 2nd Panzer and 4th Light Divisions, temporarily under the command of XVIII Mountain Corps, fought their way through the Carpathians due south of Krakow. It was here that German panzer units first encountered organised Polish armoured resistance, a brisk action being fought near Nowy Targ between elements of the 4th Light Division and the Polish 10th Mechanised Cavalry Brigade.

Units of the three Slovakian infantry divisions attacking with Fourteenth Army crossed the border into Polish Galicia, capturing a few mountain villages and effectively pinning much of the Carpathian Army along the southern frontier.

XVII Corps of the Fourteenth Army advancing from Moravia into the extreme south-west of Poland encountered rearguard elements of the 21st Infantry Division, who fell back slowly, attempting to gain valuable time for the 5th and 6th Infantry Divisions to form a cohesive defence line behind the Vistula to the south-west of Krakow. The northernmost formation of Fourteenth Army, VIII Corps, containing the 5th Panzer Division and the SS Motorised Regiment 'Germania', pushed eastwards towards Krakow along the northern bank of the Vistula. Here they ran into resistance from the Polish 23rd Infantry Division which got considerably tougher as the leading German units neared Katowice and its system of fortifications. The advance of Army Group South resumed at 6.00am on 2 September after an overnight rest to resupply the lead elements of the mechanised and motorised formations. The fighting during the next two days was to be amongst the fiercest of the whole campaign as the Eighth, Tenth, and Fourteenth Armies all attempted to batter their way through the main defence line in southern Poland.

By the end of the day, despite stubborn resistance from the 10th Polish Infantry Division, units of XIII Corps including the SS Motorised Regiment 'Leibstandarte Adolf Hitler' had managed to cross the Prosna River. Further to the south the lead elements of the 4th Panzer Division had reached the Warta north-west of Czestochowa but had not effected a crossing. The infantry divisions of IV Corps found themselves hung up on the defences of Czestochowa itself and made very little headway against the 7th Infantry Division defending the town. Further to the south XV Motorised Corps made substantial progress towards the Pilica river, only slowed slightly by the vastly outnumbered Krakowska Cavalry Brigade. By nightfall the 2nd and 3rd Light Divisions were in an excellent position to launch either an assault on the river line or swing north behind Czestochowa and envelop its defenders.

The Polish High Command, fully realising the danger of the situation, attempted to despatch as many reinforcements as possible to this area of the front. However, due to the incomplete mobilisation of many of the reserve formations and the very effective interdiction attacks of the Luftwaffe, only two provisional divisions were able to reach the front at the northern end of the defence line on the Warta.

VIII Corps of the Fourteenth Army spent 2 September attempting to smash its way through the extensive fortifications around Katowice and the smaller town of Nikotow a few miles to the south, without success. XVII Corps managed to effect crossings of the Vistula to the south-west of Krakow, the 44th and 45th Infantry Divisions pinning the Polish defenders along the river line while the 7th Infantry Division outflanked the defences from the south. The 2nd Panzer and 4th Light Divisions continued to

Men of a German reconnaissance unit survey the results of a Luftwaffe attack on a village previously held by Polish troops. (IWM.MH.13130)

A group of Polish prisoners captured by a German motorised infantry unit sit disconsolately in a village square, southern Poland, 4 September 1939. (IWM.MH.18276)

push north towards Krakow but were held up by determined resistance from Polish reservists and the armour of the 10th Mechanised Cavalry Brigade.

The final collapse of the first, and as it turned out the last, main defence line in Southern Poland came on the third day of the campaign. A coordinated attack on Czestochowa by the 4th and 46th Infantry Divisions, allied with an envelopment of the town by elements of the 2nd Light Division, led to its capture and the destruction of the 7th Polish Infantry Division; only 1,000 survivors, including the divisional commander, falling into German hands.

To the north of the town XVI Panzer Corps broke through the defensive line formed by the 28th and 30th Infantry Divisions and pushed on rapidly to the north-east in the general direction of Lodz. On its left flank troops of XI Corps established themselves firmly on the eastern bank of the Warta, forcing the 13th Polish Infantry Division and the Wolynska Cavalry Brigade to fall back in disorder.

XIII Corps of the Eighth Army also continued its north-easterly drive towards the Warta, pushing through the retreating remnants of the 10th Infantry Division, its advance becoming slowed later in the day by the 2nd Infantry Division who were moving up in support of the by now destroyed 10th Infantry Division. This was typical of the Polish defensive reaction to the German offensive. Still thinking in terms of a relatively slow-moving campaign and hampered by a woeful lack of signalling equipment, changing the orders of a formation in the field took hours, if not days. The leaders of the German mechanised formations, at the spearhead of the offensive in their ra-dio-equipped armoured command vehicles, were able to change the axis of advance of a division in minutes.

In the Fourteenth Army's zone of operations the offensive continued but at a slower pace than on previous days. By the end of 3 September VIII Corps had managed to oust the 23rd Polish Infantry Division from its positions around Katowice and Nikotow, and the road to Krakow now lay open. The 2nd Panzer and 4th Light Divisions found their way north to the city, bitterly contested by the 10th Mechanised Cavalry Brigade and elements of the 22nd Infantry Division, which had moved into the area from the general reserve. The advance was also somewhat hampered by the change late in the day of the higher command structure of the southern flank of the Fourteenth Army. Now that the mechanised units had broken through the Carpathians, control of the 2nd Panzer, 4th Light and 3rd Mountain Divisions would revert

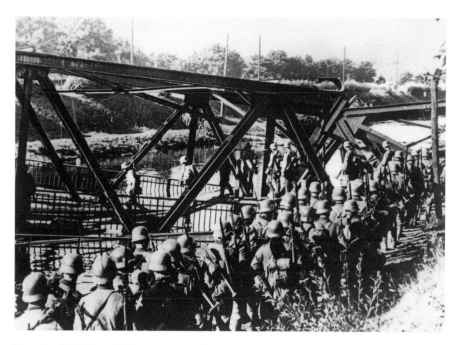

Men of the 50th Infantry Division cross the canal at the edge of the town of Bydgoszcz, 4 September 1939. (IWM.HU.39982)

to the newly mobilised XXII Panzer Corps headquarters. XVIII Mountain Corps, previously in command of these units, was now given control of the 1st and 2nd Mountain Divisions moving up from Slovakia and the three Slovak infantry divisions already ensconced on the other side of the Polish border.

The delay caused by this stubborn defence and change of command enabled most of the Polish units in the south-west corner of Poland to retreat to Krakow in good order. However, the 6th Infantry Division left behind as rearguard was smashed by the advancing XVII Corps and virtually destroyed.

So by 4 September the road to Warsaw lay open. The Polish defences meant to hold out for weeks had been irreparably breached in two days of hard fighting. Because of the speed of the German armoured spearheads there was little or no chance to reorganise a second defence line nearer the centre of Poland. The Polish High Command, already reacting to German moves a day late, lost whatever tenu-

ous grip of control over events it had. Orders issued from Warsaw from this stage of the campaign on had very little relevance to the commanders in the field. Let down by their superiors, out of contact with neighbouring formations and in constant danger of encirclement, the morale of the Polish Army dropped significantly.

This deterioration was not felt across the whole spectrum of the armed forces. Charismatic army and divisional commanders were to inspire their troops to many more heroic deeds right up till the end of the campaign but the morale of the Polish Army as a whole had suffered an irreparable blow.

All three armies in Army Group South advanced steadily through 5 and 6 September. The Eighth Army forged on towards Lodz after brushing aside the outnumbered and outgunned Polish 2nd Infantry Division. XVI Panzer Corps of the Tenth Army raced north between the Warta and Pilica rivers, overrunning the remnants of several Polish units attempting to stem the flow of the German advance. They smashed through the 29th Infantry Division, earmarked to join the defenders of Czestochowa, but forced into an *ad hoc* defence of the road to

Warsaw just north of Radomsko. XV Motorised Corps crossed the Pilica river and then swung north-east towards Radom, some 60 miles south of Warsaw. Intelligence reports had indicated that remnants of the Krakow Army and troops of the general reserve were beginning to assemble in the area for a final stand before the capital. Polish troops fought a stubborn rearguard action on the outskirts of Krakow and many of the defenders of south-west Poland managed to withdraw towards Radom before the city's capture, on 6 September. The remnants of the mountain brigades and reserve divisions that made up the Carpathian Army were forced to fall back on Lublin and Lwow as the rapid progress of XXII Panzer Corps threatened to envelop them from the north.

After the first four days of operations the Luftwaffe felt able to allocate more of its aircraft to direct ground support operations. Complete air superiority had been achieved over all of Poland except above Warsaw itself. The interdiction missions of the first few days had effectively broken up the reinforcement of front-line positions and supply columns could only move at night. Thousands of civilian refugees choked the roads, making a coordinated defence of the approaches to Warsaw virtually impossible.

While Army Group South completed its breakthrough into central Poland, Army Group North was busy consolidating its position in the north. Engineers of XXI Corps completed a series of pontoon bridges across the Vistula at Grudziadz to speed up the

Right, upper: Vehicles and guns of the SS Motorised Artillery Regiment (part of Panzerverband Kempf) cross the Narew at Govorovo, 9 September 1939. (IWM.HU.8062)

Right, lower: A car of the SS Signals Battalion pulls off the road to allow past a column of PzKpfw IIs (with a PzKpfw I in the lead) from the 7th Panzer Regiment, north-central Poland, 11 September 1939. (IWM.HU.8072)

transfer of Fourth Army troops across the Pomeranian Corridor. Units of XIX Corps completed a series of mopping-up operations against Polish troop concentrations bypassed and now trapped between the Brda and Vistula rivers. III Corps on the right (southern) flank of Fourth Army captured the last major defensive position at the base of the corridor at Bydgoszcz, defended by the Polish 15th Infantry Division.

I Corps and Corps Wodrig, having captured Mlawa, reorganised for an advance south to the Narew river, the last natural defensive barrier before the northern suburbs of the capital. Meanwhile the 207th Infantry Division and Eberhard Brigade kept the Polish naval infantry division bottled up in the far north of the country.

This apparent lack of urgency in the advance of Army Group North was deliberate. The brief rest and reorganisation of the majority of its combat forces enabled a change of plan to take place. As early as the second day of the campaign, von Bock had consulted with von Brauchitsch about the possibility of transferring the majority of Army Group North's panzer assets to the eastern flank of the Third Army. The 10th Panzer Division, originally part of Fourth Army's general reserve, had already by 3 September crossed the middle of the Pomeranian Corridor and entered East Prussia, to the north of XXI Corps. An infantry division of this corps, the 21st, was also withdrawn from the line and sent to the eastern flank of Army Group North. Together these units and the 266th Infantry Division from Corps Brand formed Kampfgruppe Falkenhorst which assembled over the next few days northeast of Nowogrod and Lomza on the Narew river. By 5 September XIX Panzer Corps had began to move across the rear of Third Army, the first unit to arrive on the left flank being the 20th Motorised Division.

On 7 September the new offensive opened with Kampfgruppe Falkenhorst attacking south towards Lomza. Two days later, with a crossing of the Narew in German hands, Guderian struck south. Within 24 hours XIX Panzer Corps was across the river in strength.

The 10th Panzer Division was now detached from Group Falkenhorst (which was renamed XXI Corps, other units of XXI Corps now being attached to II Corps, Fourth Army) and added to the armour of Guderian's Panzer Corps. XXI Corps concentrated on reducing the defence along the Narew, held in most part by the Polish 18th Infantry Division, whilst the German panzers moved south swiftly. By 11 September units of the XIX Panzer Corps had crossed the Nurczyk, a tributary of the river Bug 70 miles inside Polish territory. This deep penetration left Guderian's left flank exposed to attack from units of the Narew Group still operational in

On 16 September a strong column of Polish troops attempted to break out of the Brest Litovsk pocket. They ran headlong into the waiting 2nd Battalion of the 76th Infantry Regiment. There were precious few survivors. (IWM.MH.18254)

the Bialystok area. Units of the Podlaska Cavalry Brigade had already harried infantry units of the advancing XIX Panzer Corps quite effectively. To counter this, on 11 September Corps Brand was ordered to advance south, engage the Narew Group and push them back beyond Bialystok. The 23rd Infantry Division, formerly of Army Group North's general reserve, had moved across East Prussia behind XIX Panzer Corps and now provided much-needed support to the fortress troops and frontier guard units that made up what remained of Corps Brand.

Meanwhile I Corps and Corps Wodrig continued their attack, shifting the axis of the advance south-east, first crossing the Narew river and then on 10 September the river Bug. Elements of these forces were now within 30 miles of the north-east suburbs of Warsaw and in a position to cut off any Polish troops attempting to withdraw to the east of the city. As these forces approached from the north-east, units of II Corps pushed the remnants of the Polish forces back to Modlin, 20 miles north-west of the capital.

By 11 September the Polish government had realised that the north of the country and the capital would inevitably be lost to the advancing Germans. They therefore abandoned the city and moved south to Lwow, hoping to form a cohesive defensive line in south-eastern Poland where they could hold out until the French and British could intervene in the west.

The German High Command had already foreseen this and acted swiftly to counter the Polish plan. One of the reasons for the redirection of XIX Panzer Corps had been to prevent any enemy withdrawal east of the capital. Now Fourteenth Army was ordered to push east and north-east toward Lwow and Lublin. This would disrupt the Polish High Command's attempts to form a new defence line and prevent

A German soldier doles out rations to Polish prisoners captured after the fall of Brest Litovsk, 18 September 1939. (IWM.MH.18263)

any significant reinforcements arriving from the north and centre of the country.

The original German plan, which had envisaged a close encirclement of Warsaw and a classic Kesselschlacht battle of annihilation in the centre of Poland, was now evolving into a much larger double envelopment. An inner ring would still close around the capital, trapping a large number of Polish units, but now a second envelopment would take place east of the capital along the line of the river Bug. The speed of the German advance had taken many of the campaign's planners by surprise. Many Polish units expected to mobilise and move to the defence of Warsaw were not even ready to march by the time advancing German forces had cut off their route to the capital. Whilst there were a significant number of Polish formations trapped in or near the city, thousands of troops in the outer areas of Poland, some partially mobilised, many without orders, all paralysed by the speed and ferocity of the German offensive, had to be mopped up. A much wider envelopment carried out by the panzer formations would trap these units and allow the following infantry formations

to clear the last remaining pockets of resistance.

By 14 September the lead elements of the 10th Panzer Division had reached Brzesc (Brest Litovsk) on the river Bug due east of Warsaw. Initial German attacks forced the defenders to withdraw into the city's fortress. The 10th Panzer Division did not possess enough integral infantry to undertake an assault on the citadel itself and the 20th Motorised Infantry Division had to be called in to help out the struggling attackers. The fortress finally fell to the Germans after three days of hard fighting. Meanwhile the 3rd Panzer Division and 2nd Motorised Infantry Division pushed on south down the east bank of the Bug towards Wlodawa.

The river south from Brzesc formed the agreed demarcation line between the areas of Poland to be controlled by Germany and Russia at the end of the campaign. In the last days of the offensive, many German units engaged in mopping up the remnants of the Polish Army found it necessary to operate in what would become Soviet territory. This caused a certain amount of strain on the German–Soviet alliance and there were several instances of Russian planes 'accidentally' bombing German formations after their entry into the war on 17 September.

While XIX Panzer Corps pushed south along the river Bug, units of I Corps laid siege to the northern Warsaw suburb of Praga. Corps Wodrig completed the destruction of all the Polish forces that had managed to escape across the Vistula from the city and those immediately south of the capital.

The entry of the Soviet Union into the conflict put paid to any chances the Polish Army might have had of constructing a further defence line in south-eastern Poland. The country's eastern frontier, stripped of troops to fight the Germans, presented no obstacle to the advancing Soviets. The Red Army encountered virtually no resistance in its advance, capturing hundreds of square miles of territory a day. By the time Russian units arrived at the river Bug, German troops had completed their operations on the eastern bank, a link-up between units of XXII and XIX Panzer Corps had been effected and the new frontier sealed.

The advance of Army Group South between 7 and 17 September had had much to do with the startling success of the German campaign in Poland. After breaking through the initial defence lines of the Lodz, Krakow and Karpaty (Carpathian) Armies, the Eighth and Tenth Armies pushed on towards Warsaw from the south-west, whilst the Fourteenth Army with XXII Panzer Corps in the van headed for Lublin and Lwow.

All three of the armies made steady progress towards their objectives, each overcoming significant but largely uncoordinated resistance from Polish units, either retreating towards Warsaw, Lublin or Lwow or making a stand in their area of mobilisation due to a lack of specific orders to do anything else.

The one exception to this was the fierce Polish counter-attack launched by the Poznan Army against the northern flank of the Eighth Army as it advanced towards the capital. The Poznan Army, largely bypassed in the early stages of the campaign, withdrew in good order towards Warsaw. When on 9 September it found its way to the city blocked by units of XVI Panzer Corps on the east bank of the Bzura, an assault was launched to the south, across the same river, into the flank of the Eighth Army following in the wake of Tenth Army's panzers. By attacking the infantry divisions rather than the panzer formations, General Kutrzeba, commander of the Poznan Army, hoped to be able to break through the German lines and cut off the mechanised formations in front of Warsaw.

The brunt of the attack fell on the overstretched 30th Infantry Division and initially made rapid progress. Blaskowitz, commander of the Eighth Army, was forced to halt his advance on the capital and ask for help from Reichenau, commander of the Tenth Army. The seriousness of the situation led Reichenau to detach the 1st Panzer Division from XVI Panzer Corps and the 2nd Light Division from XV Motorised Corps, over 500 tanks in total, to halt the Polish advance. This they managed to do after two days of very hard fighting. The diversion of much of the mechanised cutting edge of Tenth Army necessarily slowed the advance on Warsaw, causing much consternation at German High Command. However, the Polish attempt to break through to the south allowed the 8th and 14th Infantry Divisions of IX Corps, Tenth Army, to strengthen their positions along the east bank of the Bzura west of Warsaw. It also enabled units from II and III Corps, Fourth Army, to move south from the base of the Pomeranian Corridor and take up positions between the Bzura and Vistula rivers. The majority of the

Hitler views the progress of the German armies in Poland on his visit to Army Group North Headquarters, 12 September 1939. (IWM.MH.13146)

Poznan Army, plus battered elements of both the Lodz and Pomorze Armies, were now trapped in a 'cauldron' some 25 miles in diameter, centred around the town of Kutno just north of the Bzura.

On 11 September General Blaskowitz was given authority to coordinate the crushing of the 'cauldron' and the destruction of the trapped Polish forces. As the ring around the Poles tightened, they were driven to ever more ferocious and desperate attacks. By this time some twelve Polish infantry divisions (the 14th, 17th, 25th and 26th from the Poznan Army, remnants of the 2nd, 10th, 13th, 28th and 30th of the Lodz Army and the remains of the 4th, 15th and 16th from the Pomorze Army) were encircled, along with three cavalry brigades (the Wielkopolska and Kresowa Brigades from the Poznan Army and the Wolynska Brigade of the

Polish prisoners, captured after their failed attempt to break out of the Kutno pocket, trudge their way to the rear, 19 September 1939. (IWM.HU.5336)

Lodz Army). These formations now represented more than one-third of the Polish Army left in the field; their destruction or capture would be a shattering blow to government hopes of continuing the fight.

On 12 September the Poles launched yet another fierce counter-attack against Eighth Army units to the south. Despite gaining some ground beyond the Bzura, the advance was effectively halted with heavy loss. German units then went over to the offensive, squeezing the Polish units into an ever smaller defensive perimeter.

For the first three days of this operation both XI Corps and XVI Panzer Corps were detached from Tenth Army and helped with the attacks on the Polish defences. This lessened the pressure on the defenders of Warsaw for a short time but on the 15th, with the Polish units reduced to a small pocket around Kutno itself, they were returned to Tenth Army control. The next day, in a last desperate attempt to break through the German lines, Gen-

eral Kutrzeba led a strong force of Poles in an assault on the German defences to the north-east in the general direction of Modlin. The attack caught the defenders by surprise and several thousand troops (including Kutrzeba himself) managed to fight their way clear into the forests between Modlin and the capital. However, the mass of Polish troops attempting to push their way through the gap presented an easy target for the Luftwaffe and most of the attackers were destroyed or forced to withdraw towards Kutno. Throughout 17 September German air attacks ceaselessly pounded the remaining troops in the pocket. Finally Polish morale cracked, and over the next two days some 40,000 prisoners fell into German hands. At the end of the operations to eradicate the Kutno pocket on the 19th, some 170,000 Polish prisoners of war (including troops captured in the Radom pocket by Tenth Army) were held by the Germans.

The speed of the Tenth Army armoured thrust gave little chance for the

remnants of the Krakow Army to link up with reserve units near Radom and form a second cohesive defence line. The Lodz Army had already effectively been brushed aside, its surviving units forced into the Kutno pocket along with the majority of the Poznan Army. By 8 September the 7th Infantry Division and Krakowska Cavalry Brigade of the Krakow Army, plus the 3rd, 12th, 19th and 29th Infantry Divisions of the general reserve, had managed to assemble in the Radom area. Of these only the 12th Infantry Division was at full strength, all the others having suffered extremely heavy losses through enemy ground and air action. Nevertheless, these forces were sufficiently strong to pose a serious threat to Tenth Army's advance on the capital, and Reichenau felt obliged to detach IV Corps and XIV Motorised Corps from the main thrust on Warsaw and send them on

an enveloping manoeuvre around Radom. While the infantry divisions of IV Corps pinned the Polish troops in front of the city, the mechanised and motorised forces of XIV Corps encircled them from both north and south. By the 11th Radom was in German hands and nearly 60,000 prisoners taken.

It was now decided that Tenth Army would operate on two fronts. The main one would be against the capital while a secondary front would be opened up by the advance of IV Corps on Lublin. XIV Motorised Corps would move to the north-east towards the Vistula, providing the link between the two advancing forces. As resistance in the centre of Poland was now slackening considerably, it was felt that the stretching of Tenth Army's forces over such a wide area presented very little risk. After crossing the Vistula south of the Polish capital, IV Corps continued with its advance on Lublin, meeting with negligible opposition along the way. Only when units of the 14th Infantry Division entered the outskirts of the city did resistance stiffen. Whilst they systematically cleared the city of its defenders, other units of IV Corps bypassed the fighting and reached the river Wieprz. By 18 September all resistance in this area, west of the Russo-German demarcation line on the Bug, had been overcome.

The main thrust on Warsaw was led by Hoepner's XVI Panzer Corps and Hoth's XV Motorised Corps, the lead elements of which had managed to reach the outskirts of the city by 8 September. After advancing over 140 miles in one week, these units were ex-

Luftwaffe prisoners shot down over Warsaw and soldiers captured during the abortive attack on the capital are put on display for the foreign press, 19 September 1939.

Left, upper: German infantry, completely exhausted after ten days of almost continuous marching, take a break by the roadside. (IWM.HU.8075)

Left, lower: Two PzKpfw I tanks of the 4th Panzer Division, in a Warsaw suburb. Note that the tank crews have learned from their earlier experiences and have partially overpainted their white crosses to make them less easy targets. (IWM.HU.8090)

hausted but determined that the capital should fall to them in another lightning strike. It was perhaps this very tiredness that led to the decision to assault the city with the 4th Panzer Division. The next day the unit, in the van of XVI Panzer Corps, attempted to capture the city with yet another armoured thrust. In its operations to date this sort of approach had paid handsome dividends but this time, with the panzers used in street fighting against an enemy determined to defend their capital and without adequate infantry support, it met with disaster. At the end of the day's fighting the division had lost 57 tanks (the white crosses on the panzers making excellent aiming points for Polish anti-tank gunners) and had been forced to re-

treat back to its previously held positions.

The defenders, units of the general reserve and the partially formed Warsaw Mechanised Brigade, were momentarily cheered by the victory. The success, along with the opening of the attack across the Bzura by the Poznan Army, held out a faint glimmer of hope. This, however, was soon to be shattered. Even though the Bzura offensive meant, at least temporarily, calling off any further major attacks on the capital, German troops from the Third and Tenth Armies were still able to link up and surround the city on 10 Septem-

The Russians invade and the German offensive continues, 15–27 September 1939.

ber. The Polish government, realising that Warsaw would eventually fall, had already wisely quit the capital and moved south to Lwow. With the slow but certain destruction of the troops trapped in the Kutno pocket, Poland's hopes of holding out faded.

While the fighting for the capital raged, units of the Fourteenth Army in south-central Poland pushed on into the interior. The mechanised formations of XXII Panzer Corps advanced rapidly north-east towards their objectives on the Bug river, while XVII and XVIII Corps advanced towards Lwow. By 10 September advance elements of both these corps were across the San river, forcing the Polish 24th Infantry Division to withdraw towards the city. The other defending unit, the 11th Infantry Division, retreated into the for-

tress town of Przemysl on the banks of the San itself. Detailing troops to invest the fortress and prevent any breakout towards Lwow, Fourteenth Army continued its advance. The Polish government, again facing the worst, abandoned Lwow and moved south-east toward the Rumanian border.

As the advance of XXII Panzer Corps on the left flank of the Fourteenth Army reached the San river south of Krasnik, Polish resistance once again stiffened and the corps found its advance at least temporarily slowed to a crawl; remnants of the elite Polish 21st and 22nd Mountain Divisions plus the 10th Mechanised Cavalry Brigade put up a spirited resistance along the river bank and in the forests and swamps around Bilgoraj to its immediate north. With the entire advance of XXII Panzer Corps brought to a standstill, it became necessary to divert units of XVII

Corps northwards from their advance on Lwow.

Fortunately, resistance further to the south had been slight and the San river line had already been outflanked. The diversion of the 44th and 45th Infantry Divisions forced a hurried withdrawal by the defending Poles, and once XXII Panzer Corps had negotiated the difficult terrain onto the central Polish plain, the speedy advance resumed once more. The 10th Mechanised Cavalry Brigade was able to withdraw quickly to the east, while the remnants of the infantry units were either captured, destroyed or dispersed.

In an attempt to capture Lwow before a cohesive defence of the city could be mounted, a special Kampfgruppe under the command of Colonel (later Field Marshal) Schoerner was formed from the motorised troops of the 1st Mountain Division. This raced ahead of the main body of the division, reaching the city early on 12 September. The unit was, however, unable to force an entry and had to content itself with preventing any further reinforcement of the garrison of 12,000 men.

Later in the day the remainder of the division arrived to bolster the Kampfgruppe. As they began their investment of the city other units of XVIII corps and units of VIII Corps continued with their mopping-up operations to the east and south.

Lwow is dominated by the Zboiska Heights to its north and north-west and if these were to fall into German hands it would only be a matter of time before the city would be forced to surrender. Kampfgruppe Schoerner began its assault on Hill 374, the tallest of the hills, on the morning of 13 September. By early afternoon the hill was in German hands and by darkness the whole of the Zboiska Heights had been captured. The mountain troops now dug themselves in to resist the furious counter-attacks that were sure to come from both the garrison attempting to break out and units retreating towards the walled city from the surrounding countryside.

During 14 September the remainder of XVIII Corps moved to support the 1st Mountain Division and cut off the last remaining exits from the city. At the same time, further north, XVII and XXII Panzer Corps were directed to continue their advance to the northeast, in the direction of Wlodzimierz and Hrubieszow and to effect a junction with units of XIX Panzer Corps, Army Group North, east of the Bug river.

The fortress town of Przemysl finally fell on 15 September after a bitter siege which cost both sides a large number of casualties. This marked the end of organised resistance in the Fourteenth Army zone of operations, ex-

The crew of a Russian BA-20 armoured car chat to German officers after the hand-over of Brest Litovsk to Soviet forces, 20 September 1939. (IWM.MH.8160)

cept at Lwow and in an area north-west of the city between Bilgoraj and Rawa Ruska.

As much of the area now being fought over by the Third and Fourteenth Armies, including Lwow, lay inside the area given over to Soviet occupation, a change of plan was needed after 17 September, with Russia's entry into the war. The Red Army crossed the border into eastern Poland with two army groups or fronts. The White Russian Front, commanded by Army Commander Kovalev and consisting of the Third and Eleventh Armies, operated to the north of the Pripet Marshes, while the Ukrainian Front, commanded by Army Commander Timoshenko and consisting of the First and Tenth Armies, advanced to their south.

The Third Army was given the objective of capturing Brzesc and Bialystok while the Eleventh Army secured Polish Lithuania and the areas adjacent to the East Prussian frontier. The First Army tasked with the capture of Lwow

was by far the biggest of the armies advancing into Poland, while the Tenth Army, which was considerably smaller, advanced in the general direction of Lublin. A total of some 20 to 24 infantry divisions, fifteen cavalry divisions and nine tank brigades took part in the offensive.

Due to the lack of resistance met by these Soviet forces, cavalry and mechanised units were able to push forward with great speed, leaving the infantry formations to follow on behind. This not only put paid to any ideas the Polish government may have had of continuing the war from south-eastern Poland (the government crossed the frontier into Rumania on 18 September) but also upset plans the Wehrmacht had formulated for the link-up of the Third and Fourteenth Armies east of the river Bug. On the 17th the 4th Light Division had managed to cross the Bug near Hrubieszow and lead elements of XIX Panzer Corps had reached Wlodawa, but there still lay a gap of some 40 miles between

Left, upper: Infantry and cavalry of the IIth Soviet Army enter Vilna (Vilnius), the capital of Polish Lithuania, 18/19 September 1939.

Left, lower: A Red Army soldier guards a crashed Polish Air Force PWS 26 light liaison aircraft, shot down over Soviet-occupied Poland.

them, inside the Soviet demarcation zone.

On 20 September Adolf Hitler ordered the withdrawal of all German units east of the demarcation line, to minimise the chances of conflict with the advancing Russians and establish a coherent frontier before the arrival of large numbers of Soviet troops. The previously agreed border ran in a roughly north–south line following the course of, first the Pisia river until it joined the Narew, then across country from the town of Ostroleka on the Narew to the river Bug. From there the border followed the line of the Bug south for roughly 200 miles, before cutting in eastwards to the San river. The frontier then ran south along the course of the San to the Slovakian border.

When the order to withdraw was received, units of Corps Brand and XXI Corps were still engaged in mopping up remaining centres of Polish resistance in the Bialystok area, which was now some 50 miles to the east of the new frontier. The 2nd Motorised Division of XIX Panzer Corps was even further east, engaged with enemy formations near Kobryn. Breaking off from contact with these Polish units, even though they were in most cases very badly mauled and without transport to pursue the Germans, presented very great difficulties. These were further magnified in the area of operations of the Fourteenth Army where XVIII Corps was ordered to disengage from the siege of Lwow.

Not surprisingly, many German commanders were reluctant to pull back from ground won at a significant cost in German lives. To ease the withdrawal to the new frontier, German

units fell back through a series of phase lines, each one supposedly at least fifteen miles in front of the advancing Soviet forces. Wounded troops were withdrawn from immediate areas of enemy activity and if necessary left behind with medical personnel to be protected by the advancing Red Army.

The Germans also took great care to remove from the battlefield as many disabled vehicles as possible and were very particular in their destruction of eleven Panzer IIIs and IVs to stop them falling into Soviet hands.

Mistakes did occur and there were skirmishes between Russian and German units, the most significant being between elements of the 10th Panzer Division and a unit of advancing Soviet cavalry in which both sides suffered several dozen casualties. On the whole, however, the withdrawal was completed as planned.

One unexpected bonus was the surprise surrender of the garrison of Lwow just as the 1st Mountain Division disengaged from the siege, the Polish troops deciding to march into

A Polish cavalry officer meets German commanders to negotiate the surrender of the garrison of Lwow, 20/21 September 1939. (IWM.MH.I339I)

captivity with the Wehrmacht rather than face the prospect of eventually being captured by the Red Army.

Polish troops continued to fight throughout this period, VIII Corps having a particularly tough fight on 23 September in the Zamosc–Tomoszow region just north of the new frontier. However, with the intervention of the 2nd Panzer Division the battle was won and a large number of prisoners were taken. The remaining Polish units retreated over the new frontier into the Soviet Army's zone of occupation.

The German Army in other areas of Poland also faced further battles with unsubdued enemy formations. At the time of Hitler's withdrawal order, Warsaw, Modlin and the Hela Peninsula were all still in Polish hands.

With the failure of the 4th Panzer Division to take the capital by storm, the battle for Warsaw quickly developed into a siege, complete with trench lines across city streets and heavy artillery bombardment. Initially German units made very little headway in their attempts to capture the city. A large part of the Lodz Army had managed to fall back on the capital and these forces, along with units from the general reserve, plus armed militia and police, put up a staunch defence. Dug-in anti-tank guns and 7-TP tanks of the Warsaw

Mechanised Brigade made sure that the German panzers played only a supporting role in the capture of the city.

On 16 September, after a leaflet drop by the Luftwaffe, a temporary cease-fire was arranged to discuss the evacuation of the city's civilian population and diplomatic colony. Talks were broken off, however, when the Polish commander, General Rommel, refused to accept a German note calling on the garrison to surrender.

A further leaflet raid called on the civilian population to quit the city within twelve hours, adding that German artillery would cease its shelling during this period. When after the drop Polish artillery continued to fire upon German positions and no significant numbers of civilian refugees appeared, the Wehrmacht bombardment recommenced.

On 18 September the German High Command ordered the resumption of offensive operations against the capital. The same day, aircraft of Luftflotte 1 attacked the city's water and power supplies and small task forces began to probe the Polish defences in preparation for the bigger assault to come.

It was decided that any offensive should be undertaken by the infantry divisions of the Eighth Army attack-

ing into the southern and western suburbs of the city. This, it was hoped, would force any major flight of refugees to head eastwards across the Vistula and towards Soviet occupied Poland. On no account was General Blaskowitz to permit civilians to pass through German lines. By hemming the population inside the city, valuable food stockpiles would be used up more quickly and the very real threat of disease would be powerful factors in influencing a Polish surrender.

Over the next few days the German artillery bombardment continued ceaselessly, with probing attacks making limited progress in forcing a path towards the city centre. Then on 26 September the final assault began. Using all the infantry resources at his command, von Blaskowitz's troops stormed the first two lines of bunkers and trenches that the Polish forces had constructed in the city's southern suburbs. At the same time units from the Third Army conducted attacks on the northern and eastern outskirts of the city, pinning a large number of the defenders in position. Major Luftwaffe attacks were carried out throughout the city, both on military and civilian targets, setting large sections of the capital ablaze.

By the end of the day's fighting the defences of the capital had been split wide open. Realising the futility of continuing the fight, General Kutrzeba sent envoys through the German lines to discuss surrender terms.

Von Blaskowitz had been instructed to accept nothing less than the total unconditional surrender of the Warsaw garrison and the envoys were sent back with this message.

Further to impress the defenders of the city, the artillery bombardment was stepped up and more threats were

German soldiers watch Warsaw burn after a series of fierce and indiscriminate Luftwaffe attacks on the capital, 18–20 September 1939. (IWM.NYP.22526)

made about fresh Luftwaffe bombing raids on the civilian population. Both the Mayor of Warsaw and General Kutrzeba, commanding the city's defences, concurred that with no electricity or running water and food stocks critically low, unconditional surrender was now the only option. Negotiations were completed on the morning of 27 September and a general cease-fire came into effect at 2.00pm local time. A total of 140,000 Polish troops laid down their arms, including some 16,000 wounded.

The fortress town of Modlin just north of Warsaw continued to hold out for a little while longer. Units of II Corps besieging the town had little luck in gaining entrance to the town or in forcing the garrison commander, General Thommee, to negotiate surrender terms. However, with the fall of the capital large numbers of heavy artillery pieces became free for transfer to support the besieging troops. By 27 September German units had managed to seize the Polish outer ring of defences surrounding the town. The intense artillery bombardment that began the next morning was enough to convince the Polish commander that

he could hold out no longer. Negotiations were opened at 7.30am and the garrison laid down its arms later that same day, having suffered some 4,000 casualties from the German assaults.

Operations at the northern end of the Pomeranian Corridor became a separate mini-campaign following the junction of the German Third and Fourth Armies. The 207th Infantry Division, Brigade Eberhard and several frontier guard units were given the task of eliminating the pocket which had formed around the Polish port of Gdynia and the heavily fortified naval

base on the Hela Peninsula. Corps Kavpisch, as it became known, initially made rapid progress driving into the pocket and cutting the link between Gdynia and Hela as early as 12 September. The corps then turned its attention to the defenders of the port, a regular naval infantry brigade and assorted militia units under the command of a Colonel Dabek, leaving an infantry regiment to close off the end of the narrow Hela Peninsula.

Although a well-planned night attack by the defending Poles caught the corps by surprise and inflicted heavy casualties, it was not enough to stall the assault on Gdynia by more than a day or two and the port fell to the advancing Germans on 14 September, Colonel Dabek committing suicide rather than surrender. Now the Germans turned their attention on the much tougher nut to crack, the heavily fortified Hela naval base.

The width of the peninsula allowed only a single infantry regiment to advance at any one time along a very

General Kutrzeba (far right), Polish commander of Warsaw, negotiates with General Blaskowitz (centre, hand on chin) for the surrender of the capital, at the Skoda motor works, eight kilometres from the city, 27 September 1939. (IWM.HU.40003)

A column of Polish soldiers marches into captivity through the streets of Warsaw watched by glum-looking civilians, 28/29 September 1939.

obvious attack route. Even with the artillery support of the 207th Infantry Division, Brigade Eberhard and the battleship *Schleswig-Holstein*, the advance was painfully slow. The first signs of success did not appear until 25 September after over a week of heavy fighting for little gain, when the Luftwaffe managed to knock out the rail system used by the Poles to wheel their heavy coastal guns in and out of the fortress. Two days later this much-needed Stuka support was lost with the transfer of all Luftwaffe ground attack assets to the west. By 30 September a regimental combat team of the 207th Infantry Division had managed to capture the tiny village of Ceynowa and was in a position to launch an attack on the fortress itself. This assault, by no means guaranteed to be successful, was scheduled for 2 October. Fortunately for the attackers, however, the fortress commander, Rear Admiral J. Unrug, feeling that further prolonged resistance would lead only to the pointless deaths of more of his men, surrendered

the base and its 5,000 defenders the day before the attack was due to be launched.

With the capture of the Hela Peninsula Adolf Hitler felt confident enough to declare the campaign against Poland at an end. On 5 October he visited the captured capital and viewed a triumphant march-past of victorious Wehrmacht troops. At the same time the last major pocket of organised resistance at Kock, south-east of Warsaw, was being mopped up by XIV Motorised Corps of the Tenth Army.

The German Army during its 36-day foray into Poland had lost 8,082 men killed, 27,278 wounded and 5,029 missing in action. This casualty rate is very low indeed when compared to Polish losses, exact figures for which are very difficult to determine. Of some 800,000 men mobilised by the Polish government during the course of the war, 694,000 ended the campaign as German prisoners of war. The remaining 106,000 were either killed in action, captured by the advancing Soviets or forced to flee across the border into Rumania.

The Germans by their own count captured 3,214 artillery pieces, 16,500

machine guns and 1,700 mortars. Although this equipment was not thought to be of high enough quality to equip Wehrmacht units, the supplies were of great value to Germany's various satellite states.

Of their valuable panzer assets, the Germans announced that they had lost 218 vehicles, 89 PzKpfw Is, 78 PzKpfw IIs, 26 PzKpfw IIIs, 19 PzKpfw IVs and 6 PzKpfw 35(t)s. The numbers given, however, indicate vehicles irrecoverable from the battlefield. The total number of tanks actually knocked out in combat was probably over 400, or 20 percent of the Wehrmacht's entire tank force. Similarly, the Luftwaffe claimed to have lost 285 aircraft but neutral sources came to the conclusion that the actual figure was much higher, also at around the 400 mark.

Overall, the campaign to conquer Poland had been a huge success, with victory being achieved at a much faster pace and with much lower casualties than had been predicted by many senior German commanders. To the satisfaction of Guderian and the other exponents of blitzkrieg, the central role played by the panzer division in the achievement of these victories ensured that this new type of strategy would be fundamental to the German campaigns against France and Russia that were to follow.

Some historians have argued that the assault on Poland was not in fact a blitzkrieg campaign and that the parameters of the offensive were determined by the traditional strategies of Vernichtungsgedanke (annihilation concept) and Kesselschlacht (cauldron battle) with the steady plodding of infantry divisions being the decisive factor. What they fail to take into account is that these ideas had been largely incorporated into blitzkrieg theory any-

Adolf Hitler reviews a drive-past of PzKpfw IIs during the Warsaw victory parade, 5 October 1939. (IWM.HU.42951)

way and also that the original plan of campaign changed radically during the offensive, from the planned encirclement and destruction of the entire Polish field army near Warsaw, to a double envelopment of enemy forces at several strategic locations and the capture of substantial proportion of the Polish forces in the field, without the need for a decisive battle.

The speed of the various armies, with the panzer formations as their spearheads, undermined the original plan, in that Polish units were unable to form cohesive defence lines or concentrate to defend the approaches to Warsaw. No Kesselschlacht could take place without this concentration and instead German forces, after having broken through the initial defensive lines, had to contend with many isolated pockets of resistance.

The very speed of the German advance also undermined the will of many of these units to fight on. With-

out clear orders, cut off from support and without supplies, many chose to surrender without a fight, the very essence of blitzkrieg. The flexibility inherent in blitzkrieg theory also ensured that German forces could react much faster at both strategic and tactical levels to take advantage of the new situa-

German heavy artillery pounds enemy positions near Modlin in northern Poland. (IWM.MH.18288)

tion as it unfolded. Guderian's insistence that modern battlefield communications be central to the teachings of modern mobile warfare paid a very handsome dividend indeed.

The Battle for France, 1940

The Rival Plans

Since September 1939 the Franco–British General Staffs had perfected a strategy known as Plan D or the Dyle Plan (after the Belgian river Dyle along which much of the Allied field armies were to deploy in the event of war).

The plan was based on the supposition that the Germans would, as in 1914, attack France via Belgium in a huge wheeling manoeuvre to outflank the Maginot Line. The strategy formulated as a counter to this move involved the deployment of the cream of the French Army, along with the British Expeditionary Force (BEF) into Belgium on the outbreak of war, where they would defend a line based on the river Dyle. The planners were handicapped by the strictly neutral attitude of the Dutch and Belgian governments who would not allow the entry of Franco–British units onto their territory before a German attack on them had commenced.

The first weakness of the Allied plan was to believe that the Dutch and Belgian Armies would be able to delay the Wehrmacht for long enough to enable the deployment to be completed. A second weakness of the strategy was to assume that the Belgian Army would have pre-prepared defensive positions along the Dyle into which the Franco–British units would slot.

The deployment of the Allied armies for the Dyle Plan ran as follows. From north to south six armies would be involved. In the far north the Dutch Army would defend 'Fortress Holland', an area of land east of a line drawn from the Zuider Zee (inland sea) to the mouth of the river Maas. The French Seventh Army would hold the Turnhout–Breda Line in south-east

Holland, thus linking the Dutch Army with the main Dyle Line to the south. The Belgian Army would hold the sector from Antwerp to Louvain, retreating to their defensive positions after delaying the German forces for 48 hours further to the east. The BEF would deploy between Louvain and Wavre, the French First Army between Wavre and Namur, and the French Ninth Army between Namur and Mezières.

Thus along with the Dutch and Belgian armies, one British and three French armies would confront the Germans on a defensive line over 100 miles in length across Belgium and into eastern Holland.

In shaping the strategy the planners had assumed that the main German thrust would be made on the Belgian plains north of Namur; the avenue of approach through the rugged forest country of the Ardennes and across the steep-banked river Meuse offering no serious threat. As a logical outcome of this thinking, the strongest French armies, the Seventh and the First, were deployed north of Namur, with the weakest, the Ninth, to the south.

This assessment by General Maurice Gamelin (the French Commander in Chief) of the probable attack route was reinforced when on 10 January 1940 a complete set of plans for the proposed invasion of France and the Low Countries fell into Allied hands.

Hellmuth Reinberger, a major in the fallschirmjäger (paratroopers) was captured while on a flight to take the top secret documents to a planning conference at the German 2nd Luftwaffe Headquarters in Cologne. His light plane, lost in bad weather, was forced to make an emergency landing

when its engine failed. The pilot unknowingly landed just across the border in Belgium and the captured plans when retrieved were passed on to the French authorities.

This unfortunate accident forced a change of strategy on the part of the Germans who had up until this point planned to strike through the Low Countries in just the manner prophesied by the Allies.

Hitler had always been uneasy about repeating the same basic manoeuvre that had opened the First World War but had gone along with the opinion of his General Staff in the first version of Fall Gelb (Case Yellow) which had been in place since mid-October 1939. Luckily for the Führer, General Gerd von Rundstedt, commander of Army Group A, and his Chief of Staff General Erich von Manstein also disagreed with the approach of the German High Command (OKH) and von Manstein had on his own initiative prepared an alternative plan of campaign. This plan

specified that the main thrust of the invasion be made not by von Bock's Army Group B across central Belgium but by Rundstedt's Army Group A through the hilly and wooded Ardennes region.

The objective of this new strategy was not to outflank the main Allied field armies and pin them against the Maginot Line (the original idea) but to slice through the French defences and race eastwards to the sea, trapping the best Allied units in Belgium and destroying them. After consulting Guderian, the father of Germany's panzer force, to confirm the practicability of the new plan, Hitler incorporated the ideas into his War Directive No. 10 of 18 February 1940.

By a combination of brilliant planning and fortuitous good luck the German attack was to fall on the weakest point of the Allied defence line, the overstretched French divisions deployed along the river Meuse. The trapping of vast numbers of Allied troops

Left: French infantry move up to the front through a Belgian village during the opening stages of Fall Gelb. They are watched by Belgian civilians and French rear echelon troops.

Right: General der Panzertruppen Heinz Guderian watches developments on the battlefront, France, May 1940. (IWM.MH.9239)

in Belgium and northern France was virtually assured from the outset of the campaign.

German Forces

For his western offensive Hitler had assembled some 117 divisions, including a reserve of 42 infantry divisions. The remainder of the units were parcelled out between Army Groups A and B, commanded by General Gerd von Rundstedt and General Fedor von Bock respectively.

Army Group B consisted of 29^1/$_2$ divisions, of which three were panzer. The armoured units were split between XVI Panzer Corps, commanded by

A column of PzKpfw IIs and PzKpfw 38(t)s of the 7th Panzer Division wend their way through the northern French countryside on their drive to the Channel coast, May 1940. Note the Swastika flag stretched over the engine deck of the PzKpfw II as an aerial recognition signal.

General Erich Hoepner (3rd and 4th Panzer Divisions), and General Rudolf Schmidt's XXXIX Panzer Corps (9th Panzer Division).

The army group had the task of attacking into Holland and northern Belgium to pin the superior forces of the French First Army along the Dyle river line, pushing them back slowly if possible.

Rundstedt's Army Group A had the decisive role of smashing its way through the weak defences of the Ardennes region and racing to the sea, thus encircling and annihilating the cream of the Allied armies.

It consisted of 45^1/$_2$ divisions, of which seven were panzer. These were split into three panzer corps. XV Panzer Corps (5th and 7th Panzer Divisions), commanded by General Hermann Hoth, was the most northerly. Under the control of General Gunther

von Kluge's Fourth Army, its task was to push on through the Ardennes as fast as possible and secure crossings of the river Meuse near Dinant.

XLI Panzer Corps (6th and 8th Panzer Divisions), commanded by General Georg Reinhardt, and XIX Panzer Corps (1st, 2nd and 10th Panzer Divisions, plus the elite Grossdeutschland Motorised Infantry Regiment), led by General Heinz Guderian, along with General Gustav von Wietersheim's XIV Motorised Corps, made up Panzergruppe Kleist. This formation, commanded by General Ewald von Kleist and consisting of units from both the Twelfth and Sixteenth Armies, was to deliver the main armoured punch against the French defence line on the Meuse at Monthermé and Sedan.

For the campaign against France the German Army managed to muster a total of 2,702 tanks, less than half the

armoured strength estimated by French intelligence, who suspected the Wehrmacht of possessing over 7,000 vehicles!

In total there were 640 PzKpfw Is, 825 PzKpfw IIs, 456 PzKpfw IIIs, 366 PzKpfw IVs, 151 PzKpfw 35(t)s and 264 PzKpfw 38(t)s. There was also a small reserve of approximately 150 vehicles to replace combat losses and 135 PzKpfw Is and IIIs that had been converted into armoured command tanks, losing their main armament.

These vehicles were not dispersed equally throughout the ten panzer divisions participating in the offensive but were distributed according to the formations' perceived roles in the battles to come.

The 1st Panzer Division (Panzer Regiments 1 and 2), 2nd Panzer Division (Panzer Regiments 3 and 4) and 10th Panzer Division (Panzer Regiments 7 and 8) each contained 30 PzKpfw Is, 100 PzKpfw IIs, 90 PzKpfw IIIs and 56 PzKpfw IVs.

The 6th Panzer Division (Panzer Regiment 11 and Panzer Abteilung 65), 7th Panzer Division (Panzer Regiment 25) and 8th Panzer Division (Panzer Regiment 1) consisted of 10 PzKpfw Is, 40 PzKpfw IIs, 132 PzKpfw 35(t)s (6th Panzer Division) or PzKpfw 38(t)s (7th and 8th Panzer Divisions) and 36 PzKpfw IVs. Panzer Abteilung 65 added an additional 19 PzKpfw 35(t)s to the complement of the 6th Panzer Division in lieu of a battery of sIG mechanised infantry guns.

The 3rd Panzer Division (Panzer Regiments 5 and 6), 4th Panzer Division (Panzer Regiments 35 and 36) and 5th Panzer Division (Panzer Regiments 15 and 31) each contained 140 PzKpfw Is, 110 PzKpfw IIs, 50 PzKpfw IIIs and 24 PzKpfw IVs.

The 9th Panzer Division was made up of 100 PzKpfw Is, 75 PzKpfw IIs, 36 PzKpfw IIIs and 18 PzKpfw IVs.

Panzergruppe Kleist (XV, XIX and XLI Panzer Corps), the force to carry

A German infantryman scurries behind a PzKpfw 38(t), using it as cover, during the 8th Panzer Division's advance across northern France, May 1940. (IWM.MH.9152)

out the main breakthrough operation on the Meuse, was given a high proportion of PzKpfw III and IV battle tanks and the army's total allocation of Czech PzKpfw 35(t) and 38(t) vehicles, the Wehrmacht's best light tanks.

In addition to the tanks that made up the panzer divisions, four other types of armoured unit took part in the Battle for France.

Each panzer division (except for the 6th) was allocated a battery of six 15cm sIG (Sfl) auf PzKpfw I Fgst 7e (a 150mm infantry gun mounted in an armoured cab on a PzKpfw I chassis) for direct infantry support operations.

There were also four independent Sturmartillerie batteries, each of six Sturmegeschutz (StuG) III assault guns (a 75mm howitzer on a PzKpfw III chassis).

Two types of independent specialist anti-armour units also took the field:

Five panzerjäger companies (two of 18 vehicles, three of 27 vehicles) equipped with 4.7cm Pak(t) (Sf) auf PzKpfw I (also known as the Marder I) tank destroyers, Czech 47mm anti-tank guns mounted on a PzKpfw I chassis, provided mobile anti-tank support for the infantry divisions.

In addition, a single company of ten 8.8cm Flak 18 (Sfl) auf Zugkraftwagen 12t, 88mm guns mounted on armoured SdKfz 7 half-track chassis, gave much-needed heavy calibre anti-tank support against the thickly armoured British Matilda and French Char B tanks.

Even with these independent formations the German panzer arm took the field on 10 May 1940 under-armoured, outgunned and outnumbered.

French Forces

The French Army which faced the blitzkrieg, along with the forces of her Allies, was divided into three army groups facing potential Wehrmacht axes of attack.

The Second and Third Army Groups, commanded by Generals Pretelat and Besson, consisting of 35 and fourteen infantry divisions respectively, held the Maginot Line from Montmédy on the Luxembourg border to Switzerland.

A sIG assault gun belonging to one of the panzer divisions of Panzergruppe Guderian passes through the village of Le Quitteur in north-eastern France, 16 June 1940. (IWM.MH.9419)

This massive system of fortifications, protecting the whole length of the Franco-German frontier, was begun in 1928 and first occupied by French fortress divisions in 1936. This formidable obstacle was supposed to be able to defeat any German attack upon it, the lines of *ouvrages* (forts) being able to exist independently of one another.

Vast barracks, magazines and stores meant that troops could exist underground for months on end. The forts had their own power stations and hospitals and even possessed underground railways to move troops long distances from one defensive position to another.

Visible above ground to any potential attackers was a system of gun emplacements, all built to give each other supporting fire and situated so as to cover every possible attack route.

By its completion the Maginot Line had cost the French government over Frs7 billion, money which would have been much better spent on improving France's field armies.

Because the line itself, for political reasons, did not cover the Belgian frontier, it was felt that any German attack was most likely to come through the Low Countries and therefore the best French divisions, along with the BEF, were placed along this stretch of border. Although viewed as a boon to France's defensive posture by allowing her to concentrate her best forces on the expected enemy axis of attack, it also acted very much in Germany's favour.

Because the French had taken up a static defensive posture on the Franco-German frontier, Wehrmacht planners were able to effectively pin down a very large portion of France's defensive assets, both in terms of men and of percentage of defence expenditure, with a relatively small number of divisions. During Fall Gelb (Case Yellow) nineteen infantry divisions of General Ritter von Leeb's Army Group C were able to pin in position more than twice their number of French troops. The Maginot Line helped Hitler to be able to concentrate the vast majority of his units for an attack through Belgium and Holland!

Not only did the Maginot Line hold down a large portion of France's forces away from the main field of battle, it also played a large part in shaping French interwar strategy. The army itself became defensively minded, with little thought being given as to how aggressive attacking tactics might have a role to play in the defeat of an invader. The linear defence also became standard French practice. If war came the French field armies would emulate the Maginot Line and form a defensive wall on which the German Army would batter itself to pieces. No thought was given as to what would be done if the line was ever breached.

Partially because of this strategy, the French High Command parcelled out its armoured assets along the whole length of the front, thus dissipating the overall advantage the Allies held in numbers of tanks. Wherever the panzer divisions struck, they were guaranteed local superiority.

When the Battle for France began, Gamelin was initially confident of success, assuming the Germans, as he had predicted, would launch their assault through the Low Countries and straight into the path of the cream of the Allied forces, the French First Army Group. Unfortunately for the French Commander in Chief, the German hammer blow did not fall on the heavily defended river Dyle as expected but instead landed on the river Meuse at the edge of the 'impenetrable' Ardennes region, a sector of the French line weakly defended by some of their worst units.

The French First Army Group contained, from north to south along their defensive line, the Seventh Army (General Henri Giraud), nine divisions strong, including the 1st DLM (Division Légère Mécanique) of 174 tanks; the BEF (Lord Gort) of nine British divisions plus the 1st Army Tank Brigade; the First Army (General Blanchard) of twelve divisions, including the 2nd and 3rd DLMs with 348 tanks; the Ninth Army (General Corap) of nine divisions, including the 1st and 4th DLCs (Division Légère de Cavalerie); and the Second Army (General Huntziger) of nine divisions, including the 2nd and 5th DLCs.

In reserve were a total of 22 divisions, including the three DCRs (Division Cuirassé) then in existence. Of these, five infantry divisions plus two DCRs had already been assigned to the French First Army Group, with another five infantry divisions deployed on the Swiss frontier, in case of a German offensive through the Alps. This left only nine infantry divisions and one DCR in the entire strategic reserve to cover for unforeseen circumstances, nowhere near enough to restore the situation should a sector of the front collapse.

The French armoured force at the beginning of the invasion of France was organised into three different types of division plus numerous independent tank battalions and companies, attached to various infantry divisions spread along the front.

Five DLCs (Division Légère de Cavalerie) existed with the allotted traditional cavalry roles of screening the deployment of infantry divisions in the field and carrying out reconnaissance and pursuit. Each division contained a single armoured battalion of twelve Hotchkiss H-39 light tanks and twelve P-178 armoured cars. A DLC also contained a dragoon regiment equipped with twenty AMR reconnaissance tanks.

Three DLMs (Division Légère Mécanique) were operational at the beginning of the invasion of France, with several more (all understrength) being raised during the campaign itself. Each division consisted of two demi-brigades, each of two mechanised cavalry regiments. Each regiment consisted of 40 tanks. The DLM was made up of two medium tank regiments equipped with Somua S-35s and two light tank regiments of Hotchkiss H-35s (H-39s in the 3rd DLM).

In addition each division possessed two mechanised cavalry reconnaissance regiments, one equipped with 40 P-178 armoured cars and one containing 60 AMR reconnaissance tanks. The role of the DLM was much the same as its lighter DLC counterpart, although the unit supposedly contained enough tanks and infantry to enable it to operate as an independent arm of decision in the field.

Three DCRs (Division Cuirassé) began the campaign in France, with a fourth being raised during the fighting. Each division consisted of two

A French light machine-gun team take cover behind the edge of the road block, thrown across a street in northern France, May 1940.

demi-brigades, each of two tank battalions. The first demi-brigade contained two light battalions, each of 45 Hotchkiss H-39 tanks, and the second demi-brigade was equipped with two battalions of 35 Char B1 or Char B1 bis heavy tanks. The 4th DCR raised during the campaign itself had a slightly different organisation. It consisted of three battalions of 45 Renault R-35 light tanks, a single battalion of 45 Char D2 infantry tanks and two battalions of 25 Char B1 bis heavy tanks. The DCR was basically an assault division with a high proportion of heavy tanks, little in the way of infantry and no reconnaissance elements at all. It was intended to be used in support of infantry divisions when attacking heavily defended sectors of the enemy line. This breakthrough tank role illustrates further that French planners were still thinking in terms of First World War battlefield strategy and tactics.

None of these armoured formations were able to act independently in the same manner as a panzer division could. Instead of being balanced all-arms units capable of a wide variety of battlefield roles, they were far too specialised. The DLCs with no integral infantry units (they possessed a mounted cavalry brigade instead) were unable to hold ground, nor could they launch effective armoured attacks. They just did not possess enough tanks but they were adept at providing fast-moving reconnaissance for infantry formations.

The DLMs had a much bigger tank complement and a motorised rifle brigade and were in a much better position to fend for themselves on the modern battlefield. However, they still were not strong enough in armoured vehicles to contend with a head-on clash with a panzer division. Again they were well equipped to carry out screening duties and delaying actions for infantry formations.

The DCRs were simply too tank heavy. With only a single mechanised infantry battalion in each division and no reconnaissance troops, they were unable to operate effectively as anything other than an armoured battering ram to smash through the enemy defensive line. Even then they were unable to hold on to any ground

Left, upper: The commander of a French P-178 armoured car asks for the latest known whereabouts of the enemy from a fellow officer. The P-178, built by Panhard, was a very modern and well-designed armoured car, its 25mm cannon being more effective than the main armament of many German battle tanks.

Left, lower: A French cavalry regiment moves up to the line in northern France, May 1940.

Below: A Renault R-35 infantry tank (nicknamed Simoun), the most numerous tank in the French Army, speeds towards the front through a Belgian town, May 1940. The R-35, although adequately armoured when compared with the German panzers, suffered, as did all French tanks, from only having a one-man turret and its 37mm gun was not up to the same standard as those found on the PzKpfw 38(t) and the PzKpfw III.

gained unless the attack was effectively coordinated with an infantry division.

In addition to these armoured formations there were 33 independent tank battalions attached to selected infantry divisions and a further twelve independent tank companies. Twenty of the battalions were equipped with Renault R-35 light tanks, two with Hotchkiss H-39 light tanks, two with FCM-36 infantry tanks, eight with obsolescent FT-17 tanks and one with the gigantic Char 2C heavy tank (these never saw action, being destroyed by a Luftwaffe attack on the train on which they were being transported). Each battalion consisted of 45 tanks, except for the FT-17 units which contained 63 vehicles (only 6 Char 2Cs were ever built).

Five of the independent companies were made up of Char B1 heavy tanks, two with Char D2 infantry tanks, three with FT-17s and two with Hotchkiss H-39 light tanks. The Char B companies contained eleven tanks, the Char D2 companies fifteen, as did the H-39 companies; and the FT-17 units comprised ten vehicles each.

If this armoury of vehicles had been organised and used effectively it is doubtful that Case Yellow would ever have succeeded. Unfortunately, the dispersal of French tanks and their outdated mechanised divisions ensured that whenever a panzer division clashed with a French armoured formation, the Germans always held the advantage.

British Forces

The BEF operated as a part of the French First Army Group and was organised into three corps, plus General Headquarters formations.

I Corps consisted of the 1st, 2nd and 48th Infantry Divisions; II Corps con-

Above: A Char D2 infantry tank on the move across soft ground in northern France, May 1940. The ace of hearts on a square background indicates that this is a tank of the 2nd Section, 2nd Company of the 4th DCR. (IWM.HU.55664)

Right: Crews of the 4th Battalion Royal Tank Regiment service their Matilda Mk I infantry tanks shortly after arriving in France, 6 October 1939. The 'Chinese Eye' insignia visible on the turret sides is peculiar to the regiment and was first used in the First World War after a Chinese labourer was heard to remark of the unit's vehicles, 'If tank has no eye, how can see?' (IWM.O.747)

tained the 3rd, 4th and 50th Infantry Divisions, and III Corps was made up of the 42nd, 44th and 5th Infantry Divisions, plus the 1st Army Tank Brigade. Also directly commanded by General Headquarters were the BEF's two armoured reconnaissance brigades, although in practice they were controlled by the infantry divisions amongst whom they were distributed.

Other British units in France during the first phase of the German invasion were the 51st Highland Division (attached to the French Third Army defending the Maginot Line) and the 12th, 23rd and 46th Territorial Divisions, initially assigned to labouring duties in the rear due to their lack of equipment and poor training. 52nd Infantry Division and 1st Armoured Division both arrived in France as Fall Gelb (Case Yellow) drew to a close.

After the end of May and the evacuation of most of the BEF, all that remained in France south of the Somme were the 51st Highland and 52nd Infantry Divisions, the 12th and 46th Territorial Divisions, the 1st Armoured Division, the Beauman Division (formed 22 May) and one brigade of the 1st Canadian Division (landed 11 June).

The 1st Army Tank Brigade, which provided the armoured backbone of the British Expeditionary Force before the arrival of the 1st Armoured Division, consisted of the 4th and 7th Royal Tank Regiments. 4th Royal Tank Regiment contained 50 Matilda Mk

1 infantry tanks and five Mk VI light tanks, while 7th Royal Tank Regiment was made up of 27 Matilda Mk 1 and 23 Matilda Mk 2 infantry tanks, plus seven Mk VI light tanks. The Matilda, the most heavily armoured tank of the campaign, ensured that the 1st Army Tank Brigade packed a big punch for its small size.

The two armoured reconnaissance brigades were made up of eight mechanised cavalry regiments, seven of them equipped with 28 Mk VI light tanks each (4/7th Dragoon Guards, 5th Dragoon Guards, 13/18th Hussars, 15th/19th Hussars, 1st Lothian and Border Horse, 1st Fife and Forfar Yeomanry, and the East Riding Yeomanry) whilst the eighth, the 12th Lancers, contained 38 Morris armoured cars.

1st Armoured Division consisted of the 2nd and 3rd Tank Brigades, each containing three tank battalions, plus a divisional support group of two infantry battalions and a combined light anti-aircraft/anti-tank regiment (the 101st LAA/ATk Regiment).

The 2nd Tank Brigade was made up of three mechanised cavalry regiments, the 2nd Dragoon Guards, the 9th Lancers and the 10th Hussars, whilst 3rd Tank Brigade contained the 2nd, 3rd and 5th battalions of the Royal Tank Regiment.

The two infantry battalions of the division, the 1st Battalion Rifle Brigade and the 2nd Battalion Kings Royal Rifle Corps, plus the 3rd Battalion Royal Tank Regiment, were sent over to France piecemeal and took part in the defence of Calais. The rest of the division landed later and took part in the battles south of the Somme alongside the French Tenth Army.

Although small in comparison with the armoured forces of the French Army, British tank units always did well in the field against their German counterparts. However, like the French DCRs they did not contain enough integral infantry support (1st Armoured Division had none) and only operated effectively when coordinated with infantry formations. The success gained

The Invasion of the Low Countries, May 1940.

by the 1st Army Tank Brigade at Arras, when only two infantry battalions of the 50th Infantry Division were present and then only for the opening stages of the attack, shows what might have been possible had Allied armoured divisions been organised in the same way as the Wehrmacht's panzer formations.

The Belgian and Dutch Armies

The Low Countries' field armies contributed a total of 26 divisions (eighteen Belgian, eight Dutch) to the defence of Western Europe, plus a further six reserve divisions (four Belgian, two Dutch) raised during the campaign itself. Under-equipped and on the whole poorly trained, these units could do little in the face of the brilliantly executed Wehrmacht offensive.

The Belgian Army contained, for its size, a fair proportion of armoured vehicles but unfortunately their tanks were not only too light (both under-armoured and under-gunned) but they were dispersed throughout the army in the same manner as the French.

Eleven Belgian infantry divisions (five of them reserve formations) were assigned T.13 light tanks, each unit receiving a single company of twelve vehicles. The two elite Chasseurs Ardennais divisions contained two such companies, plus an additional troop of three T.15 light tanks.

The two Belgian cavalry divisions each contained three twelve-tank mechanised cavalry regiments (they were called regiments even though only company-sized). Each regiment consisted of six T.13 and six T.15 light tanks.

In addition to these armoured units there existed a single Escadron d'Auto Blindées of eight French-built ACG-1 light tanks and three twelve-vehicle T.13 light tank companies, two of them

attached to independent frontier guard (cyclist) units and the third, somewhat surprisingly, attached to a Belgian fortress battalion.

The armoured force of the Dutch Army was very small indeed. Consisting of two squadrons of twelve Swedish-designed Landsverk armoured cars and one troop of five British-built Carden-Loyd tankettes, they provided the army with no significant anti-tank capability at all.

Overall, the mechanised units of the Belgian and Dutch Armies, although a minor hindrance, did little to stop the might of the Wehrmacht from crushing resistance in the Low Countries; and this with only three panzer divisions out of ten (the 3rd, 4th and 9th) operating against them.

The Invasion of France

The offensive into the Low Countries commenced at approximately 4.30am on 10 May 1940. Initial air attacks by Ju-87 and Ju-88 aircraft paralysed defenders at key points along the Dutch–Belgian border. Minutes later parachute and glider troops descended to capture strategically important bridges and airfields. Then German infantry and panzer units crossed the frontier, pushing on into the interior. Fall Gelb (Case Yellow) had begun.

For the moment France lay outside the ground fighting zone. The four armies of Pretelat's Second and Besson's Third Army Groups, manning the Maginot Line, contented themselves with holding their positions opposite the nineteen divisions of General Ritter von Leeb's Army Group C. This suited Hitler perfectly; tying down French divisions over three times the number of his own along the frontier made his penetration of Belgium and Holland that much easier. Many of these units, especially the category A infantry divisions, would have been much better deployed further north along the Meuse sector, where the German panzer hammer blow was planned to fall. Instead the region was defended by the sixteen mediocre divisions of Corap's Ninth and Huntziger's Second Armies.

In the battle-zone itself the early fighting went badly for the Dutch and Belgians. Shaken by the fury of the dawn assault, the Dutch Army under the command of General Winkelmann was forced into a precipitate retreat from the river line of the Maas and Upper Yssel. Unfortunately, in their haste to withdraw to more defensible positions from the Maastricht area, they left several river bridges unblown. This was disastrous for the Belgians who were desperately struggling to hold a defensive line along the Meuse further to the south. Tanks from Hoepner's XVI Panzer Corps were quickly across the Maas and the nearby Albert Canal in strength, effectively outflanking the Belgian defences.

As the Dutch and Belgian Armies fought to hold off their German attackers, the French First, Seventh and Ninth Armies, along with the British Expeditionary Force, put into action the Dyle Plan, the formulated strategy for the defence of the Low Countries. Wheeling into Belgium, they pressed forward to their previously assigned defensive positions along the Dyle–Meuse river line. To give enough time for the Allied armies fully to deploy,

Belgian troops were expected to hold the Germans farther east for up to a further five days.

By the end of the first day of the campaign this was beginning to look doubtful, and on the 11th, with the fall of the 'impregnable' fortress of Eben Emael, the Belgian defence line was torn asunder. The capture of these vital fortifications by an airborne assault (some of the attacking troops actually landed on the roof of the fortress in their gliders) further reinforced the French belief that the main German

Above: A German machine-gun team covers the assault crossing of the Maas from the 'enemy' bank of the river, 10 May 1940. (IWM.MH.9207)

Below: A group photograph of some of the victors of the battle for Eben Emael, taken immediately after the action, 11 May 1940. (IWM.PC.449)

thrust was to be made through northern Belgium and Holland.

However, at the very moment that fallschirmjäger (paratroops) were storming the emplacements, the cutting edge of the German mechanised offensive, Panzergruppe Kleist, consisting of Guderian's XIX Panzer Corps,

A PzKpfw III of XLI Panzer Corps passes through the Belgian village of Troyes, May 1940. (IWM.HU.8200)

XIV Motorised Corps and Reinhardt's XLI Panzer Corps (temporarily attached from Twelfth Army), were motoring across southern Belgium heading straight for the weakest link in the Allied front.

The French General Staff throughout the interwar years had thought the Ardennes unsuitable for major offensive operations. Consequently they had deployed their weakest units in the area. Described as 'mountainous' and 'heavily forested' by French military planners, they felt that there was no way that the Germans could mount a mechanised attack of any strength against the French line from this direction.

Yet the French (and for that matter the British) had totally underestimated their opponents. Through intensive training in the Eifel Mountains, Guderian had mastered the skills of manoeuvring armoured formations effectively through restricted terrain. Besides, the Ardennes were not as impenetrable as the Allies led themselves to believe. A good road net existed between Sedan and the German border, the forests were not as thick as was thought and the mountains were in reality nothing more than a series of, not too steep, hills.

Basil Liddell Hart, on touring the area in both 1928 and 1938, had declared that although the terrain was not perfect by any stretch of the imagination, it was passable for tank units. Unfortunately, visionaries such as Liddell Hart were almost totally ignored by the establishment and his advice went unheeded.

On the afternoon of 11 May the lead elements of 1st Panzer Division, in the van of the German advance, met their first significant French resistance around Arlon and Florenville, where 2nd DLC was providing a screen behind which the remainder of Huntziger's forces were deploying. They were quickly forced back, leaving 5th DLC at Libramont with its right flank in the air. This unit had also been pushed forward across the Meuse to reconnoitre the area. To make matters worse for the divisional commander, the DLCs of Corap's Ninth Army that should have been providing a screen to his immediate left had failed to appear, leaving the formation completely unsupported. Although ordered to provide a forward screen for reconnaissance and protection in front of the advancing Ninth Army to the east of the Meuse, Corap felt so confident that no major attack could be forming in his sector that he failed to order the most basic of precautions, 1st and 4th DLCs not moving onto the far bank of the Meuse until late afternoon.

The rapidly advancing panzer divisions were therefore able to push through the Ardennes with little in the way of resistance from Belgian ground forces and fall upon the still-deploying formations of Huntziger's and Corap's armies with little or no fore-warning.

The 3rd DLC, part of the Third Army of the Second Army Group, along with the 1st Spahi Brigade, had been ordered north across the Maginot Line into Luxembourg to establish blocking positions in the Esch area against any German formations moving south through the Grand Duchy.

Unfortunately for the French, as in Belgium, the Wehrmacht had pre-positioned volunteers (known as Brandenburgers) dressed in civilian clothing at strategic points along the French/Luxembourg border. An hour before regular German Army units crossed the frontier, the troops, assisted by Luxembourg fifth columnists,

changed into their uniforms and set up road-blocks.

The 3rd DLC, ordered to cross the border at 5.30am on 10 May, did not begin to move into the Grand Duchy until 8.00am, by which time fast-moving units with much-needed heavy weapons had managed to reach the Brandenburgers. The 3rd DLC were unable to breach these defences, even when the attacks were led by Hotchkiss H-39 tanks. Troops of the 1st Spahi Brigade did, however, manage to push into the Luxembourg interior, causing some consternation to General von Kleist, who ordered Guderian to detach one of his three panzer divisions and send it to the aid of the Sixteenth Army troops pushing through the Grand Duchy (an instruction which he conveniently ignored).

If a significant French force had managed to establish itself in southern Luxembourg it would have posed a serious threat to the left flank of

Panzergruppe Kleist moving through the Ardennes forests. However, due to the stubborn defence of the border area by the Brandenburgers and the failure of 3rd DLC to advance on time, this never materialised. The 1st Spahi Brigade, unsupported by any armour, aircraft or artillery, was forced to retire back across the border with 100 German prisoners.

Meanwhile the French First, Seventh and Ninth Armies and the BEF of Billotte's First Army Group continued to move forward into Belgium, confident that the deciding battle of the campaign would be fought on ground of their choosing.

Several divisions of the Seventh Army on the left of the Allied line had on the 11th reached Antwerp by rail, and elements now formed up and

A PzKpfw III of the 1st Battalion, Panzer Regiment No.1, 1st Panzer Division on the road near Bouillon, Luxembourg, 13 May 1940. (IWM.MH.9193)

headed north into Holland, to support the Dutch Army falling back before von Bock's Army Group B.

Unfortunately the advance of the German forces into Holland had been so rapid that the Dutch Army had been forced almost immediately to withdraw from the Peel–Raam and Yssel Lines, the defensive positions nearest to the German border. General Winkelmann, Commander in Chief of the Dutch Army, had to make the unenviable decision either to continue to attempt to defend the whole of the Netherlands or to begin a staged withdrawal to 'Fortress Holland', the defensive bastion in the west of the country running between the estuary of the Maas and the inland sea (Zuider Zee) east of Amsterdam. With very limited forces at his disposal he chose to fall back on the Dutch centres of population and promptly abandoned much of the south of the country to the advancing Germans. This, as has already been noted, left the left flank of the Belgian Army unprotected but it also ensured that the advance units of the French Seventh Army marched into a Holland abandoned by its troops.

In the north of the country the German 1st Cavalry Division easily penetrated the thinly held 'F' and 'Q' defence lines and by 11 May had breached the stouter Wons Position guarding the Great Dyke, separating the Zuider Zee from the North Sea. However, they then ran into Fort Kornwederzand on the dyke itself and despite constant air attack, artillery bombardment and infantry assault they could not force the garrison to surrender. The gallant defenders of the fort held out until they were ordered to capitulate on 15 May, thus safeguarding the northern approach into 'Fortress Holland' and providing the Dutch Army with its only significant victory of the campaign.

Further south things did not go nearly so well for the Dutch. The fallschirmjäger landing near the Hague

French infantrymen take cover from German fire behind an improvised road block in Luxembourg, during the opening phase of Fall Gelb, May 1940.

had quickly been rounded up but units from the 7th Parachute Division and the 22nd Air Landing Division stubbornly held on to bridges across the Maas and the Waal. This provided a route into the heart of 'Fortress Holland' which bypassed the Grebbe and New Water defence lines further to the east.

By 12 May the lead elements of the 9th Panzer Division had reached the bridges and were poised to drive on Rotterdam and The Hague. The next day the Grebbe Line fell to a concerted attack by the 207th and 227th Infantry Divisions and the SS Motorised Regiment 'Der Führer'. Things looked black indeed for the Dutch Army.

On 14 May, with panzers pushing into the heart of 'Fortress Holland' and the New Water defence line crumbling, the Luftwaffe delivered the *coup de grace* by staging a concerted bombing attack on Rotterdam, in which 100,000 civilians became casualties, over 1,000 of them being killed.

This forced the hand of the Dutch government. Although they themselves had fled Holland, they instructed the army to lay down its arms, in order to save any further civilian loss of life in a battle which was now clearly lost.

As the Dutch Army collapsed under the onslaught of the 28 divisions of von Bock's Army Group B, French and British troops continued to deploy according to the Dyle Plan. Covering the advance of the French First Army and the BEF was General René Prioux's Cavalry Corps (consisting of 2nd and 3rd DLMs) which had rushed forward into Belgium to quickly seal the Gembloux Gap, a stretch of open terrain between the Meuse and Dyle rivers, very favourable for mechanised operations.

On arrival at their predetermined defensive positions they were dismayed to find that the field fortifications promised by the Belgian Army had not been built and the area had been left virtually defenceless.

The 3rd and 4th Panzer Divisions of Hoepner's XLI Panzer Corps, having crossed the Meuse and Albert Canal in southern Holland and with their left flank protected by the German defeats of the Belgium formations in the Liège area, pushed south-east to secure the gap as quickly as possible. The first major armoured clash of the campaign took place on 12 May between the advancing panzers and the tanks of the DLMs near Hannut, twenty miles in front of the Gembloux Gap itself.

The engagement went relatively well for the French and the advance of XLI Panzer Corps was temporarily halted. The Somua S-35 tank came as a particularly nasty surprise to the Germans who found that their 37mm guns had great difficulty penetrating its thick frontal armour. However, the panzer leaders did learn that French armoured tactics were distinctly inferior to their own. The DLMs spread their tanks thinly along the whole of the front, with little in the way of coordination between units, mainly because of the lack of radio sets in French armoured vehicles. Also the one-man turrets used on all French tanks meant that their rate of fire was slower than their Wehrmacht counterparts.

However, by the end of the day's combat a roughly equal number of knocked-out French and German tanks littered the battlefield. This was where Prioux made his first mistake. His orders were to delay the onrush of the German Army, not to hold his current position at all costs. Therefore, having adjudged that he had completed his task, he ordered a withdrawal to a second line of defence between Perwez

A group of infantrymen from the SS Motorised Regiment 'Germania' take a breather before continuing with their push through the Low Countries, May 1940. (IWM.MH.225)

and Marchevolette, less than nine miles in front of the French First Army positions in the Gembloux Gap. This left the panzer divisions in possession of the field of battle, so they were able to recover and repair a significant number of their combat losses, whilst the Cavalry Corps were forced to abandon many vehicles that could have been made battle-worthy with a minimum of effort.

Meanwhile in the Ardennes the only Belgian unit offering any meaningful resistance to the advancing spearheads

of Panzergruppe Kleist, the 2nd Chasseurs Ardennais Division, was quickly brushed aside by Guderian's armour. A complete lack of coordination between the Belgian and French units operating in the area meant that little in the way of information about what German units were pressing towards the Second and Ninth Armies was getting through to their commanders. Corap, still confident that the main blow was falling further north against the First Army Group, on the night of 11/12 May ordered his 1st and 4th DLCs and the 3rd Spahi Brigade back across the Meuse, in case they were needed at a later date on his left flank. This allowed the 5th and 7th Panzer Divisions of Hoth's XV Panzer Corps to press on towards the Meuse crossings at Dinant virtually unopposed.

Huntziger, having already had his 2nd DLC mauled by German troops advancing through the Ardennes, left his cavalry screen on the northern bank of the river. They were quickly pushed back across the Meuse by XIX Panzer Corps, Guderian setting up his forward headquarters at Bouillon. However, the forced retreat of 2nd and 5th DLCs did alert Huntziger to the fact that a major German force, including a substantial number of panzers, was bearing down upon him. Unfortunately he drew the conclusion from the reports

he received from the retreating cavalry that the Germans were intent on outflanking the Maginot Line at Montmédy. Huntziger accordingly moved his best divisions to the right end of his defence line, leaving the area around Sedan, the real objective of XIX Panzer Corps, to be held by Gransard's X Corps. This, his worst formation, consisted of the category B 55th and 71st Infantry Divisions and the regular 3rd North African Division. To make matters worse, the 71st Division was still moving up to occupy its defence line along the Meuse and many of its troops were not in position when Guderian's panzers launched their attack.

Further to the north, Reinhardt's XLI Panzer Corps (6th and 8th Panzer Divisions) closed on the Meuse at Monthermé but were held up by the very narrow, twisty forest roads of the area and the fact that the 2nd Panzer Division, on the right of XIX Panzer Corps, had taken over and blocked with its own transport several roads assigned to Reinhardt.

The French XLI Corps, on the extreme right of Corap's Ninth Army, had been given responsibility for holding a

long stretch of the river Meuse between the Belgian border and Gransard's X Corps at Mezières. Most of this very long frontage was held by the 102nd Fortress Division, a formation trained for static defence and made up of elderly reservists and poorly trained foreign troops, Monthermé itself being defended by the 42nd Machine Gun Demi-Brigade (Indo-Chinese).

East of Dinant, the 5th and 7th Panzer Divisions of Hoth's XV Panzer Corps also advanced on the Meuse, their immediate opposition being formed by the 18th and 22nd Infantry Divisions, two category A units of Corap's Ninth Army, deployed thinly along a far too long stretch of riverbank. By the end of 13 May all three Panzer Corps were in a position to begin assault crossings of the Meuse on the following day.

The attacks across the Meuse were preceded and accompanied by several hours of bombardment of enemy defensive positions by the Luftwaffe. Most of the German artillery was still struggling up to the front through the Ardennes. Wave after wave of Do-17 and Ju-87 aircraft pounded the French positions and did much to undermine the morale of the defenders, who had never before been subject to such an attack.

By the end of the day's fighting each panzer corps had established a bridgehead on the far bank, Hoth's XV Panzer Corps at Houx and Dinant, Reinhardt's XLI Panzer Corps at Monthermé and Guderian's XIX Panzer Corps at Sedan. The crossings were by no means easy and in some instances only the merest of footholds had been gained by the end of the day.

At Dinant Rommel's 7th Panzer Division found it extremely difficult getting across the river, the first waves of rubber assault boats getting cut to pieces by machine-gun fire. Finally troops of his motorcycle reconnais-

A Dutch officer surrenders the garrison of Willemstad to German forces, 14 May 1940. (IWM.MH.9214.)

French Category B reservists move up to the front line on the Meuse, 12 May 1940.

sance battalion were able to gain a foothold on the far bank by using a weir to cross the river. They then gave direct fire support to the troops on the opposite side, helping them to cross and enlarge the bridgehead. Rommel showed his supreme leadership skills by personally leading the next wave of assault boats across. This gave the soldiers the morale boost that they needed and they successfully reinforced the motorcycle troops on the far bank. By the end of the day he had even managed to get a few tanks across to join the hard-pressed infantrymen tenaciously clinging on to the bridgehead.

The next morning the French counter-attacked with regular infantry of the 5th Motorised Division and tanks of the 4th DLC. Rommel, once again in the front line, organised his troops well and the potentially dangerous attack was beaten off. He even managed to turn the defence of the bridgehead into a breakout from it by leading an armoured column in an attack on Onhaye, three miles east of the river.

Early in the day Rommel had received an erroneous report indicating that his lead troops had become surrounded in the town. Taking charge of a relief column of panzers, he charged to their aid. On arrival at Onhaye he found that his troops were not in fact in danger but were in the process of capturing the town, the arrival of the panzers hastening the surrender of its defenders. During this action the 7th Panzer Division commander was slightly wounded, further enhancing his standing with his men and the charismatic control of the troops under his command.

Late in the day General Julien Martin, commander of XI Corps defending the Dinant area, asked permission of General Corap to withdraw to Philippeville, to form a second and final stop line in the hope of containing the breakout. The approval of this request was the last straw for General Gaston Billotte, commander of the First Army Group, who summarily sacked Corap, replacing him with General Henri Giraud, formerly commander of Seventh Army, for failing to act aggressively enough to stop Rommel's thrust. To be fair to Corap, even though he had made basic mistakes in his defence of the river line, much of his failure to prevent the assault crossings was the fault of Billotte who had failed to give him enough divisions to hold the front he had been assigned. He had also failed to pre-position any reserves in the area in case an attack was launched against Ninth Army.

Billotte was forced to redirect the 4th North African Division and the 1st DCR, previously moving up behind Blanchard's First Army further to the north. As the units advanced towards the new stop line on 15 May they had to push their way through thousands of fleeing civilian refugees and soldiers from the shattered 18th Infantry Division.

The infantry and heavy Char B tanks of the DCR struggled to reach the new stop line and launch a counter-attack to contain the breakout, leaving behind their artillery and support vehicles in the morass of retreating soldiers and refugees. As the day wore on the inevitable began to happen and the French tanks began to come to a halt due to lack of fuel. Ju-87 Stukas patrolling the area, creating havoc amongst the retreating columns, destroyed many of the division's stranded vehicles as they waited for their fuel trucks to catch up.

Finally they arrived and, when refuelled, armoured units were hurriedly committed to action against the advancing right flank of the 7th Panzer Division. Unfortunately, because of this piecemeal approach there were never enough heavy tanks in action at any one time to cause serious discomfort to the Germans. The Char Bs certainly came as a shock to the panzer crews who found out that their guns were ineffective against all but the rear armour of the tanks. However, by using superior numbers to work their way to the rear of the French formations and admirably supported by wave after wave of dive bombers they were able to take a heavy toll of the French armour.

Weaknesses both in the French armoured divisions' organisation and in their tank design became further apparent during the engagement. It soon became clear that the DCR did not possess enough integral infantry to allow it to fight a combined arms battle. Consequently, German infantry were able to work their way through the DCR formation. Additionally, the superiority of the French tanks' armour was in many ways offset by the very slow rate of fire from their one-man

turrets. German vehicles were able to close rapidly without taking too many casualties and from very short range were able to aim specifically for vulnerable points such as engine louvres and tracks, disabling the French tanks. Lack of radio equipment meant that new units entering the fray were unable to coordinate effectively with troops already engaged and the fight became a rather muddled but very bloody contest.

At the end of the day's combat the 1st DCR claimed to have knocked out over 100 German tanks, many of which were subsequently recovered and repaired by the field workshops which accompanied every panzer division. The French retired from the battlefield with fewer than two dozen tanks, having left behind many disabled vehicles which were easily repairable or perfectly good tanks that had just ran out of fuel.

Meanwhile the 4th North African Division had attempted to deploy across the front of Hoth's advancing XV Panzer Corps but had been caught up in the tide of retreating refugees and broken troops. The spearheads of the 7th Panzer Division hit the division just as they were beginning to organise themselves for a defence of the new stop line. They were soon carried away in the general rout that was now beginning everywhere in the sector.

To complete the victory, the German 32nd Infantry Division expanded south from the Dinant bridgehead causing the rapid collapse of the French 22nd Infantry Division on the left flank of the German advance. The panzer corps breakthrough was now total and the few organised units that remained in the area opted to retreat back across the border into France.

Reinhardt's XLI Panzer Corps found its assault crossing very tough going indeed. The initial waves of infantry attempting to cross the Meuse opposite the town of Monthermé were

cut down by a hail of well-directed machine-gun fire from several cleverly camouflaged pillboxes. By the end of 13 May they had only managed to gain a foothold on a slim finger of land formed by a bend in the river and on this they were pinned down by the accurate fire of the 42nd Machine Gun Demi-Brigade. This initial success dissuaded Corap from reinforcing this sector, directing units to other more pressed areas, such as Dinant and Sedan. This left the 102nd Fortress Division, already covering a front four times longer than that recommended, little hope of gaining a meaningful victory. Reinhardt, with his Stukas, artillery and panzer resources, could afford to slowly whittle down the defence until a crack appeared which he could exploit.

This finally happened on the 15th when troops of the 8th Panzer Division managed to gain a bridgehead just to the south of Monthermé. With both panzer divisions now on the far bank, the stubborn defence of the 102nd Fortress Division came to an abrupt end, with the unit reeling back in disorder. The 61st Infantry Division, very poorly equipped, even for a category B unit, tried in vain to plug the gap but it simply disintegrated on contact with the lead elements of XLI Panzer Corps. With the collapse of the Ninth Army's XLI Corps there were no more units in the area to attempt a counterattack, Reinhardt's panzers pushed on unimpeded into the French interior.

Right, upper: Tanks of the 7th Panzer Division push on west of Onhaye, 15-16 May 1940. The PzKpfw II nearest the camera is a vehicle of the divisional headquarters, identifiable due to the 'R' for Rommel painted on the turret side. One of Rommel's personal staff stands on the right of the frame.

Right, lower: A Fieseler Storch light observation plane overflies a halted column of tanks from the 7th Panzer Division, somewhere in the panzer corridor, 16-20 May 1940. The Storch served as the airborne eyes of the panzer divisions, helping to locate weak spots in the enemy line and calling in artillery shoots or air strikes on centres of resistance, thus helping to keep up the momentum of the blitzkrieg attack.

Guderian's XIX Panzer Corps began its crossing of the Meuse at Sedan on the afternoon of 13 May after clearing the last pockets of resistance from the town itself, which was on the German side of the river.

Supported by a continuous stream of Do-17 and Ju-87 aircraft bombing X Corps defences, especially their artillery emplacements, troops of the 1st Panzer Division and the Grossdeutschland Regiment managed to gain a foothold on the opposite bank at Sedan with relative ease. With no air support and little in the way of defensive artillery fire there was nothing the 55th Infantry Division could do to prevent the German units from expanding their bridgehead. Resistance was so light that Guderian was able to cross the river himself to view developments at first hand.

At the same time the 10th Panzer Division attempted a second crossing at Wadelincourt, south of Sedan. Without the artillery and air support available for 1st Panzer Division's attack they found the going considerably more difficult, spending much of the afternoon pinned down by accurate artillery fire from the Marfee Heights overlooking their positions. They only

Infantrymen from the 6th Panzer Division lower their pneumatic assault boat into the Meuse opposite the village of Aiglemont, 15 May 1940.

Left: Captured soldiers from the French 4th North African Division watch German transport roll by as they wait to be taken to the rear, 15–16 May 1940.

managed to gain a secure foothold when the breakout from Sedan began to threaten the left flank and rear of the 71st Infantry Division now defending this sector.

The breakthrough was completed when, late in the day, the lead elements of the 2nd Panzer Division managed to secure a bridgehead at Donchery to the west of the panzer corps' other crossing points.

The poor showing of the 55th and 71st Infantry Divisions was at least in part due to a complete lack of air support and the fact that higher command had strictly rationed the number of artillery shells that the French forces were able to fire in their own defence. The reasoning for this was that the Germans could not possibly be ready to launch a river crossing within 24 hours of securing the opposite bank and that the extensive use of artillery ammunition on 13 May would only be detrimental to the defence of the Meuse when the main attack finally came!

General Gransard, commander of X Corps, and General Lafontaine, commander of the 55th Infantry Division, did all they could to stem the tide of retreating troops from the Sedan area and in places managed to patch together secondary defence lines. However, the counter-attack launched by the two reserve regiments of the 55th Infantry Division along with two battalions of FCM tanks was a dismal failure. The units quickly got entangled with the retreating troops and, to make matters worse, the already jittery infantry, still trying to contain the breakout, took the advancing French tanks for panzers in their rear and many of them simply broke and ran. The panic quickly spread to the 71st Infantry Division, units of which also began a precipitate withdrawal from the area.

Enough of X Corps remained in the line at the day's end to force Guderian to plan another set-piece attack to finally eliminate the remaining centres of resistance and free his panzer formations for a speedy drive into the French interior. If a French counterstroke had been organised quickly and launched early on 14 May there was every chance that the Germans could have been pinned in their bridgehead and the breakout contained. Alas it was not to be.

On hearing of the initial successes of the river crossings, the French High Command lost all confidence in its ability to halt the German drive. General Doumenc, on his arrival to brief General Georges at his North-East Command Headquarters, found the general close to tears lamenting the fact that all was lost. It took much persuasion on Doumenc's part to get Georges to agree to launch a counter-attack against the German bridgeheads by the 2nd and 3rd DCRs and the 3rd Motorised Division, which were all in the vicinity.

However, valuable time had been lost and orders did not reach the troops in the field until it was too late to mount a counter-attack on the morning of 14 May. So Gransard was forced to launch his containment counter-attack with a single infantry regiment and another battalion of FCM tanks. The result was a predictable failure.

By the time XXI Corps (3rd DCR and 3rd Motorised Division) had assembled and were ready for an assault on the German positions it was midday. The commander therefore requested that he be allowed to cancel his attack and instead deploy his units in a defensive position around Stonne in order to contain the XIX Panzer Corps breakout. Huntziger agreed and the expected counter-attack never materialised. The 2nd DCR also had great difficulty forming up for the operation (the DCRs had been in existence for less than two months and their constituent units had had virtually no chance to train together) and because they were in no position to launch an attack against the bridgehead alone, they too formed a defensive line in the path of the advancing panzer divisions.

Men of the 1st Panzer Division's motorised infantry regiment set off on their assault crossing of the Meuse opposite Sedan, 14 May 1940. (IWM.MH.9417)

Guderian had in fact been rather worried about the problems he would face if a concerted counter-attack were to take place. The Luftwaffe had informed him on the night of the 13/14th that he could expect no further ground attack aircraft support and he still had very little in the way of armour across the Meuse. However, the French failure to press home any meaningful assault allowed him time to assemble and launch a series of concerted attacks to expand his bridgehead. By the end of 14 May the 1st and 2nd Panzer Divisions had pushed on a further six miles, crossing the Bar river and the Ardennes Canal, while the 10th Pan-

zer Division reached the hills around Stonne where they ran into the defence line set up by XXI Corps.

By passing the initiative to the Germans and contenting themselves with setting up a series of stop lines, trying always to maintain a linear defence, the French were allowing themselves to be consistently and predictably outmanoeuvred.

Unfortunately for the Allies, the French High Command persisted with these outdated tactics and units moving up to try to retrieve the situation were either dissipated along the defence line or sent to plug gaps that had appeared. Nowhere was there a spirit

The importance of heavy and accurate artillery fire to the defence of the Meuse river line is well illustrated by comparing the ease with which 1st Panzer Division crossed the river at Sedan with the difficulties faced by 10th Panzer Division further upstream. Here a French 75mm field gun fires in support of infantry colleagues, northern France, near the Meuse, 14–16 May 1940.

of aggression and a determination to counter-attack that might have saved the rapidly disintegrating Second and Ninth Armies.

On 15 May an *ad hoc* formation consisting of XXIII Corps, containing the 14th Infantry Division and the remnants of the 2nd DCR, plus XLI Corps, 53rd and 61st Infantry Divisions, the 102nd Fortress Division and

Right: The Panzer thrust to the Meuse.

3rd Spahi Brigade, was formed under the command of General Robert Touchon. He was promised a further three fresh divisions over the next two days and his temporary command was then to be expanded and become the new Sixth Army. This new force was somehow to stop the German advance from the Meuse.

However, if the French High Command felt that by amalgamating already beaten units with a much smaller number of as yet untested troops and calling them a new field army would somehow create a force which could miraculously halt the German offensive, it was sorely mistaken.

What was needed were fresh units from the strategic reserve backed by aircraft, artillery and armour. Alas these units had already been squandered. The Armée de l'Air had failed miserably to provide any worthwhile support for the French ground forces thus far and could be relied upon to keep up this level of commitment for the rest of the campaign. The French High Command had squandered its main armoured assets, the DCRs, by throwing them in piecemeal against the tank formations of Panzergruppe Kleist. The only tank formation of any size left, de Gaulle's 4th DCR, was hurriedly forming up east of Laon.

Throughout the next day or two the French generals worried about how they could stop XIX Panzer Corps from breaking out and heading for Paris (hence the decision to halt XXI Corps and the 3rd DCR near Stonne, blocking the southward path of Guderian's panzers). With all their attention fixed on the crossings at Sedan, Reinhardt's XLI Panzer Corps found its drive to the west and Montcornet virtually unopposed. It was not until the end of 16 May that the French High Command began to realise that the Germans did not intend to head

south for the capital but instead were headed westwards in an attempt to cut off the vast majority of the Allied units still deployed in Belgium.

Winston Churchill, who had hurriedly flown to France when he had been informed by the French Premier Paul Reynaud that all was lost, confronted Gamelin and demanded that he use his strategic reserve to restore the situation. The French Commander

in Chief could not oblige. Reserve units had already been dispersed to support the troops advancing into Belgium. All had been staked on the Dyle Plan; when this went awry, the French High Command had neither the ability nor the troops to quickly put together a coherent alternative defensive strategy.

Instead, what fresh units were still available were thrown in piecemeal in

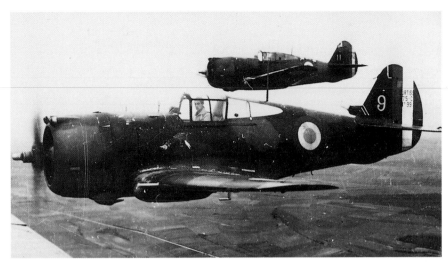

A pair of Armée de l'Air Curtiss Hawk-75C fighters on patrol over northern France. Although a relatively modern design, the United States-built aircraft was no match for the Me-109 and was not able to gain the air superiority the French Army so badly needed throughout the campaign.

an attempt to slow the German advance. On 16 May this amounted to the 9th Motorised Division, formerly of the Seventh Army, the only intact formation now in the immediate vicinity of the breakthrough. General Billotte also rushed south the 1st DLM (detached from Seventh Army) and the 1st North African Division (originally of the strategic reserve but transferred early on into the command of First Army).

The 1st DLM, with the farthest distance to travel, did not join combat that day but was ordered to prepare to attack into the right (northern) flank of the German panzer formations with the remnants of the 1st and 2nd DCRs.

The 1st North African Division, ordered to protect the right flank of First Army by holding the crossings of the Oise near Hirson, found its passage to the river blocked by elements of XLI Panzer Corps who had already secured the bridges they had been told to defend.

Meanwhile, further north, XVI Panzer Corps struggled to force a passage through the Gembloux Gap. Here the defending French units did much better, significantly slowing the German advance, the 15th Motorised Division stopping the 4th Panzer Division dead in its tracks. However, this tenacity would do them no good at all as the breakthrough on the right of First Army had already outflanked the Dyle Plan defensive positions. On the evening of 16 May units of the Ninth, First and Seventh French Armies, along with the BEF, still holding the Dyle river line, were ordered to begin a phased four-day retreat back into northern France.

Further south Rommel's 7th Panzer Division smashed into the 101st Fortress Division and the remnants of the 1st DCR defending the Maubeuge area at Solre-le-Château. Although they put up a spirited resistance, by evening their defensive line had been breached, the remaining few tanks of the 1st DCR falling back on Avesnes. By the end of 17 May Rommel had captured over 10,000 troops and 100 tanks, many of them stragglers picked up en route from French formations that had already disintegrated.

On the left flank of Reinhardt's advance Guderian's XIX Panzer Corps was also pushing rapidly westwards. On the afternoon of 16 May the 2nd DCR had attempted to launch a counter-attack against the 1st Panzer Division but logistic difficulties once again caused many of the French tanks to run out of fuel before they reached the battle area, leaving significant numbers of

Left: A rifle section of a motorised infantry regiment moves up a Belgian village street during the advance of Army Group B through the Low Countries, 10–16 May 1940. (IWM.MH.12845)

Right, upper: PzKpfw 38(t)s of the Headquarters Company, 25th Panzer Regiment, advance in close cooperation with German infantry against French positions near Avesnes, 16–17 May 1940.

Right, lower: A Somua S-35 medium tank of the 4th Cuirassiers, 1st DLM, knocked out by the roadside in the Mormal Forest, 17 May 1940.

otherwise quite serviceable vehicles directly in the path of the advancing German formations.

On 17 May Guderian received an order to halt his attacks to allow the following infantry divisions to catch up with the lead panzer formations. Hitler, worried that the gap between the two was widening to such an extent as to allow a French counter-attack to sever the panzer units from Army Group A, had directly ordered Kleist, commander of the panzergruppe, to slow down the rate of his advance.

Guderian, furious at being denied the chance to annihilate the remaining French forces to his front and press

on with the encirclement of the Allied field armies, at once tendered his resignation. Kleist was ready to accept his offer but Rundstedt, commander of Army Group A, intervened. His views on how the campaign should proceed were in accordance with Guderian's and he allowed him to continue his advance as a 'reconnaissance in force'. As this consisted of the combat elements of the 1st and 2nd Panzer Divisions it hardly constituted a lessening of the thrust at all and the advance continued at speed.

Had the Germans halted for a day or two French units may have had time to organise a further defence line along

the Somme and more Allied troops would undoubtedly have been able to pull out of Belgium. As it was, Guderian's boldness, backed by Rundstedt's judgement, was to ensure that the Battle for France was to be over in a remarkably short time and end in a glorious German victory.

On 17 May two fresh French mechanised formations joined the fray in a further attempt to slice into the flanks of the German panzer advance. Both attacks met with failure after an initial period of success. In the north the 1st DLM, which had only just reached the area, went straight into action against the 5th Panzer Division

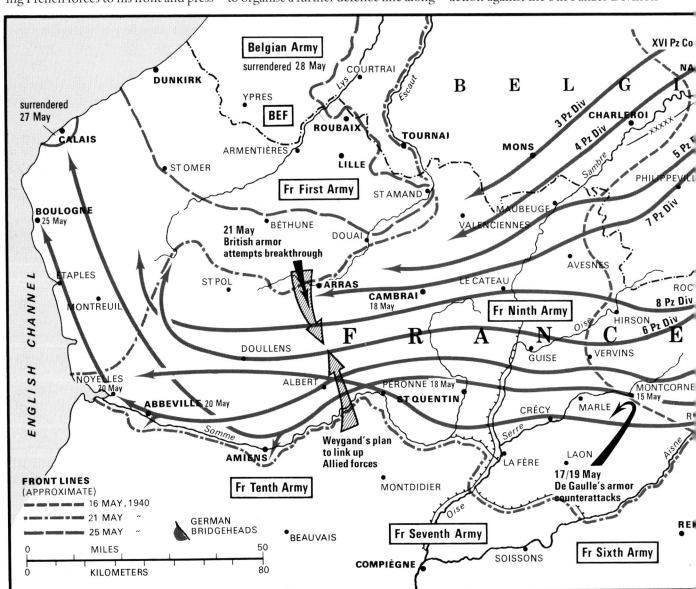

in the Mormal Forest. After 24 hours of heavy fighting the Germans managed to clear the woods, only to be re-engaged by the division on 19 May. It was not until the next day that the 5th Panzer Division was able to resume its advance to the west.

On the southern flank of the German thrust de Gaulle's newly formed 4th DCR (two battalions of R–35 and one battalion of Char B tanks) attacked northwards into the rear echelons of the 1st Panzer Division, initially catching XIX Panzer Corps by surprise and penetrating twenty miles into the German lines, recapturing Montcornet. This success was, however, short-lived.

The Panzer Corridor, 14–25 May 1940

The 1st Panzer Division pushed on westwards, leaving the 10th Panzer Division following on behind to retake the town. This it did with the extensive help of the Luftwaffe, who sent in wave after wave of Stukas against the French armour. With no air support of their own and the division being tank-heavy with not enough infantry to beat off the German assault, they were forced to retreat back to their start line.

These two armoured attacks demonstrated that fresh units properly organised could make inroads into the German advance. The pity was that higher command was never able to coordinate effectively a large enough counter-attack to halt the panzer formations and that French divisional structures militated against effective all-arms cooperation; the right balance of forces inside a French division, armoured, infantry or cavalry, was never present.

Whilst these attacks took place the German advance towards the English Channel continued. On 17 May the 2nd Panzer Division took St Quentin, the 1st Panzer Division gained a foothold on the far bank of the river Somme and the 7th Panzer Division captured Cambrai.

Up until 16 May the Allied forces in Belgium remained blissfully unaware of the disaster that had taken place at the southern end of the line. The Belgian Army had successfully withdrawn from the Albert Canal Line and had taken up position on the left of the BEF, the last of whose units had moved into position along the Dyle Line on 13 May.

The next day they had engaged German forces for the first time, repulsing attacks by IV and XI Corps. Only at Wavre did the British pull back and this was due to the retreat of French units on their right flank rather than enemy pressure on their front. The

French First Army further to the south was also doing well. Although forced to fall back at points along its line, it was very effectively slowing the advance of XVI Panzer Corps.

So when on 16 May the order went out to pull back it caught most of the units along the Dyle Line by surprise. As far as they were concerned, the German assault was being blunted. The Belgian Army was particularly disconcerted. The retreat of the Allied armies would leave Brussels undefended and leave them hanging on to only a small slice of their homeland.

On the day that the withdrawal order came through, the Germans once again attempted a full-scale assault on the Allied line in front of Louvain. The attack was repulsed by the British 3rd Infantry Division commanded by General Bernard Montgomery.

Later the same day the formation began an orderly retreat to the Senne Line, running from Charleroi to Brussels and on to the Willebroeck Canal. By 17 May all the units of the BEF and the Belgian Army had reached this new defensive position. However, they were not to stay there long, for the retreat resumed during the night of 17/18 May when the Allies fell back to the Dendre Line and then on 18/19 May they once more pulled back to the Escaut Line.

On 17 May a new British formation, 'Macforce', was created from infantry of the 42nd Division and armour of the 1st Army Tank Brigade. Their role was to protect the right flank of the withdrawing BEF should the French First Army on their right collapse under the combined weight of the attack of XVI Panzer Corps through the Gembloux Gap and the thrust of XV Panzer Corps across the Sambre towards Arras. The British had been quick to realise that they might soon be relying on themselves.

Also on 17 May Lord Gort had moved up the 12th, 23rd and 46th Territorial Divisions. These under-equipped and poorly trained units had been previously located in the rear on lines of communication duties and were now placed in the line on the Canal du Nord between the Scarpe river and Péronne, to the rear of the First and Ninth French Armies.

On the BEF's left flank a gap had appeared between the retreating British forces and the Belgian Army through which German units had begun to infiltrate. The British 4th Infantry Division had to fight its way clear to retreat back to the Escaut Line. The British government was becoming increasingly worried about the potential fate of its troops and plans were laid to evacuate the force from the beaches of northern France should the situation deteriorate altogether.

On 19 May the 4th DCR once again attempted to slow the German drive to the sea and this time hit Guderian's left rear in the vicinity of

Laon. The attack was brought to a halt by a combination of anti-tank gun fire and aerial bombardment at the town of Crécy. Once again de Gaulle's formation was left without vital air support, leaving the advancing tanks at the mercy of squadrons of Stuka dive bombers called up by the panzer division's Luftwaffe liaison officers.

Gamelin, in his last act as Commander in Chief, ordered the First Army to organise another attack into the northern flank of the advancing Panzergruppe Kleist and the Second Army to assault the base of the breakthrough at Sedan.

Men of a panzer division's motorcycle reconnaissance battalion pause in their search for weak spots in the French defence line, northern France, May 1940. These units were vitally important to the successful maintenance of the pace of the blitzkrieg offensive, seeking out the line of least resistance for the following panzer formations. (IWM.MH.9218.)

However, it was by now quite clear that the forces for these grandiose plans were just not available. On 20 May Reynaud, disillusioned with Gamelin's handling of the campaign, relieved him of command. He was replaced by General Maxime Weygand, fresh from France's colony, Syria. He promptly suspended Gamelin's plan to launch

The crew of a Bren carrier from the 3rd Infantry Division keep a look-out for enemy formations moving up the Brussels–Louvain road. A column of Belgian refugees makes its way to the rear, glad to be re-entering an Allied-controlled area, 16 May 1940. (IWM.F.4404)

A PzKpfw II crosses a road bridge over the Seine carelessly left unblown by the retreating French, 14 June 1940. A large number of water obstacles had to be crossed by the panzer divisions during Case Yellow and Case Red; with a little more planning they could have been turned into formidable defensive barriers. As it was, the Germans always had the knack of obtaining a foothold before French forces could take action.

further attacks into the flanks of the panzergruppe thrust while he made a fresh assessment of the situation.

20 May saw more disasters for the Allies with General Giraud, commander of the Ninth Army, and General Bruneau, commander of the 1st DCR, both falling into German hands.

Guderian's XIX Panzer Corps easily smashed through the British defensive line along the Canal du Nord, the 12th and 23rd Territorial Divisions, without anti-tank guns, standing no chance against the elite panzer formations.

Pushing on quickly through the British positions, the 2nd Panzer Division was able to reach the coast on the Somme estuary near Abbeville. The Allied First Army Group (Belgian Army, BEF, First French Army) was now encircled, pinned with its back to the North Sea.

The next day Weygand decided to launch assaults from both sides of the

German spearhead in the hope of cutting off the lead panzer formations. Thus after 24 hours deliberation he had fallen back on the outline of the plan adopted by Gamelin prior to his departure. General Billotte was to launch an attack southwards in the vicinity of Bapaume whilst General Besson, commanding the Third Army Group (French Sixth and Seventh Armies), was to attack northwards across the Somme.

The order to Besson was completely unrealistic. Struggling to maintain a front along the river line, he was far too busy trying to scrape his motley collection of units together to form a cohesive fighting force to be able to launch a major attack. He had no fresh armoured units available, the 3rd DCR was being rebuilt from training and depot units, whilst the 2nd DCR, with less than half of its original equipment, was in no position to launch any form of assault.

How it should be done. Infantrymen of the 2nd Battalion North Staffordshire Regiment and Matilda Mk I tanks of the 4th Battalion Royal Tank Regiment practise a combined arms assault near Hebuterne, prior to the outbreak of hostilities. (IWM.F.2105.)

Nevertheless, the northern wing of the counter-attack began to assemble as planned. The British 5th and 50th Infantry Divisions, along with the 1st Army Tank Brigade and the remaining armour of the French Cavalry Corps, moved into position during the night of 20/21 May.

The attack got underway on 21 May, hitting the 7th Panzer Division and the SS Motorised Regiment 'Totenkopf' in their right flank. Unfortunately for the British, only two battalions of infantry from the 50th Division were formed up in time to accompany the tank attack. This consisted of the 1st Army Tank Brigade with its 58 Matilda Mk 1 and 16 Matilda Mk 2 infantry tanks, and the French Cavalry Corps supporting the advance with its remaining Somua S-35 tanks but no infantry.

The sudden assault forced the 'Totenkopf' regiment into a precipitate retreat, convincing Rommel that his right flank was under attack by no less than five divisions. He quickly formed an anti-tank gun screen and deployed his 6th Infantry Regiment in the path of the British advance. However, the 37mm anti-tank guns fielded by the Germans made no impression on the thick frontal armour of the British tanks, which swept through the defence line and pushed on into the German rear.

The two British infantry battalions were at this point halted by the 6th Infantry Regiment, and the tanks, pressing on, were left without any infantry support. The Somuas of the French Cavalry Corps also came to a stop. Without any infantry support and low on fuel, they felt it more prudent to call off their assault.

When the normally impenetrable anti-tank gun screens failed to stop the British advance, Rommel halted his panzer drive to the west, diverting his 25th Panzer Regiment to attack the British formation in the flank and rear. He also deployed his divisional anti-aircraft assets in the path of the marauding British tanks. The 88mm guns

Left, upper: A SdKfz 7 half-track and its Flak 18 88mm dual purpose gun, from the 7th Panzer Division, on the move through the panzer corridor near Arras, 20–22 May 1940.

Left, lower: A burnt-out SdKfz 263 radio armoured car (foreground) and a burnt-out SdKfz 231 armoured car, both victims of British tank fire, litter the roadside near Arras, 21–22 May 1940. (IWM.RML.125)

Below: Two PzKpfw IIs of the divisional headquarters, 7th Panzer Division, cross the La Bassée Canal, 27 May 1940.

of the ack-ack batteries had been designed to be used in a ground defence role as well as for anti-aircraft fire and they were the only weapons in the German armoury capable of knocking out the Matildas of the 1st Army Tank Brigade from the front.

When the tanks reached this second defence line they were effectively halted, losing eight of their lead vehicles in the action. The 25th Panzer Regiment then commenced its assault on the British formation.

In the past this tactic of halting an advance with an anti-tank gun screen and then attacking with armour had been very effective in breaking up major French tank attacks. However, the 7th Panzer Division was to fare less well against a British armoured force with fewer tanks than the French could usually field. It must also be remembered that the main armament of the Matilda Mk 1 was nothing heavier than a machine gun whilst the Mk 2 carried the two-pounder anti-tank gun, incapable of firing a high explosive round.

Despite being outnumbered and considerably outgunned, the British gave a good account of themselves, knocking out three PzKpfw IVs, six PzKpfw IIIs and numerous light tanks and armoured cars for the loss of seven more Matildas. However, with losses mounting through 88mm anti-tank fire, no infantry support and panzers in their flank and rear, the tanks were forced to retreat to their own lines, losing more vehicles on the way. Of the 76 Matildas taking part in the attack, less than 40 made it back to safety.

This attack caused much consternation among the panzer generals who came to realise that if an uncoordinated attack such as this could be so successful, then a well-planned assault just might sever the armoured tip of the German drive. To consolidate his position, Rommel halted his panzers for the next 24 hours.

The Germans need not have worried about the prospect of a coordinated attack across their axis of advance. General Weygand was having enough trouble communicating between his two separated commands, let alone organising an effective counter-offensive. On 21 May, after completing his conference at Ypres, he found that he could no longer travel by air between the First Army Group and the main body of the French Army and had to leave by destroyer instead. To make matters worse for the French High Command, General Billotte, commander of the First Army Group was tragically killed in a car accident on his way back from the meeting to his headquarters.

His replacement, General Blanchard, formerly commander of the French First Army, was a military theoretician rather than a fighting general and failed to come up with any new ideas that might get the First Army Group out of the mess it now found itself in. To be fair to the general, he inherited a near impossible situation; the best the First Army Group could hope for was to maintain its defensive perimeter. This would only delay the Germans, not reverse the military situation. The British, realising the long-term hopelessness of the situation, continued to plan for a withdrawal to the coast and an evacuation by sea.

To this end forces had recently been despatched from England to secure and hold the Channel ports of Boulogne and Calais. The 2nd Battalion Irish Guards and 2nd Battalion Welsh Guards, along with an anti-tank battery garrisoned in Boulogne and two infantry battalions from the 30th Infantry Brigade, along with the 3rd Battalion Royal Tank Regiment and an anti-tank battery, deployed to Calais. These troops, along with the second line, second-rate French units already present in the ports, were soon to feel the full weight of a German armoured assault. Swinging north from Abbeville, the 2nd Panzer Division attacked Boulogne whilst the 1st Panzer Division quickly invested Calais.

While the thoughts of Lord Gort, the commander of the BEF, were rapidly turning to how to secure an avenue of escape from France, the French continued to launch understrength attacks against the corridor separating their two forces, in the vain hope of gaining a miraculous breakthrough.

On 22 May the French V Corps launched its planned assault in the direction of Cambrai. Once again the attack rapidly petered out. Initially envisaged as being two divisions strong, the assault was actually launched with a regiment-sized battlegroup of infantry and armour. The counter-offensive therefore became nothing more than a raid into the German positions. Nevertheless, it did manage to penetrate to the outskirts of Cambrai itself before being stopped by a combination of German infantry and anti-tank guns.

This once again showed what might have been possible had the French DCRs and DLMs been kept back and used in a coordinated fashion, with infantry support, against the flanks of the German thrust, instead of being wasted in vain piecemeal attacks against the German breakthrough points on the Meuse.

On 23 May German troops managed to force their way into Boulogne after the town walls had been demolished by artillery fire. That night, while fighting still raged in the town, eight Royal Navy destroyers began to take off the British troops, successfully evacuating 5,000 men by the afternoon of the next day. The remainder of the garrison held out until the 25th when they were finally forced to surrender.

The same fate awaited Calais. The 1st Panzer Division, which had first bottled up the British in the port, left the assault on the town to units of the 10th Panzer Division, while they

Top: A Ju-87B Stuka dive bomber flies along the Channel coast towards the Dunkirk perimeter, 27 May–4 June 1940. (IWM.MH.2469.)

Above: German heavy artillery firing on Belgian positions near Ghent, 22 May 1940.

quickly pushed north along the coast, establishing a bridgehead over the Aas Canal, only a few miles from the last remaining port in Allied hands, Dunkirk.

The attack began on 24 May and the battle was to last until the 27th, when the remaining 3,000 British troops in the town surrendered. Churchill had earlier signalled Brigadier C. N. Nicholson, the British commander at Calais, and told him that there would be no evacuation and that every hour that he could hold on to

the town would give more time for the British to strengthen their perimeter around Dunkirk. General Ironside, British CIGS (Chief of the Imperial General Staff), concurred with Churchill's view and later voiced the opinion that the stiff resistance given by Nicholson's force had been a decisive factor in enabling Operation Dynamo, the evacuation of Dunkirk, to take place.

Of much more importance to the survival of the encircled First Army Group was the fact that on 24 May Hitler gave the order that all attacks by panzer formations on the army group would cease. The Führer, conscious of the fact that his precious panzer assets needed to be preserved for the second phase of operations (Case Red, the in-

vasion of central and southern France), wanted to give them adequate time to refit and recuperate before opening another offensive.

Many of the panzer units in the field were down to 50 percent of their original strength in tanks, and after attacking non-stop now for over two weeks, the men of the divisions were near to complete exhaustion. A few days' rest would boost the fighting capability of the divisions immensely and give the field workshops time to get many of the broken-down or damaged tanks back into service.

Rundstedt concurred with Hitler's assessment and himself felt that the marshy terrain into which much of the French First Army and the BEF were now retreating would best be captured by German infantry divisions.

Besides, Göring, head of the Luftwaffe, had rashly promised the Führer that, since the Allied forces were bottled up in such a small area, they could be obliterated by aerial bombardment alone.

The only dissenting voice in this decision was Guderian, who once again was being told to halt just when he was in a position to strike at the heart of the Allied defences. This time, however, he was not given permission to continue with a 'reconnaissance in force' and the Allies gained valuable time to reinforce their defensive perimeter.

On the other side of the pocket the Belgian Army began to disintegrate under the continual pounding it was receiving from the better trained and better equipped German infantry divisions facing it. King Leopold wanted to hold on to the Ghent bridgehead for as long as possible, as another forced withdrawal would leave the Belgian Army holding on to only a tiny corner of his kingdom.

The strain on the Allied forces was immense, with the First Army Group being slowly crushed in a vice between the infantry divisions of Army Group B and the panzer formations of Army Group A. When on 26 May Hitler rescinded his order to halt the German armour, things began to fall apart rapidly.

The BEF, worried that an armoured thrust up the coast by XIX Panzer Corps could not be stopped unless the sector was significantly reinforced, decided to shrink its perimeter and at the same time thicken it. To do this it withdrew much of the BEF from the Arras area back towards the coast. This rather left the French First Army in the lurch as its right flank now hung in the air.

The British argued that the perimeter of the pocket was over-extended and that to survive longer the defence line would have to shrink. The French, still hoping beyond hope for a counter-attack to sever the German-held corridor south of First Army Group, turned on the British, accusing them of abandoning the First Army. General

Weygand took the opportunity to blame the failure to launch a significant counter-attack on the British strategy of a slow withdrawal to the beaches.

It is difficult, however, to give credence to these cries of betrayal. The British government had a duty to save as many of its troops as it could. It was patently obvious that the French field armies had neither the will nor the manpower, with the possible exception of the French Seventh Army, to successfully launch a counter-offensive.

In truth, the French Commander in Chief fully realised that not only was a formidable counter-stroke not an option but that the French Army was rapidly disintegrating in its defensive positions. Since the Meuse breakthrough tens of thousands of French soldiers had either given themselves up without a fight to the first German unit that came along, or had simply thrown away their weapons and joined the hordes

of refugees heading south into central France.

The morale of the French Army, never particularly high, had collapsed with the failure of the Dyle Plan. The French nation and its soldiers had placed their faith in a clique of generals who still thought of war in terms of the trench conflict of 1914–18. When they failed to stop the Wehrmacht at the French frontier with their outdated linear tactics, they simply could not come up with an alternative plan of campaign.

This outdated thinking went some way to explain why the French armies to the south of the Somme failed to put in any counter-attacks worthy of the name against the southern flank of the panzer corridor. It is true that the French Sixth Army, made up of the remnants of Ninth Army and First

Captured Belgian infantry carry a wounded comrade to the rear, 25–28 May 1940.

Army units that had fled south, was in no condition to undertake an immediate offensive, but the Seventh Army, which had managed to withdraw from Belgium on the whole intact, also failed miserably to put in any concerted counter-attacks.

The French units were tired and many were disorganised after their hurried withdrawal, but only as tired and disorganised as the German infantry divisions that had had to march equally hard to keep up with them.

By 24 May the formations guarding the northern bank of the Somme were strung out along a very long front. Three German infantry divisions (the 9th, 33rd and 62nd) and the 13th Motorised Division held the river line between Amiens and the junction of the Oise and Somme rivers (two further infantry divisions, the 27th and 87th, were held in reserve in the centre of the corridor).

This meant that the divisions were defending stretches of territory comparable with those held by the thinly deployed French divisions along the Meuse ten days earlier. In contrast to the French units, the German infantry had no pre-prepared defensive positions and had not previously exercised over the ground they would have to defend. Yet the Seventh Army failed to launch a single meaningful attack across the river until it was far too late. This confirmed the complete lack of confidence of both officers and men in their ability to turn back the German tide.

The situation got worse for the First Army Group when on 27 May King Leopold informed the Allies that the Belgian Army, completely exhausted and on the verge of collapse, would be surrendering to the Germans the next day.

The BEF was forced to shrink its defensive perimeter yet again, moving Montgomery's 3rd Infantry Division to the left of the British line. The ca-

A trawler packed with British troops leaves Dunkirk harbour during the last days of the evacuation. (IWM.HU.2108.)

pitulation of the Belgian Army, plus the further withdrawal of the BEF, now left many French First Army units in danger of becoming completely cut off.

Guderian's and Hoth's panzers continued to make some inroads into the southern flank of the pocket, although spirited British resistance slowed down their advance to a fraction of what it had previously been. The two days' respite given to the BEF had been spent well, tightening up their defensive line.

On 26 May, sensing no other alternative, Churchill sanctioned the beginning of Operation Dynamo. Forty British destroyers, later augmented by fifteen French warships and over 800 smaller vessels, ranging from large merchantmen to small yachts, crossed the Channel and began to evacuate the BEF. Between 27 and 29 May about 72,000 men withdrew by sea.

On the 29th Hitler finally called off his panzer attacks on the pocket, giving some respite to the beleaguered rearguard. They moved south, away from the battle zone, to rest and refit for the coming invasion of central France.

After this the evacuation gathered pace, with between 53,000 and 68,000 men taken off the beaches or from the port of Dunkirk daily until the end of May. The operation continued until 4 June, with the number of soldiers be-

ing rescued tailing off down to 20,000 on the last day of the operation.

Much of the credit for the success of the evacuation must go to the French forces of the First Army, who as the evacuation went on provided more and more of the perimeter defence. A new sense of purpose seemed to invigorate the men; they realised that the battle was lost but that by buying time for the BEF and a significant number of their comrades to escape, they were ensuring that the Allies would stay in the war against Germany. Eventually on the afternoon of 4 June the remaining 40,000 man rearguard, virtually all of them French troops, surrendered.

III Corps of the BEF (four divisions) had been evacuated between 29 and 30 May, II Corps (three divisions) departed on the 31st and the three divisions of I Corps had been taken off by 3 June. By the time the evacuation came to an end, over 330,000 men, one third of them French, had been rescued.

The Royal Naval and volunteer vessels that bravely came in to the beaches to pick up the troops, often under intense aerial bombardment from swarms of Ju-87 and Ju-88 bombers, took heavy losses, over 240 vessels being sunk during the operation.

Despite this the operation was a tremendous success, far more troops being saved than had been expected. The ordeal of Dunkirk was seen in Britain as a sort of victory and gave a tremendous boost to the nation's flagging morale. Winston Churchill, however, was quick to point out that 'Wars are not won by evacuations' and for the British forces still left on mainland France the worst was yet to come.

During the days leading up to the Dunkirk evacuation the British troops south of the Somme did not stand idle.

Initially widely dispersed, the formations were drawn together and placed under the command of the French Seventh Army.

The infantry backbone of the force was made up by the 51st Highland Division which, although part of the BEF, had been stationed on the Maginot Line under the command of the French Second Army. The mechanised element of the new British grouping was provided by the 1st Armoured Division which had arrived in Cherbourg on 23 May and moved up to join the British force south of the Somme. The final unit to make up the new for-

mation was an *ad hoc* division, named after its creator General A. B. Beauman. The general scraped together every rear echelon unit he could find, requisitioning Matilda Mk 2 tanks sent as replacements for the trapped 1st Army Tank Brigade and taking abandoned guns from airfields for his artillery.

Below left: British troops huddle on the deck of HMS Vanquisher, waiting to be evacuated after climbing aboard from the mole in Dunkirk harbour, 27 May–4 June 1940. (IWM.HU.1153.)

Below: A French soldier runs for cover through heavy German shelling that destroyed much of central Dunkirk and left this abandoned truck ablaze, 27 May–4 June 1940.

The 2nd Tank Brigade, the first unit of the 1st Armoured Division to arrive at the front, soon found itself in action. On 24 May it launched an attack against the German bridgeheads south of the Somme, west of Amiens.

Even though the Germans had heavily defended these areas, expecting counter-attacks, the brigade still managed to eliminate one of the positions, even getting infantry across the river and into the town of St Sauveur. Unfortunately the captured bridge was too damaged to take the weight of anything other than light vehicles, and the infantry, unsupported by armour, were eventually forced to fall back south of the river.

The brigade again saw action when on 27 May a major assault was finally launched by Allied units south of the Somme. 1st Armoured Division led the attack supported by the reconstituted 2nd and 5th DLCs of the newly formed Tenth Army. The attack was, however, launched too late and against the wrong section of the German line. By waiting till the 27th the initiative had been handed back to the Wehrmacht who had several more days to prepare and consolidate their defensive positions.

By the 27th the Dunkirk evacuation was in full swing and an operation to penetrate the panzer corridor was in any case futile as the pocketed First Army Group had already decided to relinquish the field to the Wehrmacht. It was perhaps for this reason that the assault was aimed initially at the German bridgeheads south of the Somme near Abbeville, the strongest point in their defence line. The bridgehead, a potential breakout point for any future panzer thrust, was defended by the best infantry and panzer divisions along the entire river line (the 2nd and 29th

Two British soldiers lie dead on the beach on the Dunkirk seafront, 4 June 1940. Note the abandoned ambulance and stretcher which indicates they may be Royal Army Medical Corps personnel. (IWM.HU.2287)

Motorised Divisions, with the 4th and 9th Panzer Divisions in reserve).

The Allies would have been much better advised to launch their attack to the east, not west of Amiens, where several very tired and overstretched infantry divisions held the line with no armoured support in reserve. They might then have sliced deeply into the panzer corridor, forcing the Germans onto the defensive north of the river.

The 1st Armoured Division suffered heavy casualties in the attack, losing 110 out of 257 tanks, 2nd Tank Brigade ceasing to exist as a viable combat formation. Many of the vehicles lost were in fact repairable but had to be abandoned on the battlefield due to fierce German counter-attacks.

The French doggedly persisted with the counter-offensive, continuing the assault the next day with the 2nd and 5th DLCs and the reformed remnants of the 4th DCR. They also took heavy punishment and failed to throw the Germans back across the river.

On 29 May the French High Command requested that the 51st Highland Division be assigned to the continuing assault on the bridgehead. The British, recognising the futility of further attacks, declined, although they did permit the inclusion of two Scottish battalions in the renewed fighting. The French themselves reinforced their forces with the 31st Alpine Division and the reformed 2nd DCR. After another day of heavy fighting the French had still failed to achieve their objective.

The battle continued until 4 June with the Germans gradually moving over to the offensive, pushing back the French divisions, sensing the gradual crumbling of the forces in front of them.

The next day brought the launch of Case Red, the invasion of central France, which saw the rapid collapse of the French Army and spelled the beginning of the end for the French forces in the field.

The destruction of the First Army Group left the Germans in complete control of the Low Countries and a small part of northern France, north of the Somme and Aisne rivers. Case Red called for Army Groups A and B to smash through the French river defences and push south into the French interior; they would then execute a wide wheeling manoeuvre, pinning the majority of the remaining French field units against the Maginot Line.

The German High Command calculated that the French would not abandon these fortifications and fall back south, as to do so would allow von Leeb's Army Group C free rein to cross the Rhine at any point it so chose. Its loss would further undermine the already shaky morale of the French Army.

As the offensive by Army Groups A and B developed, Army Group C was to ensure that the troops in the Maginot Line stayed inside their defences by launching attacks across the Upper Rhine (Operation Bear) and into Alsace-Lorraine (Operation Tiger). For the opening of the offensive von Bock's Army Group B was repositioned, taking up a front from the Channel coast to the river Oise. Von Rundstedt's Army Group A was to hold the sector between the river and the northern end of the Maginot Line.

Before the offensive could begin the Germans had to give their panzer divisions a few days to rest and receive reinforcements. On 31 May, General Halder, Chief of the General Staff, had reported that only 50 percent of the army's tanks were still operational. By 5 June, through the heroic efforts of the panzer field maintenance service, this figure had risen to 70 percent. However, this still necessitated drawing on all of the army's reserve vehicles, mostly out of date PzKpfw Is and even this did not make up the shortfall.

Not only did the panzer formations need a rest to refit, they also had to reorganise themselves for the offensive to come. Panzergruppe Kleist was now placed under the control of Army Group B, with the newly formed XIV

A French 25mm anti-tank gun and crew lie in wait by the roadside for advancing German armour. (IWM.HU.55668)

A Cruiser Mk IV of A Squadron Queen's Bays knocked out near Quesnay, 30 May 1940. This particular tank managed to penetrate the German lines and caused a lot of damage before being hit six times. The crew managed to bail out and escape. (IWM.F.4605)

reorganised XXXIX Panzer Corps, now consisting of the 1st and 2nd Panzer Divisions, plus the 29th Motorised Division and XLI Panzer Corps, still containing the 6th and 8th Panzer Divisions, with the addition of the 20th Motorised Division. These formations were to strike south across the Aisne from the vicinity of Rethel and Attigny.

Many of the panzer units in the new offensive had to travel 150 miles or more to join their new formations. The disengagement from combat, travel, restructuring and re-equipping of the panzer divisions in such a short space of time, all demonstrated the superb efficiency of German staff work at all levels of command.

On their new defensive line along the Aisne and the Somme the French could only muster 40 infantry divisions plus another ten or so mechanised or

Panzer Corps, consisting of the 9th and 10th Panzer Divisions, in position to strike south from Amiens.

Meanwhile XVI Panzer Corps, still made up by the 3rd and 4th Panzer Divisions, attacked south from the Péronne bridgehead to the east of the city. Also under the command of von Bock, XV Panzer Corps (5th and 7th Panzer Divisions) was positioned in the Abbeville bridgehead, near the mouth of the Somme, ready to turn the recent successful defence of the area into an equally successful breakout.

The panzer units of von Rundstedt's Army Group A were formed into two new corps formations called Panzergruppe Guderian. They comprised the

motorised formations, mostly badly mauled units well below strength. This new position, known as the Weygand Line, could not be defended in a linear fashion as traditional French doctrine dictated, so the Allied forces were deployed in a series of 'hedgehogs' along the front. These were small defensible areas, such as woods and villages, which for the most part stood astride roads needed for the German advance. A mix of arms would defend these hedgehogs, infantryman, anti-tank gunners and artillerymen, who would be mutually self-supporting, equipped with a wide array of weapons to defeat whatever the Germans might throw at them.

They were to hold out even if the German troops bypassed them; there was to be no further retreat. Wherever possible the hedgehogs were to be made suitable for all-round defence, becoming island bastions in a sea of German troops. The idea was that this form of defence would seriously slow the rate of advance of the German mechanised forces. The front would not now be a defensive line but a quadrillage (chequer-board) of interlocking defensive positions.

What remained of the French mechanised and motorised formations would provide units to plug gaps that appeared in the line and counter-attack any significant German forces that made their way through the maze of hedgehogs.

On the opening of Case Red the French Army was deployed as follows: The Third Army Group (Besson) held the line of the river Somme from the coast to the Oise. The Tenth Army, along with what remained of the BEF, was positioned on the left of the line from Abbeville to Amiens and the Seventh Army held the sector from Amiens to the junction with the Oise.

The Fourth Army Group (Huntziger) held the line from the Oise to its junction with the Second Army Group (Pretelat) defending the Magi-not Line. The Sixth Army defended the left flank, along the Aillette Canal and the Aisne as far as Neufchâtel, whilst the Fourth Army defended the remainder of the river line and the stretch of ground between Attigny and Montmédy where the fortifications commenced.

Each division on the Weygand Line held a front of up to ten miles, about twice the normal divisional frontage, hence the need for the hedgehog defence. The original intention for this new form of defence was that the individual island bastions would be near enough to each other to give mutually supporting artillery and even small arms fire. However, the great length of front to be defended meant that many hedgehogs were isolated from the very beginning of the offensive and the large gaps between them meant that it was only a matter of time before the reconnaissance units of the panzer divisions found a way through the quadrillage defence line.

To counter this de Gaulle had called for the withdrawal of all the remaining tanks from the divisions still in the field (of which there were 1,200 in his estimation) and the formation of several new armoured divisions, which would form a mobile reserve ready to counter-attack any German breakthroughs. However, Weygand vetoed the idea, considering that the infantry scattered in their hedgehogs would need local tank support to hold their positions. Thus the mechanised forces available for a counter-attack were reduced to the remnants of the 2nd, 3rd and 4th DCRs (a total of 150 tanks) and the newly created 7th DLM with another 174 vehicles. This force would find it difficult holding back a breakthrough by a single panzer division; it was to stand no chance against the full-blooded assault of a panzergruppe.

Instead of relying on his armour, Weygand felt that the Armée de l'Air could provide the force needed to stall any panzer breakthrough. General Vuillemin had managed to scrape together just over 1,000 combat aircraft for the battles to come, with the RAF providing a further 100 machines. Again this was a paltry total when compared with the number of available German aircraft, and the air superiority needed to operate effectively over the battlefield was unachievable from the very beginning of the offensive.

When the attack opened on 5 June the French forces put up a surprisingly stiff resistance to the initial German mechanised thrusts; XIV Panzer Corps attacking south from Amiens was slowed significantly, only managing to advance six miles during the first 24 hours of the offensive. XVI Panzer Corps had no more success breaking out of its Péronne bridgehead.

Fortunately for the Germans, Hoth's XV Panzer Corps, with Rommel's 7th Panzer Division in the van, made better, although still comparatively slow, progress. Whereas the attack of Panzergruppe Kleist was to virtually stall over the next two days, Hoth's divisions gradually increased their momentum. By 8 June XV Panzer Corps had created a deep wedge in the Tenth Army's positions, threatening the left flank of the Seventh Army, successfully holding Panzergruppe Kleist at bay.

The French IX Corps, along with the British 51st Highland Division, were now becoming increasingly isolated with their backs to the Channel coast. The remaining units of the British 1st Armoured Division had been forced to flee south of the Seine. The next day, despite the blowing of the bridges across the river, troops of the

Right, upper: A wounded soldier from the motorcycle reconnaissance battalion of the 1st Panzer Division is brought to the rear to receive medical attention, Le Quitteur, 16 June 1940.

Right, lower: Two German soldiers inspect an abandoned French FT-17 tank that had been defending the entrance to the main square of Rouen, 10–12 June 1940. (IWM.STT.4073)

7th Panzer Division managed to gain a foothold across the Seine south of Rouen. They then handed over their positions to the 5th Panzer Division. Rommel's formation then turned north-west and raced along the northern bank of the Seine, reaching the sea on 10 June and effectively encircling the 51st Highland Division and IX Corps.

Hearing from a British prisoner that another mini-Dunkirk was to be attempted from the port of St Valery-en-Caux, Rommel pushed hard for the town, capturing it on 12 June after only 2,000 British troops had been rescued. The 7th Panzer Division captured nearly 40,000 prisoners, of which 8,000 were British, including General Fortune, the commander of the 51st Highland Division.

The only armoured counter-attacks of any note against Army Group B in the early days of the offensive took place between 8 and 11 June. On reaching the Seine the lead unit of von Manstein's XXXVIII Corps, the 1st Cavalry Division, was attacked by a concentration of 100 French tanks, bringing the advance to a temporary halt. However, with extensive Luftwaffe support the advance was able to resume the next day, with the 6th and 46th Infantry Divisions of von Manstein's Corps launching an assault crossing of the Seine. By 10 June footholds had been obtained on the far bank.

The next day the remaining 60 or so tanks of the French force reappeared and attempted to dislodge the infantry clinging to the river bank. Again, with extensive Luftwaffe support the attack was beaten off. The Armée de l'Air, unable to gain even temporary air superiority over the battle area, could not give the French armour the support it so desperately needed.

Panzergruppe Kleist, operating against the French Seventh Army, made considerably less progress than those

General Erwin Rommel smugly surveys the captured British and French garrison of St Valery-en-Caux, 10 June 1940. Next to him stands Major General Fortune, commander of the 51st Highland Division.

units on its right flank. On 6 June von Bock, commander of Army Group B, decided to pull the stalled XIV Panzer Corps from its bridgehead at Amiens and move it to join XVI Panzer Corps trying to forge forward from its Péronne bridgehead.

However, by 7 June it was becoming clear that XVI Panzer Corps was itself beginning to grind to a halt, so the next day a decision was made by Adolf Hitler to redeploy Panzergruppe Kleist entirely and launch a fresh attack from a position on the right flank of Panzergruppe Guderian, against the weaker infantry divisions of the French Sixth Army.

This once again highlights the combat effectiveness of the largely intact French Seventh Army and further demonstrates that these divisions, if they had been launched in a concerted counter-attack against the panzer corridor before 26 May, might have had a decisive effect on the outcome of Case Yellow.

Army Group A had much more success with its attacks across the Aisne which were launched on 9 June. Even so, by the end of the first day's operations only XXXIX Panzer Corps had obtained substantial footholds across the river, west of Rethel at the village of Château Porcien.

Over the next two days the Germans expanded their bridgeheads south of the river, the mechanised formations slowly threading their way through the French hedgehogs and the following infantry divisions laying siege to any strategic centres of resistance.

After 48 hours of intense fighting the stubborn defence of General Jean de Lattre de Tassigny's 14th Infantry Division was overcome by the armoured thrust of the 1st Panzer Division and the siege tactics of the following 2nd Infantry Division. This left a gaping hole in the French line south of Rethel and it seemed that the German breakout was about to begin in earnest.

However, on 10 June, just as the lead elements of the 1st Panzer Division deployed out of the gap near the village of Juniville, they were met head

on by the remaining 86 tanks of the 3rd DCR and a fiercely fought armoured battle began. The French tank crews, realising that this was their last chance to stem the German advance, fought fanatically, knocking out over 100 panzers in the action. The panzer commanders, although superior in their tactical handling of their units, just could not knock out the French Char B tanks in a face to face gun duel. It was not until the German tanks, with their superiority in numbers, managed to work their way round the flanks of the DCR that they began to destroy the vehicles, forcing a withdrawal first to La Neuville and then east towards the edge of the Argonne Forest.

The 1st Panzer Division continued to push south, with its sister unit, the 2nd Panzer Division, swinging southwest and heading for the regional capital of Reims. On 12 June French armour put in its last serious attack against the advancing XXXIX Panzer Corps when 50 tanks of the 7th DLM counter-attacked the 1st Panzer Division at Suippes. Weight of numbers soon told and the French unit, outmanoeuvred and under constant aerial attack, was soon forced to withdraw.

On the same day XLI Panzer Corps, which had crossed the Aisne behind the 2nd Panzer Division and then swung east towards the Argonne Forest, ran into the remnants of the 3rd DCR and the reformed 3rd DLC. The units, both seriously understrength, and the 3rd DCR, increasingly battle weary, were pushed aside with relative ease.

To make matters worse for the French High Command, the lead divisions of Panzergruppe Kleist, which had redeployed from the Somme front, also came into action on the right flank of Panzergruppe Guderian, making immediate gains south of the Aisne.

With the Weygand Line in tatters (the lead elements of the 1st Panzer Division had established a bridgehead over the Marne at Châlons by the end of 12 June) the end was in sight for the French Army.

The government had already sensed the inevitable and quit the capital on 10 June, heading for Tours. With the capture of crossings over the Marne on the 13th they declared Paris an open city. The Germans marched in triumphantly the next day. Resistance was crumbling everywhere; the German mechanised formations were now able to push 30, 40 or even more miles a day across the undefended central plains of France. There were no French reserves left; the defence of the Weygand Line had been the last gamble of a desperate High Command.

Renault R-35 infantry tanks wait under the cover of a copse to go into action against the advancing panzers. (IWM.HU.55663)

On the 14th, with the French capital in German hands, Churchill ordered the withdrawal of the remnants of the BEF from France. The 1st Armoured Division, 52nd Infantry Division and the Beauman Division were all safely evacuated from Cherbourg, the first units embarking on 15 June. Two days later the last British units in the front line, the 3rd Tank Brigade, a brigade of the 52nd Infantry Division and elements of the Beauman Division disengaged from the enemy, leaving units of the French Tenth Army to cover their retreat.

By 18 June the evacuation from the port was complete with a total of some 31,000 troops eventually reaching Britain. The majority of these were British but some French units also made their escape. The 1st Canadian

Division, recently landed, was evacuated from Brest between 16 and 17 June and a further 57,000 troops were taken off from Nantes and St Nazaire by the 18th, the majority of them Frenchmen, Czechs and Poles. Convoys continued to leave the free ports in the south and south-west of France until the armistice and by the end of this second phase of evacuations a total of 136,000 troops had made it to safety in England.

On 17 June Hoth's XV Panzer Corps began a new offensive, vigorously pursuing the rapidly withdrawing Allied forces. The 7th Panzer Division rushed headlong onto the Cotentin Peninsula in the hope of catching the BEF before they escaped. Fortunately for the British, the French commander in the area ordered his troops

to try to slow the rampaging panzers, despite Weygand's statement, issued on the 17th, that because of Britain's 'betrayal' French units no longer had any obligation to protect the BEF. Cherbourg did not fall until the 19th, 24 hours after the last British troops had left, the French garrison surrendering after a token resistance. With a rumour that an armistice was to come into effect any day, there was no point in defending a strategically unimportant port for a lost cause, now that the British had gone.

On 16 June von Manstein's XXXVIII Corps had defeated the last coordinated Allied armoured attack of the campaign north of Le Mans, when the surviving remnants of the French DLMs left in the field attempted to halt the formation in its drive to the Loire.

Lacking numbers, low in morale and unsupported from the air, the assault was easily defeated. On 19 June the corps was in Le Mans, by the 22nd they were across the Loire.

Meanwhile on 14 June von Leeb's Army Group C had joined the fray when it became apparent that Weygand had ordered the withdrawal of most of the divisions manning the Maginot Line southwards. To pin them in position, an attack by the First Army was launched against the Sarre Gap, part of the Maginot Line (Operation Bear), whilst the Seventh Army launched an amphibious assault across the Rhine on the following day (Operation Tiger).

Both operations met with considerable success, not only holding seventeen French divisions in position but also penetrating through the fortifications in several places.

The First Army, having broken through the Sarre Gap relatively easily, then smashed into the French XX Corps, which was defeated in a two-

day battle at Lagrand, between 17 and 18 June. The 1st Polish Division, under-equipped and badly outnumbered, fought fanatically against the hated occupiers of their homeland and was virtually destroyed in the battle.

On 18 June XLI Panzer Corps captured Belfort after a brief engagement between corps artillery and the fortified towers and citadel of the town. Further north the 6th Panzer Division captured Epinal, pushing the remaining units of the French Second Army Group into a pocket, sandwiched between the advancing Seventh Army on one side and Panzergruppe Guderian on the other. The encirclement was completed on 19 June when troops from the two formations linked up east of Belfort and units of the First Army sealed the last exit from the pocket in the north. The remaining divisions of the French Third, Fifth and Eighth Armies, some 200,000 men, were now trapped and were to remain so until the end of the war.

A PzKpfw II from Kampfgruppe Koppenburg, an ad hoc formation raised to push ahead of the main body of XLI Panzer Corps and effect a junction with von Leeb's infantry divisions, races down a road near Belfort, 19 June 1940.

A column of German infantry triumphantly enters Paris down the Champs Elysées, 14 June 1940. (IWM.MH.11115)

The Battle for France was now all but over. Three days had passed since the resignation of French Premier Paul Reynaud and his replacement by Marshal Philippe Pétain, the collaborationist leader. On 17 June he had begun his new reign of office by announcing that an armistice was being sought with Germany at the earliest opportunity.

Even after this date, in isolated cases French units still fought courageously. On 19 June, the cadets of the cavalry school at Saumur valiantly brought the advance of the 1st Cavalry Division to a complete standstill. They were, however, forced to surrender the next day when their meagre supplies of ammunition ran out.

In various forts along the Maginot Line troops refused to give up even after the armistice had come fully into force on 25 June. It was not until the first week of July, when French government officials visited the fortifications, that the last units could be induced to surrender.

On 20 June a ten-vehicle column left the seat of the French government at Bordeaux (Tours having been hurriedly evacuated in the face of the German advance) and headed north through the German lines. The final destination of General Huntziger and his staff was to be a railway carriage in the Compiègne Forest. On 22 June 1940 the surrender of France was formally signed in the very same spot that 22 years previously had seen the French receive the German capitulation.

During the campaign France had lost 100,000 men dead, 120,000 wounded and a million and a half prisoners. Losses of equipment and material were immense and unquantifiable. German casualties totalled 200,000, of whom 40,000 were killed.

To be fair to Weygand there was little he could have done to prevent France from suffering defeat. The beginning of the end had begun as early as 15 May with the successful German assault crossings of the Meuse. By the time he took over, the fate of the trapped First Army Group had been sealed and the defence of northern France with an understrength and unenthusiastic French Army was a near impossibility.

France was defeated by a combination of a well-led German Army, willing to put to the test new and revolutionary theories of blitzkrieg warfare and its own backward-looking leaders, who still attempted to fight the Battle for France with outmoded linear tactics and a naive belief that all that was necessary to achieve victory was to dig in and defend.

CHAPTER FIVE

Operation Barbarossa
The Invasion of Russia, 1941

German Strategy and Deployment

Three traditional routes of advance existed into Russia from Germany and her recently acquired Polish territory. The northernmost skirted the Baltic Coast to Leningrad from East Prussia. The second, taken by Napoleon in 1812, runs through central Russia, just north of the Pripet Marshes to Moscow, via the cities of Minsk and Smolensk. The third, lying between the Pripet Marshes and the Carpathian Mountains, is the route from southern Poland deep into the Russian interior, via the 'bread-basket' region of the Ukraine and its capital city Kiev.

Apart from the natural barriers that defined these three broad avenues of approach (the Baltic, the Pripet Marshes and the Carpathians) there were no major geographical obstacles standing in the way of a German invasion of Russia. True, there were several major river lines running north/south across the interior but the very length of these obstacles made it difficult to defend them comprehensively.

Prior to the First World War Alfred von Schlieffen, the chief planner of the Imperial German Army, had considered an invasion of Tsarist Russia

A German light machine-gun team dash forward under enemy fire during the opening stages of the campaign.

should a two-front war break out involving Germany, Russia and the Western Powers. A major factor in his decision to concentrate his blow on France and not Russia was the fact that there existed a lack of geographical features against which a defending Russian army could be pinned, encircled and destroyed. The Russian soldier was not the problem, field armies could be beaten over and over again but their defeat on the battlefield would only bring 'ordinary victories'. The vast Russian Army could always retreat further into the interior to reorganise for yet another stand. With the advent of mobile panzer warfare came the opportunity to outflank and encircle slow-moving Russian armies, destroying them utterly. Adolf Hitler reasoned that the time was now ripe for a successful invasion of the Soviet Union.

Russian forces, outdated, ill-equipped, badly led and corrupted by communism, would be easy meat for a triumphant Wehrmacht and their blitzkrieg strategy. As Hitler told von Rundstedt, 'You only have to kick in the door and the whole rotten structure will come crashing down.' As events were later to show, the Führer seriously underestimated the resilience of the Red Army.

Hitler had made up his mind to attack Russia as early as July 1940, with the successful conclusion of the campaign against France. Detailing both General Alfred Jodl, head of OKW (Wehrmacht High Command, Hitler's personal staff) and General Franz Halder, head of OKH (Army High Command), to come up with plans for an attack, the OKH strategy formulated by Halder's deputy General Erich Marcks was the first to be presented to the Führer for perusal on 5 August 1940.

Rather optimistically, Marcks felt that the Germans would be able to outnumber the Red Army in any invasion. He estimated that the Wehrmacht would be able to field some 110 infantry, 24 panzer and twelve motorised divisions compared to 96 Russian infantry (rifle) divisions, 23 cavalry divisions and 28 armoured brigades.

The bulk of the German army was to be concentrated into two central army groups for two thrusts from Poland, one directed towards Moscow along the traditional invasion route into Russia, the other to aim southeast for Kiev in the heart of the Ukraine. Once these two objectives had been captured the army groups would swing south and north respectively, encircling and destroying the main Russian field armies between the Dvina and Dniepr rivers. Two subsidiary attacks would be made, one from East Prussia along the Baltic coast to Leningrad and the other east into the

A field artillery battery move forward to a new firing position near Rhyezh, 15 October 1941.

southern Ukraine from Rumania. These would protect the flanks of the main advance and ensure that no large concentrations of Soviet forces were left in areas not encircled by the main thrusts.

This plan, although much amended later, formed the basis for Operation Barbarossa, at least in the eyes of the Army High Command. The OKW plan, revealed at the slightly later date, envisaged the formation of three main army groups. The objectives of Moscow and Kiev were maintained, with the addition of Leningrad in the north. To provide the requisite number of troops for the new northern thrust, the attack from Poland to Kiev was to be weakened. However, the subsidiary thrust from Rumania into the Ukraine was maintained and this, it was hoped, would contain enough Soviet formations to enable the attack on Kiev to succeed. The other notable difference between the OKW and OKH plans

was that OKW foresaw the three army groups advancing abreast of one another, ensuring that no Russian formations were left behind their flanks. This would only ensure a series of 'ordinary victories', as Red Army units would be free to fall back to regroup after each successive battlefield defeat. It was hoped that the cumulative effect of these would be to render the Red Army incapable of fighting on, due to exhaustion and lack of supplies.

OKH put both these theories to the test in a large-scale war game later that November and came to the conclusion that Marcks's plan was the more sound but that the addition of Leningrad to the list of priority objectives was also desirable. Halder therefore recommended that three army groups be formed: Army Group North to attack Leningrad through the Baltic States; Army Group Centre to advance on Moscow via Minsk and Smolensk and Army Group South to capture Kiev,

German infantry clear a typical steppe hamlet of Russian troops, after first subjecting it to an artillery bombardment, July/August 1941.

two of its armies advancing from Poland while a third attacked from Rumania. A total of 105 infantry divisions and 32 panzer divisions would take part in the offensive.

From these findings OKW and OKH prepared a joint final directive on the invasion of Russia which was presented to the Führer on 17 December 1940. Hitler, however, could not resist tinkering with the plan and when he issued his Operational Directive No. 21 outlining the strategy for the invasion of Russia major changes had taken place.

The capture of Leningrad had been elevated further from being an objective of equal importance with Moscow and Kiev to being the primary objective. The division of forces between the three army groups remained as outlined by the joint directive, but as soon as the corridor to Moscow through Smolensk had been opened, a large portion of Army Group Centre's assets were to swing north and help in the attack on Leningrad. Only when this city was captured would the advance on Moscow resume. Thus the capture of the Russian capital, seen to be the most decisive manoeuvre of the invasion by OKH, was relegated to a secondary objective on the whim of the Führer.

In addition to these changes a German mountain army was to operate alongside Finnish forces in the far north of Russia and two Rumanian armies would now form the backbone of Army Group South's advance across Bessarabia.

The eventual boundary of the German offensive was fixed on a line from Archangel south along the course of the river Volga. Any remnants of the Red Army retreating beyond this line could, Hitler felt, be held in check by Wehrmacht forces and the Luftwaffe would be given the task of destroying the small amount of Soviet industry left east of the Ural mountains.

A total of 1,160 bombers, 720 fighters and 120 reconnaissance aircraft, split into three Luftflotten, were used for the support of Operation Barbarossa. Luftflotte I, commanded by General Karl Koller, supported the operations of Army Group North. Luftflotte II, commanded by General Albrecht Kesselring, supported the operations of Army Group Centre, and Luftflotte IV, commanded by General Alexander Loehr, the operations of Army Group South.

The three German army groups lined up for the opening of Operation Barbarossa as follows: Army Group North, commanded by Field Marshal Wilhelm Ritter von Leeb, assembled in East Prussia on the Lithuanian border. Consisting of the Sixteenth (Küchler) and the Eighteenth (Busche) Ar-

mies, totalling eighteen infantry divisions, plus General Erich Hoepner's Panzergruppe IV, it was the smallest of the three army groups to attack Russia. The panzergruppe, which provided the armoured spearhead for the advance on Leningrad, contained a total of 812 tanks. It was made up of XLI Panzer Corps, commanded by General Georg Reinhardt, consisting of the 1st and 6th Panzer Divisions and the 36th Motorised Infantry Division; and LVI Panzer Corps, commanded by General Erich von Manstein, consisting of the 8th Panzer Division and the 3rd Motorised Infantry Division. The SS Motorised Division 'Totenkopf' formed the panzergruppe reserve.

Army Group Centre, commanded by Field Marshal Fedor von Bock, assembled on the 1939 Polish/Russian frontier, both north and south of Warsaw. Consisting of 42 infantry divisions of the Fourth (Kluge) and Ninth (Strauss) Armies and Panzergruppen II

and III, it contained the largest number of German infantry and panzer divisions in all three army groups. The cutting edge of Army Group Centre, Panzergruppe II, commanded by General Heinz Guderian, consisted of three panzer corps, XXIV, XLVI and XLVII, totalling some 930 tanks. XXIV Panzer Corps, commanded by General Leo Geyr von Schweppenburg, contained the 3rd and 4th Panzer Divisions, the 10th Motorised Infantry Division and the 1st Cavalry Division. XLVI Panzer Corps, commanded by General Heinrich Vietinghoff-Scheel, was made up of the 10th Panzer Division, the SS Motorised Division 'Das Reich' and the elite Motorised Infantry Regiment 'Grossdeutschland'. Finally, XLVII Panzer Corps, commanded by General Joachim Lemelsen,

An MG 34 machine gun on a sustained fire mount gives supporting fire to an infantry assault on a burning village, July/August 1941.

made up the panzergruppe. It contained the 17th and 18th Panzer Divisions and the 29th Motorised Infantry Division.

The second panzergruppe of Army Group Centre, Panzergruppe III, containing 840 tanks and commanded by General Hermann Hoth, was slightly smaller in size, consisting of only two panzer corps. XLIX Panzer Corps, commanded by General Rudolf Schmidt, consisted of the 7th and 20th Panzer Divisions and the 10th and 14th Motorised Infantry Divisions. LVII Panzer Corps, commanded by General Adolf Kuntzen, contained the 12th and 19th Panzer Divisions and the 18th Motorised Infantry Division.

The two panzergruppen were deployed on the flanks of the army group, Panzergruppe III in the north, on the East Prussian/Russian frontier, north of Bialystok; and Panzergruppe II in the south, on the Polish/Russian border opposite Brest Litovsk (formerly known as Brzesc).

Army Group South, commanded by Field Marshal Gerd von Rundstedt, had by far the longest stretch of contiguous border with Russia along which it could deploy. The front, reaching from central Poland to the Black Sea, was held by one panzergruppe, three German and two Rumanian armies, plus a Hungarian motorised corps, under German control. The German armies, the Sixth (Reichenau), Seventeenth (Stulpnagel) and Eleventh (Schobert), contained a total of 33 German, two Italian and two Slovak infantry divisions. The two Rumanian armies, the Third (Dumitrescu) and Fourth (Ciuperva), possessed a total of fifteen infantry divisions. The Hungarian Motorised Corps (Szombathelyi) was made up of a cavalry division and two motorised divisions, containing a total of 160 tanks (65 Italian CV-33 tankettes and 95 Hungarian built Toldi light tanks) under the control of Stulpnagel's Seventeenth Army.

Panzergruppe I provided the armoured support for Army Group South's advance into the Ukraine. Commanded by General Ewald von Kleist, it contained a total of 750 tanks and consisted of III Panzer Corps, commanded by General Eberhard von Mackensen, and XIV Panzer Corps, commanded by General Gustav von Wietersheim. III Panzer Corps contained the 13th and 14th Panzer Divisions, along with the SS Motorised Divisions, 'Leibstandarte Adolf Hitler' and 'Wiking'. XIV Panzer Corps contained the 9th and 16th Panzer Divisions, plus the 16th Infantry Division. The 25th Motorised Infantry Division formed the panzergruppe reserve.

Army Group South's offensive into Russia was to be made along two main axes of advance. The northernmost and strongest in terms of tanks and men, was to be made from southern Poland towards Kiev. It comprised the Sixth Army on the left of the German line, just south of the Pripet Marshes, with the Seventeenth Army on the right flank, west of Lwow. In between these two infantry armies lay Panzergruppe I.

The Hungarian Motorised Corps deployed along the national border with Russia, south-west of Lwow. Its role was to pin as many Soviet units in the border region as possible, while the northern advance of Army Group South cut them off from their rear. The other Army Group South advance, from Rumania across Bessarabia into the Ukraine, was to be undertaken by three armies. The Rumanian Third Army, deployed in the far north of the country with the German Eleventh Army on its right and the Rumanian Fourth Army, assembled at the southern end of the Rumanian/Soviet frontier on the Black Sea.

German war industry was unable to provide enough tanks to re-equip the already existing panzer divisions, let alone kit out the further eleven formations called for in Operation Barbarossa. The required number of divisions were therefore raised by the simple expedient of halving the number of panzer regiments in each division from two to one. Although many of the Panzer Is and IIs which had formed the majority of German front-line tank strength in the Polish and French campaigns had been withdrawn from service, more than half of

A PzKpfw IV Ausf E pushes on into the interior through a Soviet village, August/September 1941. (IWM.MH.19585)

the tanks participating in the invasion of Russia were light tanks of German or Czech manufacture. A total of 3,332 German tanks took part in Operation Barbarossa, 410 PzKpfw Is, 746 PzKpfw IIs, 149 PzKpfw 35(t)s, 623 PzKpfw 38(t)s, 965 PzKpfw IIIs, and 439 PzKpfw IVs.

So the panzer divisions opening the invasion of Russia were much weaker in numbers than their predecessors of 1939 and 1940 and they still relied to a large extent on obsolescent light tanks to provide their armoured punch. During the French campaign this weakness had begun to become apparent in tank versus tank combat but deficiencies in French vehicle design, notably their lack of radio equipment and reliance on one-man turrets, had still given German armour the overall battlefield advantage.

Most Soviet tanks did not have radios and many were of poor quality when compared with current German designs but steps had been taken to remedy these deficiencies and the new Russian vehicles, the T-34 and KV-1, were far in advance of anything the Wehrmacht could field. Armed with high-velocity 76.2mm guns, they could easily destroy even the heaviest German tanks. The KV-1 carried 90mm frontal armour, making it impossible to be knocked out by most of the anti-tank guns in German service. The T-34, with its good mobility and well sloped 45mm frontal armour, was almost as difficult to stop. German panzer commanders were soon to lament that without vehicles of comparable combat capability the tank war in the east would be lost.

So the new 1941 panzer division contained one tank regiment of two, sometimes three, abteilungen (companies) totalling 150-200 tanks; two motorised rifle (schützen) regiments, each of two battalions, whose soldiers were carried in armoured half-tracks or similar vehicles, and a reconnaissance

Red Army KV-Is wait to move forward against the advancing Germans. The slogans painted on the side of the tank turrets were a common sight on Soviet vehicles, exhorting soldiers in the field to heroic deeds to rid the motherland of the Fascist aggressors. (IWM.STT.889)

battalion of three companies (two armoured car, one motorcycle). The divisional artillery consisted of two field, one medium and one anti-tank regiment and an anti-aircraft battalion, all motorised to enable them to keep up with the fast-moving panzers.

The motorised infantry divisions accompanying the panzer divisions in the panzergruppen were similarly organised but lacked the tank element and had an additional rifle regiment.

The infantry divisions, as in previous campaigns, had to rely on horse-drawn transport for their supplies and artillery, and the infantrymen themselves had to rely on their own two feet

to get them across the vast Russian steppe.

By June 1941 the Sturmartillerie had been expanded from the four assault artillery batteries that had seen action in the Battle for France. Each army group was now provided with two assault artillery battalions and a varying number of independent batteries, supplementing these formations with new vehicles as the campaign pro-

gressed. By the late summer of 1941 some 250 Sturmgeschutz (Stug III) assault guns were in action on the Eastern Front.

Again as in the 1939 and 1940 campaigns, the panzer arm could only provide the armoured spearhead of the advance. The vast majority of the Axis units committed to the invasion were infantry formations. Although panzer units could and did race ahead of the main body of each army group, the speed of the offensive into Russia was always regulated to a greater or lesser extent by the rate at which the infantry could advance.

This speed became even more important when the start of the campaign against Russia had to be delayed by a crucial five weeks. It was originally due to commence on 15 May 1941 but the Italians' disastrous campaign against Greece and the anti-fascist coup in Yugoslavia forced Hitler to divert troops earmarked for Barbarossa into a short-lived campaign in the Balkans.

This new offensive began on 6 April and lasted until 26 May, ending with the airborne operation to capture Crete. By this time most of the units participating in Barbarossa had begun to return to the eastern frontiers of the Reich. The delay incurred, however, meant that the offensive into Russia could not begin until late June.

Hitler was irritated by this loss of time but was at no point deterred in giving the go-ahead for the campaign to begin. Operation Barbarossa, named after the twelfth-century Germanic emperor who led a crusade against the heathen Slavs, was to be the ideologi-cal struggle to the death that the Führer had long planned for. His hatred for communism and the 'sub-human' Jews and Slavs of the east lead him to declare that this new campaign 'will have to be conducted with unprecedented, unmerciful and unrelenting harshness . . . The commissars (Red Army political officers) are the bearers of ideologies directly opposed to National Socialism. Therefore all commissars will be liquidated. German soldiers breaking international law . . . will be excused. Russia has not participated in the Hague Convention and therefore has no rights under it.' The war for Russia was to become the bloodiest and most savage the world has ever known.

The Soviet Army and Its Defensive Strategy

Hitler's belief that the Red Army could be defeated with ease lay in part in his assessment of the pernicious effect of communism on the Soviet military. In many respects his evaluation was correct in that during the interwar years the Communist Party had striven to maintain control of the Red Army at every level. This had ruinous effects on the competence and initiative of the officers corps, particularly at a junior level.

When in 1937 Stalin began his great purge of the Soviet military, an already inefficient army became an incompetent one. By the time the purge was over at the end of 1938, the Red Army had lost the vast majority of its experienced officers, thousands of them having been executed or sent to a slow death in the Siberian gulags.

The ones who survived, especially in the higher echelons, were yes-men who owed their lives and position to Stalin. One or two, such as Zhukov and Timoshenko, were to prove capable field commanders in the coming campaign (in Zhukov's case he was to become the most outstanding Russian general of the war). However, most were either out of touch traditionalists, such as Marshal Semyon Budenny, who wanted to fight the Germans in the same manner as he had fought the Whites in the civil war, or complete incompetents such as Marshal G. I. Kulik who had no idea at all of military professionalism. Promoted to Head of Ordnance after the execution of Marshal Grigori Tukhachevsky in 1937, he ordered the suspension of all further manufacture of anti-tank and anti-aircraft guns and the withdrawal of all automatic weapons from the Red Army for redistribution to the police! Not content with disrupting the production and distribution of the Red Army's hardware, he also ordered the disbandment of the large armoured formations built up by Tukhachevsky and the redistribution of the tanks amongst infantry formations in small units.

The commissar, throughout the interwar period, played a central role in the command structure of the Soviet Army. It was through this political officer that the Communist Party maintained its ascendancy over the military at every level. Each military commander had a political counterpart and this commissar was able to veto any of the commander's decisions or even force the commander to execute his own orders if these were deemed to be in the interest of the Communist Party. This system stifled any thoughts of individual initiative, as all important command decisions were referred to and made by the 'omniscient' party.

During Tukhachevsky's brief reign as head of the Red Army's mechanisation programme this party straitjacket was removed and modernisation went ahead at lightning speed, Stalin's forced industrialisation policies enabling a startling growth in tank numbers. From a starting point of 92 vehicles in 1928 the Red Army grew to 15,000 tanks by 1935 and 24,000 by June 1941.

Left, upper: A dramatic photograph of a Wehrmacht supply wagon coming under artillery fire in a Russian street. In the haste to get to safety one of the wagon's rear wheels has come off and its load appears to be about to spill over the road.

Left, lower: A Sturmgeschutz (StuG) III assault gun pushes on into the Russian interior near the village of Sarasova, July/August 1941. Note the rings round the gun barrel, indicating that this vehicle has knocked out six Soviet tanks so far in the campaign.

Left: A Red Army 45mm anti-tank gun goes into action against German armour from its camouflaged emplacement, July/August 1941. (IWM.RUS.372.)

Right: A medical officer treats an infantryman wounded in an assault on a village on the road to Kiev, 1–7 July 1941.

ising at last that Soviet Russia needed a modern efficient army to defend her borders, reinstated many of the reforms called for by Tukhachevsky. Separate mechanised corps and tank divisions were re-raised, the commissar was relegated to the role of political adviser and the operational independence of the military commander was re-established. Officers who had languished in the gulags as a result of the purge were released and reinstated.

Unfortunately the executions of thousands of professional military officers left equal numbers of inexperienced and incompetent soldiers in positions of influence and authority. Used to being subjugated to the rule of the party, they did not know what to do with their new-found autonomy. By June 1941 the Red Army may have been capable of defending itself with the equipment in its armoury but its officer corps was certainly not able to meet the intellectual challenges of modern warfare. These lessons they would have to learn through bitter experience.

The Soviet Army in the spring of 1941 had in its order of battle between 230 and 240 divisions, not including reserve divisions that could be raised in time of war. Of these some 170 were within operating range of the western frontier. The majority were rifle (infantry) divisions, each of about 14,000 men, containing little transport and completely unmechanised. The tank divisions, of which there were at least 32 and perhaps as many as 60, each consisted of two tank regiments, a lorried infantry regiment and an artillery regiment. Motorised divisions, of which there were at least thirteen, con-

Although the numbers of tanks produced continued to rise during and after the great purge, the doctrinal changes called for by the modernists, such as Tukhachevsky, died with them. This lamentable state of affairs continued until the very serious reverses suffered by the Red Army during the winter war against Finland in 1940 forced Stalin to re-examine the way the Soviet military was organised. That war, which began on 30 November 1939 with the invasion of the Karelian Isthmus north of Leningrad, went disastrously for the Russians. The Red Army, vastly outnumbering the tiny Finnish Army in both men and equipment, was not only unable to capture the small amount of territory claimed by Stalin but was defeated again and again on the battlefield. The Red Army was only able to force the Finns to accede to Soviet demands after widening the conflict along the entire frontier and amassing an army of nearly a million men against them.

The disaster in Finland reinforced Hitler's belief that the Red Army was rotten to the core and that a swift victory was easily achievable. Stalin, real-

The North-East Front, defending Latvia east of Riga and Leningrad, consisted of four rifle divisions under the command of General Markian Popov.

The North-West Front, commanded by General Vasili Kuznetzov (later by Sobennikov), consisted of the Eighth and Eleventh Armies, commanded by Generals Sobennikov and Morosov and was deployed in Lithuania. In total the two armies contained 20 rifle divisions and four tank divisions.

The West Front, commanded by General Dimitri Pavlov, ran from Kaunas in Lithuania south to Brest Litovsk in White Russia (occupied since 1939). It contained the Third Army (General V. I. Kuznetov), the Tenth Army (General K. D. Golubev) and the Fourth Army (General Korobkov), totalling 30 rifle divisions and eight tank divisions.

The South-West Front, commanded by General Mikhail Kirponos, ran from Brest Litovsk to the Lower Ukraine. It contained the Fifth, Sixth, Twenty-sixth and Twelfth Armies, commanded by Generals Potapov, Muzychenko, Kostenko and Ponedelin respectively and totalled 40 rifle divisions and sixteen tank divisions.

The South Front, commanded by General Ivan Tyulenev, ran from the Lower Ukraine to the Black Sea. Made up of the Eighteenth Army (General Smirnov) and the Ninth Army (General Cherevichenko), it totalled twelve rifle divisions and four tank divisions.

The Red Army looked able, at least on paper, to acquit itself well should the Germans decide to attack. With the reformation of mechanised corps, tank divisions and motorised divisions, the Russians could field far more armoured formations than could the Wehrmacht. Even with the inexperi-

tained a single tank regiment, two lorried regiments and an artillery regiment.

The air force, part of the Red Army, suffered from exactly the same drawbacks in terms of officer quality as did the ground forces. In addition it was plagued with obsolete and inferior aircraft, with no war-winning designs (as the army had with its T-34 tank) coming into service. At the beginning of the campaign the Soviet Air Force had in service on the western front some 1,350 bombers (only 500 of which were not obsolete), 200 fighters, all inferior in combat to the German Me-109, and 800 old-fashioned reconnaissance aircraft.

In June 1941 the Red Army defending the western frontier was deployed in a series of five fronts from the Baltic coast to the Black Sea. After the first series of battlefield defeats these were reduced to three fronts, under the commands of Marshal Kliment Voroshilov (North-West Front), Marshal Semyon Timoshenko (West Front) and Marshal Semyon Budenny (South-West Front).

However, at the outset of the campaign they were organised as follows:

A rare sight indeed. A Russian nurse treats a wounded SS infantryman captured during the opening stages of Operation Barbarossa. As the Soviet Union was not a signatory of the Geneva Convention and Hitler viewed all Slavs as 'sub-humans', the campaign on the Eastern Front rapidly degenerated into a savage conflict with little quarter given by either side, especially to captured SS. (IWM.RUS.579)

ence, inefficiency and incompetence of many of the Soviet commanders, the overwhelming numbers of Red Army units should have been enough to stop an invasion in its tracks.

However, three other factors worked decisively against the Red Army in its defence of Russia. First of all, the quality of the armoured vehicles making up the majority of these new mechanised formations left a lot to be desired. Indigenous tank production increases had meant that more and more vehicles had been made available but a large number of these home-grown designs were notoriously unreliable, many of a tank division's vehicles being out of commission at any one time due to mechanical failure.

The tanks themselves were on the whole not of a particularly good design. The Soviet multi-turreted heavy tanks, the T-35 and T-28, were unwieldy and prone to breakdown, the Germans contemptuously referring to them as Kinderschrecken (things to frighten children) due to their bizarre appearance. The T-26 was well armed with a 45mm gun but suffered from a lack of armour and was again mechanically unreliable. The BT series of tanks were armed with the same gun, were

fast and able to traverse very difficult terrain due to their Christie suspension system but their armour was paper-thin. The Soviet light tanks, the T-37, T-38 and T-40, were little better than tracked machine-gun carriers, only the T-60, armed with a 20mm gun, making a promising reconnaissance vehicle. To counterbalance this the Soviets were beginning to supply their forces with increasing numbers of the new T-34 and KV-1 tanks. By June 1941 867 T-34s and 508 KV-1s, with their 76.2mm guns and heavy armour, were in service with the Red Army. This was equivalent to more than one-third of the entire tank force of the Wehrmacht attacking Russia!

The other qualitative factor that let down Soviet armour was the severe shortage of radio equipment. The cumbersome size of a mechanised corps (two tank divisions, each of two tank regiments with 200 tanks each, plus a motorised rifle regiment and an artillery regiment) was due, at least in part, to the lack of communication equipment in the Red Army. Unit sizes had to be kept large because there were not enough radios to permit a more flexible stance. In tank units it was rare for a command net to be established at

below regimental level. Commanders had very little control over their troops once committed to action. Tank formations relied heavily on rehearsals and drills, whole regiments attacking in line abreast. Changing the direction of an attack once launched was impossible and the formation of *ad hoc* battle-groups (kampfgruppen) could not even be contemplated. Armoured attacks therefore tended to be made in straight lines with strictly limited objectives. This lack of flexibility enabled the much smaller panzer units to run rings round their opponents.

Finally, the entire deployment of the Red Army in the West was highly suspect. Most of the blame for this must be shouldered by Stalin himself.

With the expansion of the Soviet empire in 1939 and 1940 large new tracts of land came under communist control. In October 1939 half of Poland had been annexed, followed in the next year by the occupation of the Baltic States and the annexation of Bessarabia from Rumania. Stalin viewed these acquisitions as increasing the buffer zone between potential enemies and the Russian heartland. However, if anything, it made the Soviet Union easier to attack. The Red Army was forced to abandon the old frontier defences which had been heavily fortified over the previous two decades and move several tens, in many cases several hundreds, of miles forward to defend the new border.

An open frontier, without strong fixed defences and without formidable natural obstacles, demands a defence in depth, by forces able to wage mobile warfare in a flexible manner.

Left: Soviet T-34 tanks move forward to engage the enemy, October 1941. On the 4th of the month the first major engagement took place between these tanks and German panzers. The T-34, with its well-sloped armour and 76mm gun, shocked the Germans, and, with its good cross-country mobility and low ground pressure, it came into its own in the severe weather of the Russian winter. (IWM.STT.902)

Right, upper: A good photograph of a Red Army BT-7 fast tank towing a damaged staff car to safety through a Ukrainian village, August 1941. (IWM.RUS.616)

Right, lower: The charge is rammed home into a German 210mm K-39 heavy gun bombarding Soviet positions, June 1941. (IWM.HU.5076)

The Red Army was caught almost totally by surprise, even though Winston Churchill had passed on Enigma intelligence to Stalin forewarning him of the planned German assault. Marshal Timoshenko had gleaned some information from the dictator and had on his own initiative issued an alert to the staffs of the various Soviet military districts several hours before the attack commenced. However, by the time the assault opened very few, if any, of the front-line Soviet commanders had been informed of what was about to happen.

The Red Army units in the immediate path of the attacking German formations were easily overwhelmed and soon the armoured spearheads of the advance were pushing on into the interior. The linear defence of Soviet territory played straight into German hands.

Army Group Centre, assigned the task of advancing along the Minsk–Smolensk road, the main highway to Moscow and the traditional invasion route of Russia, made rapid progress, even though its initial advance involved the assault crossing of the Niemen and Bug rivers. Von Bock's initial strategy was quite simple. The panzergruppen of Guderian and Hoth would advance as rapidly as possible, forming the jaws of a trap into which the Soviet units defending the immense Bialystok salient (the Tenth Army, the Third Army

The Red Army, ponderous and slow-moving, was the exact opposite of what was required.

The situation could have been remedied somewhat by the deployment of large numbers of reserve units at key communications centres behind the front. They would then have been ready to move to any breach in the line and stem the enemy's advance. Unfortunately for the Russian commanders, Stalin insisted on a forward defence of all Soviet territory, spreading the Red Army formations along the entire frontier at equidistant intervals, with no strategic reserve. This invited disaster and when the campaign began it came as no surprise to many of the generals in the field (even the inexperienced ones) that their commands were almost immediately cut off and surrounded.

The Invasion of Russia

Operation Barbarossa opened at 3.30am on 22 June 1941 with an intense artillery barrage of Soviet defensive positions along the border. Three-quarters of an hour later the first German infantry units crossed the frontier. The Battle for Russia had begun.

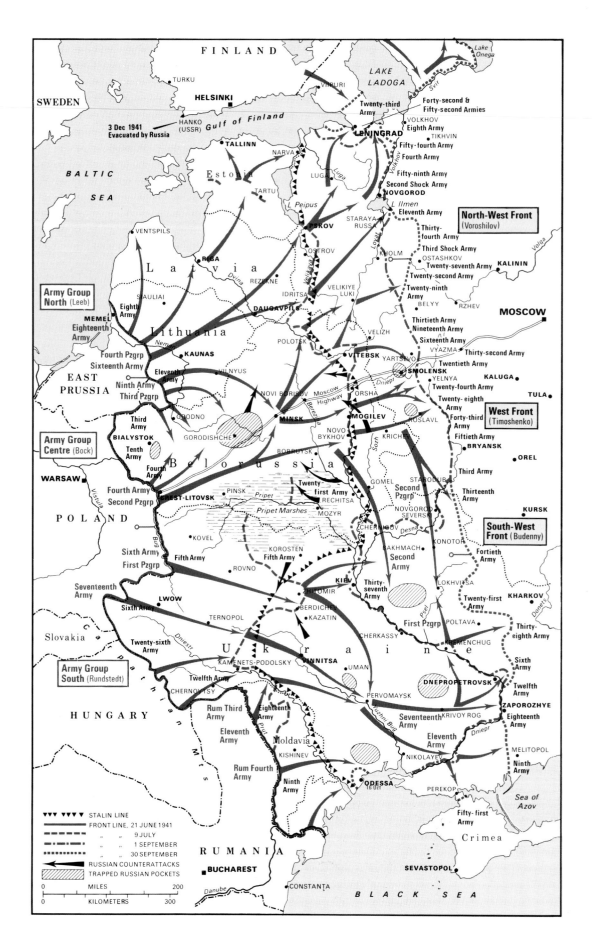

FINLAND

SWEDEN

TURKU

HELSINKI

3 Dec 1941
Evacuated by Russia

HANKO
(USSR) Gulf of Finland

LAKE LADOGA

VIIPURI

Svir

Lake Onega

Twenty-third Army

Forty-second & Fifty-second Armies

VOLKHOV

Eighth Army

TIKHVIN

LENINGRAD

Fifty-fourth Army

Fourth Army

Fifty-ninth Army

Second Shock Army

NOVGOROD

BALTIC SEA

TALLINN

NARVA

Estonia

L Peipus

TARTU

Luga

LUGA

PSKOV

OSTROV

Velikaya

L Ilmen

Eleventh Army

STARAYA-RUSSA

North-West Front
(Voroshilov)

Thirty-fourth Army

VENTSPILS

Lovat

KHOLM

Third Shock Army

OSTASHKOV

Twenty-seventh Army

KALININ

Latvia

RIGA

Dvina

REZEKNE

IDRITSA

VELIKIYE LUKI

Twenty-second Army

Volga

Twenty-ninth Army

BELYY

RZHEV

Army Group
North (Leeb)

SAULIAI

Eighth Army

DAUGAVPILS

VELIZH

MOSCOW

MEMEL

Eighteenth Army

Lithuania

Nemen

Thirtieth Army
Nineteenth Army
Sixteenth Army

POLOTSK

VITEBSK

YARTSEVO

VYAZMA

Thirty-second Army

KAUNAS

Fourth Pzgrp
Sixteenth Army

Eleventh Army

VILNYUS

NOVI BORISOV

Moscow Highway

ORSHA

Dniepr

SMOLENSK

Twentieth Army

KALUGA

TULA

EAST PRUSSIA

Ninth Army
Third Pzgrp

GRODNO

MINSK

Berezina

MOGILEV

Twenty-fourth Army

Twenty-eighth Army

Forty-third Army

West Front
(Timoshenko)

Third Army

BIALYSTOK

Tenth Army

GORODISHCHE

NOVO BYKHOV

ROSLAVL

Fiftieth Army

BRYANSK

Belorussia

BOBRUISK

KRICHEV

Sozh

OREL

Army Group
Centre (Bock)

WARSAW

Fourth Army

Twenty-first Army

RECHITSA

GOMEL

Second Pzgrp

Third Army

KURSK

Fourth Army
Second Pzgrp

BREST-LITOVSK

PINSK

Pripet

MOZYR

NOVGOROD-SEVERSK

Thirteenth Army

Pripet Marshes

POLAND

Bug

KOVEL

KOROSTEN

Fifth Army

CHERNIGOV

Desna

KONOTOP

South-West
Front (Budenny)

Sixth Army
First Pzgrp

Fifth Army

ROVNO

BAKHMACH

Second Army

Fortieth Army

Seventeenth Army

LWOW

Sixth Army

TERNOPOL

ZHITOMIR

BERDICHEV

KAZATIN

KIEV

Thirty-seventh Army

LOKHVITSA

Twenty-first Army

KHARKOV

Slovakia

Dniestr

Twenty-sixth Army

KAMENETS-PODOLSKY

VINNITSA

First Pzgrp

POLTAVA

CHERKASSY

KREMENCHUG

Psel

Thirty-eighth Army

Donets

Carpathian Mts

Army Group
South (Rundstedt)

CHERNOVTSY

Twelfth Army

UMAN

PERVOMAYSK

DNEPROPETROVSK

Sixth Army

Twelfth Army

HUNGARY

Rum Third Army

Eighteenth Army

Uzhni Bug

Seventeenth Army

KRIVOY ROG

ZAPOROZHYE

Eighteenth Army

MELITOPOL

Eleventh Army

Pul

Moldavia

KISHINEV

Eleventh Army

NIKOLAYEV

Dniepr

Ninth Army

Rum Fourth Army

Ninth Army

ODESSA

16 Oct

PEREKOP

Sea of Azov

RUMANIA

Fifty-first Army

Crimea

BUCHAREST

SEVASTOPOL

Black Sea

▼▼▼ ▼▼▼▼ ▼ STALIN LINE
——————— FRONT LINE, 21 JUNE 1941
— · — · —   " " 9 JULY
— ·· — ·· —   " " 1 SEPTEMBER
·········   " " 30 SEPTEMBER
◀━━━━ RUSSIAN COUNTERATTACKS
▨▨▨ TRAPPED RUSSIAN POCKETS

0   MILES   200
0   KILOMETERS   300

Danube

CONSTANTA

BLACK SEA

and most of the Fourth Army) would fall. The two panzergruppe pincers were to close for the first time around Minsk, west of the Beresina river, to prevent the escape of Soviet troops across the Dvina and the Dniepr rivers farther to the east. The infantry divisions of the Fourth and Ninth Armies, following up, would then help eliminate any centres of resistance left behind the advancing panzer formations.

Left: Operation Barbarossa, 22 June–30 September 1941.

Below: A PzKpfw IV Ausf F Tauchpanzer presses on into the Russian interior after crossing the river Bug near Patulin, 22 June 1941. Note the Swastika flag used as an aerial recognition symbol. The Tauchpanzer was a specially converted submersible PzKpfw IV originally designed for Operation Sea Lion, the planned invasion of Britain. (IWM.STT.520)

Thereafter the panzer divisions were to secure the 'land-bridge' to Moscow between the head-waters of the Dvina and Dniepr rivers.

Luftflotte II, supporting the ground advance, was able to provide Army Group Centre with immediate air superiority, destroying vast numbers of Soviet planes on the ground and easily defeating the few fighter and bomber sorties directed against von Bock's forces.

Only at Brest Litovsk did the Russians manage to hold on to any of their frontier defences for any length of time, the fortress town holding out until 9 July. Although inconvenient for the advancing Germans, the siege did not hamper the advance of Army Group Centre. An infantry division was simply detached from the Fourth Army to hold the defenders in check while the offensive continued.

The ease with which Army Group Centre had broken through the Russian lines led von Bock to suspect that the Red Army was putting into effect a pre-planned strategy to withdraw from the indefensible new frontiers and fall back on a prepared defence line along the Dvina and Dniepr rivers. Accordingly he requested that Panzergruppen II and III be allowed to abandon their mission to close their pincers around Minsk, 200 miles inside Russia, and push on to Smolensk, a further 125 miles into the Soviet interior.

This request was refused as OKH (Army High Command) felt that the

German field artillery pounds Red Army defensive positions during the opening phase of Operation Barbarossa. (IWM.HU.5073)

risks of extending the pincers was too great. The isolation of a single panzergruppe could prove disastrous to the progress of the offensive. Only when the jaws of the trap had been closed around Minsk would von Bock be allowed to direct a second such operation around Smolensk.

This, as it turned out, was a wise decision. The Red Army units retreating from the Bialystok salient were not in fact falling back to a secondary defence line but were blindly attempting to find their way out of the impending encirclement.

In the French campaign the very threat of envelopment was often enough to cause entire divisions to capitulate.

However, Soviet units not able to withdraw at anything like the speed of the advancing panzers (who averaged over 50 miles a day in the opening phase of the campaign) tended to try to batter their way through the pincers of the advancing panzergruppen. This they began to do with limited success against the flanks of Guderian's Panzergruppe II, some Red Army units breaking out south-eastwards towards the Pripet Marshes. If von Bock had been allowed to stretch the jaws of the pincers a further 125 miles to Smolensk, many more units would have been able to break free, creating a significant 'stay behind' problem on the German lines of communication.

As it was, infantry divisions from the Fourth Army were able to staunch the flow of Soviet units with a relatively slight loss of speed for the advancing panzergruppe.

By 25 June, only three days after the beginning of the offensive, Army Group Centre found itself fighting three battles of encirclement, the smallest being the battle for Brest Litovsk. Around Bialystok six Russian divisions had been surrounded and further to the east near Volkovysk six more divisions,

Left: The crew of a Red Army 76mm infantry gun man-handle their weapon forward into a new firing position, June/July 1941. (IWM.RUS.547A)

Right: German supply wagons trundle across the pontoon bridge over the Dniepr at Smolensk, July 1941. (IWM.HU.5086)

which had managed only a partial withdrawal, were trapped.

Four days later Army Group Centre was fighting to close the largest pocket so far created, around the city of Minsk. Containing fifteen Soviet divisions, some of them refugees from the western frontier, others reserve units caught up in the retreat, they put up a fierce resistance in an area centred just west of the city itself. It took until 9 July to eliminate the last resistance in the pocket, with the assistance of infantry divisions from the Fourth and Ninth Armies, who arrived having dealt with the smaller envelopments further west.

Orders for the next stage of operations had already been issued by OKH on 1 July, together with a directive reorganising Army Group Centre. General Gunther von Kluge, previously commander of the Fourth Army, was now redesignated commander of a new formation, the Fourth Panzer Army, controlling both Panzergruppe II and Panzergruppe III. The Fourth Army, now redesignated Second Army, was to be commanded by General von Weichs.

The first order von Kluge received was to prepare to 'break through in the direction of Moscow'. Accordingly Panzergruppe II was ordered to force a crossing of the Dniepr south of Smolensk and seize the Yelna Heights in the bend of the river Desna; whilst Panzergruppe III was to remain on its present axis of advance and proceed along the upper Dvina to Vitebsk, where it was to cross and capture the territory north of Smolensk.

The Second (ex-Fourth) and Ninth Armies were to follow up as quickly as possible, eliminating any stubborn centres of resistance in the path of the advance. The Luftwaffe would continue to support the advance with Kesselring's Luftflotte II, Fliegerkorps II supporting the armies in the south of Army Group Centre's advance, while Fliegerkorps VIII supported those forces in the northern arm of the pincers.

The operation began on 3 July, before the infantry divisions of the Second and Ninth Armies had finished clearing the Minsk pocket, leaving the panzergruppen with only their own integral infantry to support them.

Almost immediately the panzergruppen encountered heavier opposition than any met so far. Panzergruppe II was halted on the banks of the Beresina near Borisov and although subsidiary crossings were forced at Rogadev on the Dniepr and Polotsk on the Dvina, neither was considered acceptable as alternative axes of advance. Von Bock was faced with the dilemma of either waiting for the infantry divisions to catch up with the panzers, then forcing a crossing with a traditional-style infantry assault, or continuing to press for a breach with

his mechanised forces, thus exposing them to the danger of substantial losses in men and material.

He bravely chose the latter option, calculating that speed was of the essence and that any major delay could be fatal to the offensive as a whole.

Initially it looked as though von Bock had made the wrong decision as the Russians stubbornly resisted any

attempt by Panzergruppe II to gain a foothold on the opposite bank.

Fortunately for the Germans, Panzergruppe III had managed an effective breakthrough further north. Hoth had quickly established a bridgehead over the Dvina at Vitebsk and was now pushing his armoured formations through the gap as fast as he could. So extensive was his breakthrough that

von Bock considered abandoning the southern attack and moving all the panzer units towards Moscow on the northerly route. This, however, would have meant abandoning the encircling strategy hitherto employed with such great success, so von Bock continued to push for a breakthrough across the Dniepr. Finally on 10 July, one week after beginning their crossing attempts, units of Panzergruppe II managed to gain a foothold on the far bank. At the same time further north units of Panzergruppe III raced on towards Smolensk.

By 13 July Panzergruppe II had not only managed to retain its bridgehead but had began to break through the Soviet defences. On the 14th Panzergruppe III was able to place a division across the Moscow-Smolensk road, cutting off the main source of supply for the Russian divisions further west. Incredibly, the next day a single German division was able to capture the city of Smolensk itself in a surprise assault.

Over the next two days the two panzergruppen continued to push towards each other, finally linking up on the 17th at Yelna, 50 miles south-east of Smolensk. Inside the pocket were some 21 Soviet divisions, in three different defensive groups. Six or seven divisions were trapped near the town of Mogilev, near to the start line of Panzergruppe II's assault across the Dniepr. A further three or four were

Left: A Soviet infantrymen ties together five grenades to produce a crude but effective (if the soldier could get close enough) anti-tank weapon. He has already completed two other bundles, one on the lip of the trench, the other on its floor. Lying in the corner of the foxhole are two even cruder anti-tank weapons, Molotov Cocktails. Basically empty bottles filled with petrol and a rag stuffed in the top, they could and did knock out German panzers but only if a Russian soldier was brave or foolhardy enough to approach close to the enemy vehicle and smash it over an engine louvre or other weak spot. (IWM.RUS.375)

Right: German soldiers round up Soviet prisoners in the Smolensk pocket, July 1941.

cornered just south of Vitebsk near to the breakthrough point of the northern panzer thrust. The final group, consisting of some twelve to fourteen divisions, was trapped to the east of Smolensk, strung out along the road to Moscow.

Normally the infantry divisions of the Second and Ninth Armies would have moved in to eradicate the pocket and mop up any remaining centres of Soviet resistance. However, because of the time needed to eliminate the troops in the Minsk pocket, many infantry units were up to 200 miles behind the advancing panzers and it was not until 27 July that the Smolensk pocket finally became watertight.

For much of the intervening time the cordon had to be held by tank and motorised infantry units stretched very thin indeed. Because of this some Soviet units were able to break out and make their way farther east to take up

yet another stand. However, what worried the German commanders even more was the fact that Red Army troops and supplies continued to battle their way into the pocket, even after it had been sealed.

Although this indicated that Soviet commanders were tactically naive it did prove to the Germans that the Battle for Russia was not going to take exactly the same course as had the Battle for France. Red Army units when resupplied would often have to be almost totally eradicated before the survivors would even contemplate surrender. Only through stifling the flow of munitions to trapped Soviet divisions could they be induced to surrender en masse. The fighting in the Smolensk pocket was to continue until 5 August, when the last centres of Soviet resistance were finally eliminated. By this time the offensive into Russia had moved on and infantry formations

found themselves once more many miles behind the front line. The stubbornness of Red Army units surprised Hitler and the OKH, heightening their apprehension about leaving large enemy troop concentrations trapped in the rear of the advancing German armies.

Stalin was not slow to appreciate that something had gone dramatically wrong at the strategic level but as with most dictators he discerned no personal mistakes and laid the blame for the disastrous opening of the campaign on his generals. General Pavlov, commander of the West Front opposite Army Group Centre, was recalled to Moscow early in July, along with his chief of staff and chief signals officer. All three were summarily executed.

Because of the failure of the military to stem the German advance Stalin felt that a reimposition of party discipline could only be of benefit to the

The two Russian infantrymen inspecting the knocked-out PzKpfw 38(t) in the lower half of the photograph, found the photograph shown above it, the same vehicle before the beginning of the campaign, on the dead body of one of its crew members, who presumably appear in the top photograph. (IWM.RUS.424)

by the Red Army, the problem of how to replace the massive losses in men and material suffered during the opening phases of the invasion was by far the most pressing problem confronting the Soviet High Command.

By mid-July the German Army had captured over 300,000 Russian prisoners, plus 1,400 artillery pieces and 2,500 tanks. OKH estimated that 89 of the 164 Red Army divisions facing them had been destroyed. This total was to double with the sealing of the Smolensk pocket, a further 310,000 prisoners, 3,100 guns and 3,200 tanks being captured. The Soviet Air Force had by this time been almost completely wiped out, losing nearly 6,000 aircraft, half of them in the first five days of the campaign.

True, the Germans had yet to meet any significant numbers of the new T-34 and KV-1 tanks but the infantry divisions being raised to support these tank units were increasingly having to recruit from the partially trained Osoaviakhim, the Soviet equivalent to the Home Guard/Territorial Reserve. In addition the government had begun to raise Opolchenie (People's Militia) units. These were armed with whatever old and obsolete weaponry they could get their hands on and their uniforms generally consisted of civilian clothing, often, but not always, with the addition of an identification arm band.

As units of Army Group North pushed on towards Leningrad, German troops encountered more and more of these units. Surprisingly, they fought with the same grit and determination as did their regular counterparts, only being let down by their inferior equipment and complete lack of tactical

Red Army. On 16 July the principle of 'dual command', in which the commissar was given equal command status to the military officer, was reintroduced. In addition Stalin also set up the Stavka, a new High Command structure consisting of both party functionaries and military officers, to direct operations and to ensure that the direction of the campaign stayed firmly under political control.

At the same time the front structure of the Red Army was reorganised, the number of fronts being reduced from five to three, each of the new fronts roughly opposite the three German army groups. The North-West Front, opposite von Leeb, was commanded by Marshal Voroshilov, the West Front, opposite von Bock, was now commanded by Marshal Timoshenko, and facing von Rundstedt was the South-West Front commanded by Marshal Budenny.

Although this restructuring helped alleviate some of the difficulties faced

Stalin's eldest son, Yakov Djugashvili, at a Russian aerodrome awaiting his transfer to the rear and further interrogation by the Wehrmacht, Smolensk, 16 July 1941. (IWM.MH.11434)

training. Army Group North, numerically the smallest of the attacking forces with only twenty infantry divisions and a single panzergruppe, had also managed a spectacular advance in the opening stages of Operation Barbarossa.

Advancing in three columns, the Eighteenth Army along the Baltic coast, Panzergruppe IV in the centre and the Sixteenth Army on the right flank, the army group easily smashed through the Lithuanian border defences, which consisted of a single rifle division stretched out along a 40-mile front. The army group passed quickly through the Baltic state, being greeted in many places by enthusiastic citizens as the liberators of occupied Lithuania. By 4 July the lead elements of Panzergruppe IV had reached Ostrov, part of the fortified Stalin line along the pre-1939 Soviet–Latvian border. Ten days later, having bypassed whatever Russian concentrations stood in its way, XLI Corps of Panzergruppe IV stood on the line of the Luga, the last important river obstacle before Leningrad and only 60 miles from the city.

Von Rundstedt's attack into Russia was like Army Group Centre's, in that it followed two main axes of advance. In the north the Sixth and Seventeenth Armies, headed by Kleist's Panzergruppe I, thrust towards Kiev, the Ukrainian capital, via Lwow, from southern Poland. Further south the Eleventh Army, along with the Rumanian Third and Fourth Armies, attacked across Bessarabia, striking east to Odessa and north-east of Kiev. Thus Army Group South was attempting a pincer move on the city, much like von Bock's encirclements of Minsk and Smolensk. The problem von Rundstedt faced was that the jaws of his trap were much wider and that only the northern pincer of the attack contained a concentration of armour able to move at speed. However, it was hoped that Axis units would be able to outmanoeuvre the Red Army at a more local level and create a series of smaller envelopments as they pushed for Kiev.

T-26 tanks and infantry of the Soviet Sixth Army advance against German positions near Kazatin, west of Kiev, July 1941. (IWM.RUS.273)

A Sturmgeschutz (StuG) III assault gun pushes into a Ukrainian village past a PaK 36 anti-tank gun, July/August 1941.

The plans for a wide encirclement of the Soviet Twelfth and Twenty-sixth Armies suffered a set-back during the opening weeks of the campaign when the Red Army at last staged a coordinated a large-scale counter-attack against the northern pincer of Army Group South.

The Fifth Army, which had retreated north into the Pripet Marshes, and the Sixth Army ,which had fallen back into the steppe south-east of Lwow, attacked into the flanks of Panzergruppe I, advancing eastwards on Kiev. The attack was a failure. Soviet forces did not manage to penetrate the German flank defences, indeed they were quite easily repulsed by the motorised infantry and anti-tank guns screens they ran into. However, the delay to the advance caused by these attacks enabled both the Twelfth and Twenty-sixth Armies to withdraw beyond the jaws of the trap set by Army Group South.

This is not to say the advance of the northern pincer of Army Group South had been unsuccessful. By 11 July leading elements of Panzergruppe I were within ten miles of Kiev. It was just unfortunate that Army Group South had not been able to emulate the actions of Army Group Centre and capture vast numbers of Soviet troops.

To both Hitler and his staff at OKW and the Army General Staff at OKH the campaign seemed as good as over. All that was needed was a plan to defeat the broken remnants of the Russian armies.

From this point on, Adolf Hitler began to actively involve himself in the operational planning of the campaign, much to the annoyance of the field commanders involved. The opening phases of the offensive had been carried through as planned by OKH and had met with great success. However, the Red Army had failed to act like the Polish and French had in previous campaigns and continued to fight on, even when badly mauled and trapped behind enemy lines. In particular the Fifth Army, operating out of the Pripet Marshes, posed a considerable risk against the flanks of both Army Group Centre and the northern pincer of Army Group South.

To counteract this, Hitler in a supplement to his War Directive No. 33, issued on 23 July, ordered that the attack on Moscow be temporarily suspended. No further advance towards the Soviet capital was to be made until the Smolensk pocket had been totally eradicated and the infantry divisions of Second and Ninth Armies, some of which were over 250 miles behind the front line, had caught up with the lead mechanised elements.

Furthermore, in the original directive issued on 19 July, Hitler had stated that the two panzergruppen leading the advance of Army Group Centre should prepare for a new offensive. This was not, however, to continue the attack eastwards in a concentrated thrust but to split the armoured formations, Panzergruppe III turning north to help in the advance on Leningrad, and Panzergruppe II turning south to attack the Russian Fifth Army in the Pripet Marshes. Guderian's panzers were to link up with units from Kleist's Panzergruppe I and infantry divisions from the Sixth Army. These formations were to attack northwards, encircling the Fifth Army and also cutting off several Soviet reserve divisions that had moved westwards from the Kiev area.

Guderian, horrified at what he saw as the gross misuse of his panzer formations, did all that he could to delay the transfer of his units to the south. He remonstrated with his superior von Bock, arguing that the terrain in this area was unsuitable for armoured operations and that the panzergruppen should be used as the spearhead of the German advance and not as some mobile force for mopping up the rear areas. The commander of Army Group Centre had much sympathy with Guderian's views and was already upset with Hitler for suspending his push on Moscow. Conniving with the panzergruppe commander, he allowed Guderian to get himself involved in a

A German infantry brigade commander consults with his staff on how best to continue with the Kiev encirclement, outside a recently captured Red Army bunker, 11–12 July 1941.

Left: A light machine gun fires on a suspected sniper's position in the advance across the steppe near Gelenovka, August 1941.

Right: A Russian M-1931 203mm howitzer prepares to fire against Army Group North positions, September 1941. (IWM.RUS.638)

battle with several Russian divisions at Roslavl, 70 miles from Smolensk, thus pinning them in the van of the army group. Luckily for the German generals, Timoshenko, commander of the Soviet forces facing Army Group Centre, chose this moment to launch a heavy but totally inept counter-attack on the forces arrayed on the Smolensk–Moscow road.

This strengthened Guderian's case for a freezing of the redeployment of the panzergruppe away from the main axis of advance of Army Group Centre, and Hitler partially concurred with his view. In Führer Directive No. 34 he accepted the need for panzergruppe forces to remain at the forefront of

Army Group Centre for another ten days, enough time for them to see off the Soviet counter-attack. However, he still expected Hoth and Guderian to prepare their forces so that when the attacks petered out they could resume their previously ordered operations. Hitler re-emphasised this on his visit to Army Group Centre headquarters at Novi Borosow on 4 August. Hoth diligently began to prepare to move his troops north. Guderian did nothing of the kind, only edging a few units a little further to the south in an attempt to placate the Führer.

The Russian High Command seemed to share Guderian's view that Moscow was of prime importance, as

it sent Timoshenko the most plentiful reserves. However, reinforcements at this stage in the campaign rarely meant anything more than collections of hastily trained men, stiffened with cadres from survivors of earlier debacles.

Budenny, Soviet commander in the south, with a smaller share of the Red Army's manpower resources, appealed to the Stavka to be allowed to withdraw the Fifth Army from the Pripet Marshes to help maintain a cohesive north–south front. The Soviet High Command correctly adjudged that the, at least temporary, slowing down of the offensive on Moscow was due to worries about Red Army operations behind the German flank and refused Budenny's request.

To fill the gap that was rapidly developing between units of Timoshenko's front west of Moscow and Budenny's forces retreating south-east into the Ukraine, Stalin created the new Bryansk Front, a grand-sounding army group that in fact consisted of a few half-trained reserve rifle divisions without a single tank to its name.

Both OKH and OKW battled hard to change Hitler's mind about the redeployment of Army Group Centre's panzer assets and for a while it looked as though they had succeeded in placing the drive on Moscow back on the Wehrmacht's priority list. However, Hitler's Directive No. 34, temporarily

Left: Field Marshal Walther von Reichenau (left with binoculars), commander of the German Sixth Army, consults with one of his divisional commanders, Lieutenant General Stapt, during the drive on Zhitomir, July 1941.

Right: The commander of a Sturmgeschutz (StuG) III assault gun uses his anti-aircraft machine gun in an attempt to winkle out the Russian defenders of a thatched hut, near Gelenovka, August 1941.

suspending the switch of the panzer-gruppen, was overridden on 12 August when local set-backs in front of Leningrad yet again changed the Führer's mind.

Issuing yet another set of orders, he directed the two outer army groups to press on towards Leningrad and Kiev and ordered 'a concentric operation from the inner flanks of Army Groups South and Centre, against the Soviet Fifth Army'.

The chiefs of the German Army finally acquiesced in Hitler's demands, Halder immediately setting off for the front to pass on the bad news to von Bock. Guderian received his new orders on 23 August and still refused to believe that he had lost his argument. With Halder's agreement he immediately set out to see the Führer face to face, to try to persuade him to change his mind.

On arrival at Hitler's headquarters, von Brauchitsch forbade him from mentioning Moscow to the Führer but luckily Hitler brought up the subject himself, at which point Guderian launched into his well-rehearsed plea for the resumption of the Moscow offensive. It did not change the Führer's mind. When the panzergruppe commander saw that no senior officer was prepared to speak up in his defence he realised that the High Command had been browbeaten into submission and he reluctantly agreed to swing his forces south.

He set out immediately for his headquarters, arriving the next day, where he threw himself into organising his new task. The objective now was not to take Moscow but to advance south, encircle Kiev and the Soviet armies in central Ukraine and be back in a position to launch an offensive against the capital before winter set in. He had two and a half months.

Army Group South was now to play the major role in the destruction of the Red Army planned by Hitler for the late summer of 1941. Up until this point in the campaign von Rundstedt's armies had not achieved spectacular successes comparable with those of Army Group Centre farther north. This failure to achieve a quick and deep penetration was due in part to its lack of armour, only Panzergruppe I being allotted to support the advance. The great width of the front, nearly 600 miles in total, and the diversity of objectives within southern Russia, also militated against a series of decisive thrusts, as used by von Bock's forces.

The northern wing of Army Group South, after breaching the frontier defences, was forced to split into two groups. The first, containing Kleist's Panzergruppe I and the Sixth Army, headed for the Dniepr below Kiev, whilst the Seventeenth Army advanced south-east to reach the Bug below Vinitsa. This ensured that no significant Soviet formations were left behind the inner flanks of the two advancing wings of the army group.

Units from the northern group were then to swing south whilst the Sixth Army continued its eastwards drive. The projected link-up near Uman would trap any Soviet formations that had managed to place themselves between the two thrusts of the northern wing of the army group advance.

The southern wing of Army Group South had as its objective the securing of the Black Sea coast, especially the Soviet naval base at Odessa, the capture of the Crimea and the formation of a cohesive front along the Dniepr, to the south of the army group's northern thrusts. This was asking an awful lot of a force which, apart from the Eleventh Army, was made up of formations from satellite countries, armed in the most part with obsolete equipment. Apart from the Eleventh Army, the southern wing of Army Group South consisted of a Slovakian motorised division, a Hungarian motorised corps (of three brigades), the Rumanian Fourth Army (of thirteen divisions) and a corps of the Rumanian Third Army.

General Kirponos, the Soviet commander of the South-West Front at the beginning of the campaign, tried in vain to take advantage of the weakness of Army Group South caused by this dispersal of effort but the Red Army formations proved themselves to be far too unwieldy to use in anything but set-piece assaults or static defence. Not lacking in imagination, Kirponos tried on several occasions to launch counter-attacks to sever the thrusts of the northern wing of Army Group South. Unfortunately the handling of the Soviet tanks used in these operations left a lot to be desired.

German troops found it relatively easy to counter the text book attacks by Red Army armour, often made in line abreast like the cavalry charges of old. The Germans would let Soviet tank units pass right through them before remanning their positions and destroying the vehicles with anti-tank gun fire from the rear. As Russian infantry-tank cooperation was extremely limited and coordinated attacks very rare, it was quite easy to separate the tank units from their supporting infantry, eliminating each piecemeal. The other tactic adopted by the Germans, which invariably succeeded, was to withdraw their panzer forces in the face of an attack, luring the Russian armour onto a secondary defence line of well-camouflaged 88mm guns, where they were easily destroyed.

Soviet commanders could also be relied upon to make disastrous mistakes

Left, upper: Two Soviet infantrymen watch a T-26 tank attack go in against German positions. These assaults, often with no infantry support, cost the Red Army dear in armoured vehicle losses. (IWM.RUS.598)

Left, lower: The crew of a camouflaged 37mm anti-tank gun lie in wait on the flanks of the German advance through the Ukraine, August/September 1941. (IWM.HU.5072)

Left, upper: A German tank column pushes through the town of Zhitomir, 31 July 1941.

Left, lower: German infantrymen flush out the defenders of a rail-yard south of Kiev, 30–31 July 1941. Note the KV-I captured while still on its railway transport flat wagon.

without the Germans taking any part in the process. Corps Commissar Vashugin, ordered to counter-attack the advancing Germans with one and a half tank divisions from IV Mechanised Corps, managed to direct his entire unit into a swamp where all the vehicles had to be abandoned. Vashugin later committed suicide rather than face the wrath of Stalin.

Faced with an ever mounting number of irreplaceable tank losses Stavka ordered Kirponos to retire 'on the 1939 Stalin Line', where fortifications and river obstacles would allow him to conduct a static infantry defence.

Shortly thereafter, the reorganisation of the Front system led Kirponos to be replaced by Budenny. However, one final armoured counter-attack was launched in the second week of July, by units of the Fifth Army operating from the southern edge of the Pripet Marshes and the Sixth Army pushing north towards Berdichev, in an attempt to cut off Panzergruppe I from the following German formations near Zhitomir. Although this too was an abject failure, the Soviet forces being pushed back to their start lines with relative ease, it was the attack that finally convinced Hitler that the Soviet will to resist would not be broken by deep armoured penetrations, as had the French in 1940. If Russian formations were capable of launching offensives when outflanked and even surrounded, then the plan of campaign would have to be altered. Accordingly Hitler, much to the annoyance of his generals, ordered the redeployment of the panzergruppen from Army Group Centre.

The Battle for Russia would not now be one of deep thrusts for strate-

Left, upper: An SS medium machine-gun team engage the enemy north of Uman, early August 1941.

Left, lower: Red Army infantrymen captured in the Uman pocket wait to board trains to take them to the rear, Pleshow, 21 August 1941. (IWM.HU.8958)

the Russian field armies in the Ukraine.

The northern wing of von Rundstedt's forces continued to press south-eastwards towards the lower reaches of the Bug and Dniepr rivers. He had already made the decision that Kiev itself would not be assaulted unless the Red Army weakened its defence of the city considerably. Accordingly he directed the 13th and 14th Panzer Divisions, on the northern flank of the Army Group South advance, to watch for any withdrawal but to seek a crossing of the Dniepr south of the city. With the change of direction of Panzergruppe II, a future envelopment of the area, with an Army Group South–Army Group Centre link-up east of the city, made a direct attack unnecessary.

The majority of Panzergruppe I's mechanised assets were shortly thereafter diverted southwards, when reconnaissance reports suggested that the Russian front line south of the city along the Kiev–Dnepropetrovsk railway was only thinly held. By 30 July the railway line was in German hands. Pressing their advantage, the panzers pushed south down the Kiev–Uman highway, reaching the town two days later. This breakthrough not only presented the northern wing of Army Group South with an advance route into the interior, south of Kiev, but also cut the main supply routes for the Sixth, Twelfth and Eighteenth Soviet Armies, facing the attacking German Seventeenth (pushing south-east from Poland) and Eleventh (advancing east across northern Moldavia) Armies.

The only escape route now open for these troops was to withdraw southwards along the eastern bank of the

gically important cities but a series of giant encircling manoeuvres ending in battles of annihilation, physically destroying the enemy. This reversion from blitzkrieg strategy, as propounded by Guderian and other armoured commanders, to a more classic Vernichtungsgedanke approach, did indeed result in the elimination of vast numbers of Soviet units but at the cost of suspending the drive on Moscow.

Both Guderian and von Bock were confident that by continuing the advance on the capital all the available Soviet reserves would be sucked in to provide for its defence. The envelopment of the city would then be a massive blow to Soviet morale. It would deprive the forces in the field of a vital communications centre and, most importantly, break the back of the Red Army by capturing hundreds of thousands of Russia's best troops. This, however, was not to be. Guderian was now directed south to assist Army Group South in its envelopment of Kiev and

Bug to the Black Sea at Nikolaev. At this point Budenny hesitated fatally, unable to make up his mind whether to pull back or feed more reinforcements into the area.

By 3 August, Schobert, commander of the Eleventh Army, had managed to gain a foothold across the Bug at Pervomaysk, severing this last line of retreat. Tanks of XIV Panzer Corps battered their way south through the Russian lines, the lead elements linking up with Schobert's troops only a day after they had crossed the Bug. It was to take until 8 August, however, before the Uman pocket could be finally sealed shut.

At last von Rundstedt had achieved a battlefield victory comparable with those of Army Group Centre. Trapped in the pocket were the remnants of fifteen rifle and five tank divisions. By the end of the mopping-up operation Army Group South had netted 103,000 prisoners.

The German success in the northernmost region of the army group front now unlocked the southern coastal sector for the Rumanian Fourth Army. Without interference from the Russian field armies further north, they were able to force a passage of the Dniestr and reach the outskirts of Odessa on 5 August, IV Rumanian Corps completing the investment of the port by the 14th.

As soon as the war had begun, the Soviet High Command had ordered the construction of a ring of fortifications around the city. By the time the Rumanians arrived, a defensive perimeter over three miles deep and manned by over a hundred infantry battalions had been built. The siege of Odessa was to cost the Rumanians dear. The Special Maritime Army of General Petrov, made up in large part of sailors of the Black Sea Fleet pressed into service as infantrymen, was to hold out until 16 October, inflicting over 100,000 casualties on the besieging Fourth Army.

After the city's capitulation, as a prize for participation in the campaign, it was incorporated into Rumania as the capital of the new province of Transniestria.

While the siege of Odessa was getting under way Stavka had once again reorganised the number of fronts facing the Germans. The new Bryansk Front, consisting of two infantry armies, was raised with General Andrei Yeremenko in command and was deployed between Timoshenko's West Front and Budenny's South-West Front.

At the same time Budenny was allowed by Stavka to order a withdrawal of all his remaining forces to the east bank of the Dniepr. Too late to save the vast majority of units already trapped in the Uman pocket, this nevertheless enabled the South-West Front to re-establish a cohesive defence line with which to face Army Group South. The Soviet Thirty-seventh Army was ordered to remain in Kiev on the west bank of the river and the Fortieth Army, a scratch formation made up of amalgamated remnants of destroyed units, and the Fifth Army ordered back from the Pripet Marshes, were to form a second line of defence in the Konotop–Chernigov area. This was a precaution against a major German attack, should OKH not realise that the widening gap between Timoshenko's and Budenny's commands had been filled by the brand-new but still weak Bryansk Front.

By mid-August, with no German attack materialising, the Soviet High Command felt itself able to order Yeremenko to go over to the offensive. Stavka did not realise that the halting of the German advance in this sector had more to do with strategic quarrels between the field commanders, OKH and Hitler, than with the success of the Red Army in the field.

Stalin offered Yeremenko several T-34 tank battalions and Katyusha rocket

batteries, along with the newly raised Thirteenth and Twenty-first Armies, if he launched his counter-attack soon.

Unfortunately, Yeremenko was placed under the impression by Shaposhnikov, the Soviet Chief of the General Staff, that as well as launching the new offensive he was now responsible for the southern approaches to Moscow (which was not true, as Timoshenko still held that responsibility). This misunderstanding was typical of poor Soviet staff work during the opening phases of the campaign. Accordingly he split his force, placing the majority of his best units on his northern flank and launching the offensive on 29 August with the Twenty-first Army, a new untried formation with very few tanks.

Even though the attack was supported by the 500 remaining aircraft of the Red Army Air Force, it failed dismally. A lack of mechanised and motorised vehicles enabled Guderian's XXIV Panzer Corps easily to outmanoeuvre their opponents, turning their flank almost as soon as the offensive began. Von Kluge's Second Army followed suit, getting around the Soviet left flank a day or so later. Forced into a hurried retreat, the Twenty-first Army carried away several supporting Soviet units moving up behind the main body of the advance and left a gaping hole through which the mechanised and motorised elements of Panzergruppe II passed with relative ease. Guderian's southward thrust had begun in earnest.

While Guderian was breaching Kiev's northern defences, Kleist, whose Panzergruppe I had played a major role in the Uman encirclement, was busy redeploying his forces to attack northeastwards on a convergent course with Panzergruppe II. Reconnaissance units of several panzer divisions had already managed to gain footholds across the Dniepr between Cherkassy and Kremenchug, a stretch of front defended by the poorly equipped and below-

Right, top: The Germans were greeted as liberators in many parts of the Ukraine, whose populace hoped that the Nazis would prove to be more enlightened rulers than the communists. Here villagers give directions to an infantry patrol, August/September 1941. (IWM.HU.5063)

Right, centre: A transport column of the 97th Infantry (Jäger) Division receives the attention of the Red Army Air Force, August/September 1941. Note the knocked-out T-28 tank on the right of the photograph. (IWM.HU.3418)

Right, bottom: A knocked-out PzKpfw III Ausf F and SdKfz 251 half-track of the 3rd Panzer Division are examined by Red Army soldiers, September 1941. (IWM.PC.366)

strength Thirty-eighth Army. Soviet planners had left the area lightly defended, having considered a crossing at this point unlikely because of the great width of the river (at some places several miles across).

While Kleist consolidated and expanded his bridgeheads Guderian's panzers pushed south. Organised resistance, when it was encountered, was stiff but it was all too easy for the German mechanised columns to avoid contact with the immobile, uncoordinated Red Army defenders, leaving them in the wake of the advance to be mopped up by the following infantry divisions. The advance of Panzergruppe II southwards, east of Kiev, was a risky business, in that an ever longer exposed left flank was left hanging in the air, positively inviting a counter-attack. Fortunately for Guderian, the Red Army was so confused by this unexpected axis of attack that they failed to organise a cohesive counter-stroke.

Guderian's panzers struggled south for the next eighteen days, hampered both by the enemy and fierce rainstorms that turned the dirt roads into quagmires and rivers into raging torrents. At times Panzergruppe II's rate of advance was as slow as the infantry formations of the Second Army, pressing the Red Army back further to the west.

As the advance continued, it became increasingly clear to Stavka that a massive encirclement of Kiev was under way, yet Stalin continued to strip reserves from other, no less vital sectors of the front and send them to bolster the defence of the Ukrainian capital. Budenny, the South-West Front commander, repeatedly requested that he be allowed to withdraw from the area while he still had time but was persistently refused permission. Finally, on 13 September Budenny was 'transferred' to the Reserve Front, leaving Stalin to deal with a much more pliable commander. In fact the change of leadership did nothing to stem the German advance; it only served to heighten the confusion of the field commanders in the area.

By 12 September Kleist had finally secured an adequate passage across the Dniepr for his panzergruppe and in the process had virtually destroyed the Soviet Thirty-eighth Army. After crossing the river the panzers pushed north, covering over 100 miles over the next four days, and on 16 September, at the town of Lokhvitsa, they linked up with the lead reconnaissance elements of Guderian's Panzergruppe II.

As the mechanised infantry of the panzergruppen began to tighten the cordon around the trapped Russian armies, infantry formations began to squeeze the pocket from the north and west. The Second Army was driving south on the right flank of Panzergruppe II, the Seventeenth Army advancing north on Kleist's left and the Sixth Army advancing eastwards from the area north of Uman, pushing in the pocket from its western side. Added to these attacks was the constant bombing from Kesselring's Luftflotte II and Lohr's Luftflotte IV, which caused thousands of casualties in the ever

tightening pocket in which the Soviet armies were now trapped.

By 26 September the battle for Kiev had to all intents ended. The Germans captured 665,000 prisoners, 884 tanks and 3,718 guns. Right up until the last moment Stalin had continued to feed reinforcements into the area, in the vain hope that they could somehow stem the German advance. It was not as if the Soviet troops had no other option other than to stand and fight; withdrawal had been possible. Nikita Krushchev, the political commissar of the South-West Front, had managed to organise the evacuation of much of the area's heavy industry. If whole factories could be removed then surely infantrymen could have marched out.

Whatever Stalin's reasoning, he forbade any retreat until it was too late. Only 24 hours after the closure of the pocket did he give permission to withdraw. Thousands of troops attempting to break out were killed, including General Kirponos, former commander of the South-West Front.

As the catastrophe of the Kiev encirclement became apparent to Soviet High Command, von Manstein, now commander of the Eleventh Army, gave the Red Army another significant strategic defeat further to the south. Between 21 and 29 September, units under his command were able to force a crossing of the Dniepr estuary and advance as far as the neck of the Crimean peninsula. This potentially cut off thou-

Right, upper: A Soviet defensive position on the east bank of the Dniepr, August/September 1941. (IWM.RUS.769)

Right, lower: Ju-87 dive bombers return from an attack on Red Army positions, overflying a German armoured column pushing across the steppe. (IWM.HU.40710)

sands of Russian soldiers and naval personnel in the Sevastopol area and, more importantly, threatened to turn the southern flank of the Red Army altogether.

Because of the intense fighting around Kiev, before Leningrad and in front of Moscow, there were virtually no reserves available at the southern end of the Russian defence line. If German troops could push on eastwards and capture Rostov they would have effectively turned the Soviet flank. They would then be in a position to roll up the defence line and capture the great industrial centre of the Donets basin.

As Army Group South celebrated its dramatic victory in southern Russia,

Army Group North began to find itself bogged down before its main objective, Leningrad.

Things had initially gone well for von Leeb's forces, the smallest of the three army groups forging into Russia. Consisting of the Sixteenth and Eighteenth Armies, plus Hoepner's Panzergruppe IV, it totalled some twenty infantry divisions, three panzer divisions and three motorised divisions. Because of the relatively narrow axis of advance of the army group through the Baltic States, von Leeb doubted whether he would be able to bring off anything in the way of a major encirclement.

Additionally, the Niemen and Dvina rivers running across the army group's

line of advance provided the Russians with two strong natural defensive barriers. Farther north on the approaches to Leningrad, two lakes, the Peipus and Ilmen, further constricted the advance route. To reach the city von Leeb's forces would have to pass either through the narrow opening between the northern tip of Lake Peipus and the Baltic Sea or force a passage of the slightly wider gap between the southern tip of Lake Peipus and the eastern end of Lake Ilmen.

To make planning even more difficult, the Red Army had deployed no less than three armies, the Eighth, Eleventh and Twenty-seventh, across the path of Army Group North; in total some 28 infantry divisions and three mechanised corps, containing just under 1,000 tanks. The North-West Front, to which all of these formations were allotted as soon as hostilities began, was commanded by General Kuznetzov, a competent if not outstanding officer.

Von Leeb's solution to these problems was to form up the army group with Panzergruppe IV in the centre and the two infantry armies on either flank. Instead of conducting a series of enveloping manoeuvres Army Group North would advance with a series of armoured pushes along a single axis of attack. The following infantry formations would mop up centres of resistance left behind the advancing panzers and would shore up the sides of the thrust as the advance continued. If any major obstacles presented themselves, then infantry divisions could be brought forward to conduct set-piece assaults. The problem of significant Soviet troop concentrations being left behind the advancing flanks of the

Left, upper: A group of Russians surrender to SS infantry of the Motorised Division 'Wiking', near the Dniepr, late August/early September 1941.

Left, lower: A Soviet 85mm anti-aircraft gun is loaded, somewhere on the steppe, July/August 1941. (IWM.RUS.187)

Left, upper: A German mortar team in action against a Russian village, August/September 1941.

Left, lower: A light machine-gun team assess the next avenue of advance through the Soviet-held village of Malaya Kochnovka, August/September 1941.

Above: A Sturmgeschutz (StuG) III assault gun advances through a Baltic town, July/August 1941. (IWM.PC.399)

army group was solved by placing the northern flank of the assault actually on the Baltic itself. Any Red Army formations to the south would be faced with the possibility of being trapped between Army Group North and the northern wing of Army Group Centre. Thus the drive to Leningrad was to be conducted in a more deliberate manner than the other thrusts of the invasion. This suited the infantry general von Leeb perfectly.

This is not to say, however, that panzer formations did not play a vital role in the advance. They formed the spearhead of Army Group North's attack, attaining their first major objective, the

bridges across the Dvina, only four days after the beginning of the offensive.

By launching the attack into Lithuania from the recently annexed territory of Memelland, von Leeb was able effectively to outflank the Soviet first line of defence along the river Niemen. However, the vital bridges over the Dvina still lay another 150 miles on to the north-east. With von Manstein's LVI Panzer Corps in the van, Panzergruppe IV sped on towards its objective.

A major armoured clash was narrowly avoided on the first day of the campaign when LVI Panzer Corps passed through the border town of Kedaynyay only a few hours after a Red Army armoured column, seeking the spearhead of the army group assault. Von Manstein pressed on with his corps into the Lithuanian interior, leaving XLI Panzer Corps to deal with the Russian tanks left behind the right flank of the advance. When the Soviets realised their mistake they turned

about and headed back to Kedaynyay. However, XLI Panzer Corps was waiting and the Red Army tanks were stopped dead in their tracks by intense anti-tank fire, then enveloped and destroyed by the corps armour.

On 26 June the 7th Panzer Division, in the van of the LVI Panzer Corps advance, seized the first crossing over the Dvina at Daugavpils. The speed of its advance, averaging over 35 miles per day, had stunned the Soviets who had failed to prepare the bridges for demolition. By 1 July XLI Panzer Corps had seized further crossings to the south of the town and an eighteen-mile stretch of the far bank of the river was securely in German hands.

The very next day a new offensive began to capture the 'land-bridge' to Leningrad, the stretch of territory between Lake Peipus and Lake Ilmen on the old Latvian-Russian frontier. The panzergruppe's immediate problem was to capture crossings over the river Velikaya which flowed into the south-

A team of Soviet stretcher bearers wait to go forward to recover casualties near the Dniepr, August 1941. (IWM.RUS.857)

ern end of Lake Peipus. Major bridges spanned the river at (from north to south) Pskov, Ostrov and Opochka.

The first of the crossings to be captured was at Ostrov, which was taken unopposed on 4 July, the Russians having massed nearly all their armour to the north round Pskov, expecting Army Group North to take the most direct route towards Leningrad. When the Red Army swung its tanks southward the next day they ran into the anti-tank screen of XLI Panzer Corps on the outskirts of the town and lost over 140 tanks in pointless headlong charges at the German positions.

Counter-attacking, XLI Panzer Corps was able to take Pskov with ease. At the same time LVI Panzer Corps attacked and captured the third crossing point at Opochka.

Panzergruppe IV had now made over half the distance to its main objective, Leningrad. It was here, however, that things started to go wrong for Army Group North and the advance began to slow down.

The difficulty in maintaining the momentum lay in part in the lack of motorised transport available to bring supplies of petrol and ammunition to the lead panzer formations. It had taken all the resources of Army Group North to launch the second phase of the advance to the 'land-bridge' and when the bridgeheads across the Velikaya had been obtained, the supply situation had worsened considerably. The gap between the lead panzer elements and the following resupply units was now too wide to maintain the prodigious rates of advance obtained thus far.

A Red Army 85mm anti-aircraft gun deployed in an anti-tank role, northern Russia, September 1941. (IWM.RUS.728)

However, the main problem slowing the further advance of Panzergruppe IV was a wide belt of marshland beyond the Velikaya on the old Latvian–Russian border. It was least passable east of Opochka, the projected route of advance for von Manstein's LVI Panzer Corps, who had been ordered to take Novgorod on the river Luya, the first main line of defence before Leningrad. Several attempts were made to push through the difficult terrain and all met with failure.

LVI Panzer Corps was then diverted northwards to Ostrov, the crossing point of XLI Panzer Corps, from where it was to open its attack on Novgorod. However, it, too was having difficulty progressing through the swampland, and the two panzer corps attempting to operate on the same limited axis of advance caused chaos, bringing both formations to a standstill.

It was then decided to transfer XLI Panzer Corps north of Lake Peipus to make its advance on Leningrad along the Baltic coast. Although this created enough room for both formations to operate effectively, it split the armoured thrust of Army Group North. The two panzer corps were now operating at each end of Lake Peipus with all the diminution of coordinated attacking power that this brought about.

To make matters worse, from mid-July onwards von Leeb was ordered to strip infantry units from the Sixteenth Army on the right flank of the Army Group North, to support the advance of the left wing of Army Group Centre. This in turn forced him to order von Manstein to undertake no deep penetration, even if the opportunity should present itself, as there was not sufficient infantry support available.

In the face of this difficult terrain and hardening Soviet resistance, the advance slowed to a crawl, although LVI Panzer Corps was now clear of the Velikaya Marshes. By the beginning of August von Leeb had decided to abandon the plan of a lightning thrust to capture Leningrad itself. Instead he devised a strategy to envelop the city using the two panzer corps in the south and the German–Finnish Army in the north.

Finland had declared war on Russia three days after the launching of Operation Barbarossa and its small army; along with the German Norwegen Armee of General Dietl (six infantry divisions in total), had immediately gone over to the offensive. Hitler hoped that the Finns would fight alongside the Wehrmacht in the battle to crush communism and obliterate the Russian state. However, Marshal Karl Mannerheim, the Finnish leader, proposed to fight a purely limited war to regain the territory lost to Stalin in 1940. When these objectives were achieved he aimed to stand fast and consolidate his gains. Von Leeb counted upon the cooperation of the Finns in his plans. For his envelopment of Leningrad to succeed they had to advance

Russian infantry defend a Baltic river line, August 1941. (IWM.RUS.751)

southwards down the Karelian Isthmus and south-eastwards round the inner shore of Lake Ladoga past their pre-1939 frontier.

For the Germans the opening phase of this plan was to break through the last major obstacle on the road to Leningrad, the river Luga, which flowed from Lake Ilmen to the Baltic Sea.

The Russian forces manning the river line were divided into three groups: The first, near Lake Ilmen, consisted of an *ad hoc* rifle division and an infantry brigade. The second, along the Luga, was made up of three rifle divisions. The third, containing another three rifle divisions, held the area around Kingisepp, a town near the coast, through which ran the main Leningrad to Tallinn railway line.

This small stretched force was by no means enough to prevent German forces from breaking through the river line defence. By 11 August, three days after the opening of the assault, a breach had been created in the Kingisepp sector through which troops began to pour.

To give extra impetus to the attack, von Leeb ordered Manstein's LVI Panzer Corps to disengage from the enemy at the southern end of the line (its place being taken by infantry divisions from the Sixteenth Army) and move north to help exploit the gap created.

Just as the panzers arrived at Kingisepp a totally unexpected threat appeared at the southern tip of the Army Group North advance. The Soviet Thirty-eighth (Cavalry) Army sweeping round the southern edge of Lake Ilmen crashed into the right flank of the Sixteenth Army. Although it did not manage to penetrate far into the German lines, the attack caused von Leeb to redirect LVI Panzer Corps back to its original position, a round trip of nearly 200 miles for no gain in territory.

It was not only von Leeb who was surprised by the sudden appearance of cavalry on his flank. General Popkov, commander of the Luga defence line, had no idea that the Thirty-eighth

Left, upper: A German MG 34 machine-gun team in action against Soviet troops, Verno Leninsk, 17 August 1941. (IWM.STT.2864)

Left, lower: An infantrymen crawls back into cover after being wounded at the entrance to a Soviet-held village. A PzKpfw IV and accompanying infantry prepare to move forward to flush out the defenders. (IWM.PC.413)

Right: Men of the 44th Engineering Battalion rest by the roadside during their advance into the Ukraine, July/August 1941. (IWM.HU.8895)

(Cavalry) Army was in the vicinity either. The formation was officially earmarked for the defence of Leningrad from the Finns in the north. The army commander had moved his troops south on his own initiative, neglecting to inform higher command that he had done so!

Once the panzers had returned to their previous zone of operations, the marauding Soviet cavalry were easily contained and pushed back beyond Lake Ilmen. Nevertheless, the assault had slowed down Army Group North's advance from its Kingisepp bridgehead and brought temporarily to a halt the advance on the southern flank of the drive for Leningrad.

With the repulse of the Thirty-eighth (Cavalry) Army's attack, the German offensive once more regained a modicum of impetus. Novgorod, at the northern end of Lake Ilmen, was reached on 16 August and Chadowo, 50 miles further north, fell four days later. German troops were now within 30 miles of the outer suburbs of Leningrad. The lead elements of XLI Panzer Corps were positioned to the south-west of the city at Krasnog-vardeisk and LVI Panzer Corps farther east at Chadowo. Hoepner's forces had additionally been boosted by the addition of XXXIX Panzer Corps from Hoth's Panzergruppe III, part of the redistribution of armour ordered by Hitler. This unit lay on the right flank of Manstein's formation.

Instead of pressing on to Leningrad immediately, von Leeb adjudged he had sufficient time to envelop the Red Army divisions still left on the Luga defence line, now caught in between and to the rear of XLI and LVI Panzer Corps. Accordingly he ordered XLI Panzer Corps to move south-east on Novgorod to complete the encirclement. The fighting to close this pocket was quite bitter, the Russians defenders fighting fanatically to break out and reach the comparative safety of their second city. However, by 31 August all resistance had come to an end and 20,000 Soviet prisoners had been taken.

The final phase of the battle to encircle Leningrad now began. For it to be successful the Finnish Army had to be persuaded to advance past its pre-1939 frontiers. After much wrangling, which involved Keitel flying to Mannerheim's headquarters to plead with the field marshal in person, the Finnish leader agreed to move his troops south to the line of the river Svir just inside the Soviet Union. No

amount of cajoling, however, could persuade him to advance on Volkhov as von Leeb wished.

Army Group North was therefore left to complete the envelopment of Leningrad, using only units it possessed currently under its control. These at first glance seemed ample for the task. But even though only 50 or so miles of territory had to be captured to complete the encirclement, the attacking German units would have to penetrate three fortified defence lines surrounding the city.

The outer ring had already been breached in its south-west corner by the onrush of XLI Panzer Corps during its operation to capture Krasnogvardeisk. But the others still stood in the general line of advance of Army Group North. The fortifications in total consisted of over 600 miles of earthen walls, 400 miles of anti-tank ditches, 370 miles of barbed wire and some 5,000 pillboxes, manned by tens of thousands of Red Army soldiers.

To make matters worse on, 5 September Hitler ordered Panzergruppe III south to assist in the new drive on Moscow, leaving XXXIX Panzer Corps, relatively new to the region, as the only source of armoured support for the infantry divisions making the assault.

Nevertheless the attack through the defences, initially at least, went well and by 11 September German troops had penetrated the first line of defence and captured Schusselberg on the southern shore of Lake Ladoga. This cut Leningrad off from the Soviet interior.

The only way left of getting into and out of the city was by boat across the lake itself. On the same day German infantry managed to battle their way to the top of the Dudernof Heights just seven and a half miles south of the city.

From this commanding position observers could overlook and direct artillery fire onto its defenders and inhabitants.

By 14 September German troops had managed to capture Krasnoe Selo, the 'Versailles of Leningrad' and key to the second line of defence in front of the city. Three days later they breached the final fortified defence line before the city, when the Pulkovo Heights were captured after a long and bitter fight. The loss of these strategically important positions did not, as the Germans had hoped, lead to a drop in morale amongst the defenders of Leningrad, indeed it seemed only to stiffen their resolve to hold out.

From this point on, the battle for Leningrad became a continual hard slog for a few yards of ground gained every day. When, on 17 September, the last units of Panzergruppe III pulled out of the line and headed south, the attack ground to a halt.

Leningrad, birthplace of the revolution, was a highly politicised city with a highly efficient and well organised Communist Party apparatus. Nearly one in six of its inhabitants belonged to either the party itself, a trade union or other workers' association with

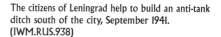
The citizens of Leningrad help to build an anti-tank ditch south of the city, September 1941. (IWM.RUS.938)

strong party links. Through these organisations the Leningrad leadership was able to galvanise its citizens effectively for the defence of the city.

As early as 27 June the Leningrad City Soviet had issued a decree mobilising the entire population of men between 16 and 50 and women between 16 and 45 for defence work. By early July thousands of civilians were at work constructing the triple ring of defences around the city. Often under enemy air attack and sometimes even overrun by sudden German thrusts, they worked twelve to fifteen-hour days to ensure that Army Group North

would not be able to seize the city by direct assault.

In addition to providing manpower to work on Leningrad's fortifications, the city leadership drew up a plan to form a militia army of 200,000 men organised into fifteen divisions. Although this was never realised, a total of eight Opolchenie divisions had been raised by 13 August, all of which were sent immediately to the front. The troops of these units had no military training at all and were led by Communist Party officials, a few of whom were reserve officers. They often went into battle without uniforms and in

some units men shared rifles with a comrade.

These efforts by Leningrad's citizenry helped to slow the German advance and convinced Hitler that the city could not be taken by a direct assault. Already dubious as to the viability of fighting his way through a western-style city, with many well-constructed stone buildings and a maze of canals, von Leeb concurred with the Führer's judgement.

Instead Leningrad was to be invested and gradually reduced to rubble by artillery fire and aerial bombardment. Hitler reasoned that as the populace had helped defend the city against the German invader, then its inhabitants were to be eliminated along with its Red Army defenders. Those not killed by German bombs and shells were to be allowed to starve to death in the winter to come.

Even before Leningrad had been encircled and Kiev had fallen, Hitler had once more turned his thoughts to the capture of the Russian capital. Führer Directive No. 35 conveyed the news of Hitler's change of mind to his army group commanders.

In it he called for a renewal of the attack on the Soviet West Front, commanded by Timoshenko, guarding the direct route to Moscow. The offensive was to begin at the earliest possible date, which Hitler estimated would be towards the end of September. It was vital to begin no later than early October to give the German forces in the field sufficient time to envelop the capital before the winter prohibited all offensive action.

To enable the offensive to take place both Army Group North and Army Group South lost much of their panzer force, transferred to von Bock's command, Hoepner's Panzergruppe

IV and Guderian's Panzergruppe II bolstering Hoth's Panzergruppe III. In addition to these armoured formations Army Group Centre was assigned three infantry armies, the Second, the Fourth and the Ninth, with which to undertake the attack.

Their immediate aim was to encircle as much of Timoshenko's force as possible before Moscow itself. The attack was to take the form of a double envelopment, with Panzergruppe III forming the northern and Panzergruppe IV the southern wings of the attack. Units of the Ninth Army would advance on the inner flank of Hoth's formation, shoring up the side of the pocket and eliminating any centres of resistance left behind the advancing panzers. The Fourth Army undertook a similar operation on the left flank of Hoepner's force. The two pincers were to meet east of Vyazma. This would bring the leading edge of Army Group North to within a hundred miles of the capital.

Guderian's Panzergruppe II (which had been renamed the Second Panzer Army) was to attempt a similar envelopment further south around Bryansk, by advancing north-eastward from the Konotop area and linking up with infantry units of the Second Army advancing due east of the town.

Above: Russian Opolchenie (People's Militia) train near Leningrad, July/August 1941. (IWM.RUS.531)

Left: : A PzKpfw IV of the 1st Panzer Division fires at a suspected enemy position during a night action between Bryansk and Viasma, 9 October 1941. (IWM.HU.39660)

These objectives and dispositions were set out in the plan of attack code-named Operation Typhoon, issued by von Bock on 19 September.

After a delay of nearly two weeks, during which time Army Group Centre managed to cobble together a ramshackle but reasonably effective supply system for the coming operation, the offensive began.

It was not only the rear echelon units that were suffering from the rigours of a prolonged campaign. All German front line formations were also well below strength. Panzer divisions averaged between 25 percent and 50 percent of their tank establishment, while most of the mechanised infantry units that accompanied them had also sustained around 50 percent losses. The German infantry divisions fared somewhat better, remaining on average at 65 percent of their establishment strengths. Nevertheless Operation Typhoon began more or less on time, Guderian's Panzergruppe II beginning its attack on 30 September, with the other formations following suit on 2 October.

Facing the German onslaught were three recently reorganised Russian fronts: the West Front, deployed astride the main highway to Moscow, was now commanded by Marshal Ivan Koniev (Timoshenko being transferred to the Southern Front facing von Rundstedt); the Bryansk Front, commanded by Marshal Andrei Yeremenko, was stationed in the path of Guderian's offensive, further to the south; and the Reserve Front of four armies, commanded by Marshal Georgi Zhukov, formed the final defensive barrier in front of Moscow, to the rear of the other two army groups.

In all the Russians held the front against Army Group Centre with fifteen armies. This sounds an impressive total but it most be remembered that nearly all of these formations were badly understrength, either through combat losses or because of the lack of availability of new recruits. Many of the units were made up entirely of green

A KV-I passes through Moscow on its way to the front, October 1941. (IWM.RUS.1229)

conscript troops who had little or no training; artillery and tanks were scarce and air support was non-existent.

Despite their lack of armour the panzergruppe thrusts went well. The front line was soon penetrated and by 7 October the main forces of the West and Reserve Fronts, the Nineteenth, Twenty-fourth, Thirtieth and Thirty-second Armies, had all been surrounded, trapped between Vyazma and Smolensk.

At the same time Guderian pulled off another major encirclement in the Bryansk area. The lead elements of his panzer thrust linked up with the marching infantry of the Second Army on 9 October, thus surrounding and eventually subduing the Third and Thirteenth Soviet Armies.

By the end of the first phase of operations the German Army had captured a further 657,000 prisoners, 1,241 tanks and 5,396 artillery pieces.

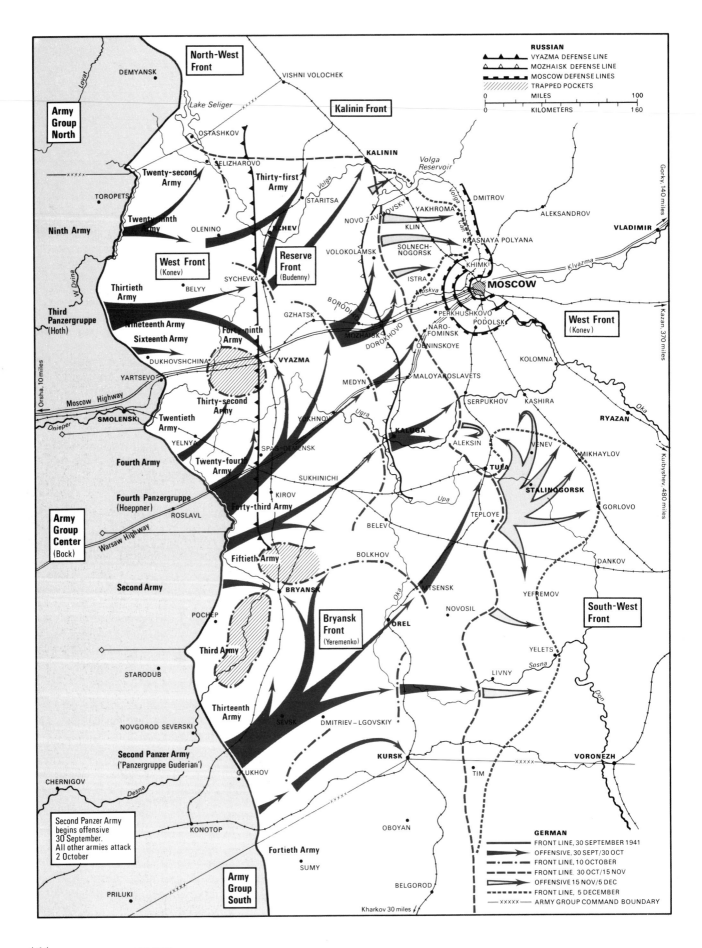

As a result of these staggering losses Zhukov was forced to admit that to all intents and purposes the road to Moscow was open.

Despite this major defeat German field commanders were beginning to notice a new tactical awareness starting to appear amongst their Red Army counterparts. Guderian, visiting his 4th Panzer Division after its first engagement against Soviet T-34s on 4 October, noted that the Russian armour was no longer being used in linear frontal assaults but was concentrated against the flanks of the advancing German units. As current German anti-tank guns were unable to penetrate the frontal armour of the new types of Russian tanks, these attacks were gaining an unexpected measure of success. New up-to-date equipment and long months of bitter experience had begun to pay dividends for the hard-pressed Soviets.

On 6 October the Red Army gained another ally in its battle to save Moscow, the first heavy snowfall of the campaign. It melted quickly, turning the roads into quagmires of liquid mud. The Russian Autumn with its heavy rain, sleet and snow had arrived. The German advance began to slow.

For the Soviet High Command these encouraging signs were overshadowed by the huge losses it had so recently suffered. As a response to the disaster, the forces defending the capital were once more reorganised. The West Front guarding the immediate approaches to Moscow was turned

Left: Operation Typhoon, the assault on Moscow, 30 September–5 December 1941.

Right, upper: A German MG 34 machine-gun team guard a junction on the Leningrad–Moscow railway line, near the Baltic city, captured 9 September 1941. (IWM.HU.39627)

Right, lower: The repeated snowfalls and thaws of October and early November turned the Russian countryside into a sea of mud. Transport of all types floundered helplessly. Here a Wehrmacht supply wagon is stuck fast.

Left, upper: German soldiers surrender to a Red Army patrol, November 1941. The soldier's chances of survival in a Russian PoW camp were slim (as they were for Soviets captured by the Wehrmacht) but some preferred it to trying to survive the severe winter with no special clothing and meagre supplies. (IWM.RUS.719)

Left, lower: A Sturmgeschutz (StuG) III assault gun and accompanying infantry push on towards Moscow, early December 1941. (IWM.HU.39726)

over to Zhukov. Timoshenko was recalled to command the South-West Front south of the capital, and Koniev was given command of the newly formed Kalinin Front to the north of the city. A new 'final' defence line (the Mozhaisk line) was declared 40 miles west of Moscow, although there was little in the way of field defences in existence.

It was plain to Zhukov that the Germans would once again try a double pincer attack to envelop the capital. He did his best to marshal his forces to defend against such an attack, although the brunt of the armoured attack was to fall on Koniev's and Timoshenko's formations.

His main hope was that the German infantry armies would become bogged down and unable to shore up the sides of the panzergruppe thrust. The Fourth and Ninth Armies were already having difficulty pushing down the main Moscow–Minsk highway because of the continued resistance of many Soviet units trapped in the Vyazma pocket. Panzergruppe IV, unable to count on any significant infantry support, was finding it tough going in its attempt to batter a way through the Mozhaisk Line farther to the east.

Things went significantly better for the Germans in the north against Koniev's forces. On 14 October Hoth's Panzergruppe III broke through the Soviet defensive line and entered Kalinin, cutting the Moscow–Leningrad highway and the main north–south railway line.

This serious situation threatened to undermine morale in the capital but a series of stirring speeches by Stalin helped restore the population's confidence and a deterioration in the weather helped slow the German advance even further. Between mid-October and the first week of November a continuous series of snowfalls and thaws seriously hampered the German Army's attempts to get into a position from which it could launch a final offensive against the capital. Roads remained liquid mud, motorised and horse-drawn transport floundered helplessly and the advance of the panzer units slowed to a crawl. As well as losing the momentum of the attack, vehicle breakdown losses mounted alarmingly. The mechanised and motorised units forming the cutting edge of the offensive against Moscow were now all at less than half strength.

The first sharp frosts of the year gave a last opportunity for the German High Command to launch a decisive thrust for the Russian capital.

However, it became clear at a meeting of Army Chiefs of Staff, held at Army Group Centre's headquarters on 13 November, that von Bock was the only army group commander who wanted to press home the assault. Fortunately, Hitler concurred with his views and the offensive began on 16 November. However, the incident illustrates the misgivings many of the German field commanders had about launching an attack with seriously depleted units, when only a few weeks of already bad weather remained before the Russian winter blizzards set in.

The new offensive opened with Panzergruppen IV and III (now commanded by General Georg Reinhardt, Hoth having been elevated to command Seventeenth Army) attacking north of Moscow towards Klin and Istra. At the same time Panzergruppe II (Second Panzer Army) pushed north-east towards Stalinogorsk and Kashira. The objective, which was plain to both German and Soviet commanders, was to encircle the Russian capital by a double envelopment.

Despite the arrival of reinforcements of men and material from the interior, the Red Army initially gave ground to the German attack. Panzergruppe III was the most successful of the attacking panzer formations, capturing Klin

A French-built Hotchkiss light tank with accompanying infantry during an anti-Partisan sweep behind the lines, early December 1941. (IWM.MH.8515)

Red Army infantry, well equipped to fight in the sub-zero temperatures of the Russian winter, counter-attack a German-held town, 5/6 December 1941. (IWM.RUS.982A)

and breaching the Volga Canal defence line north of Moscow on 28 November. It is an indication of the difficulties of advancing against determined Russian opposition, with seriously understrength mechanised units, in appalling weather conditions, that the infantry formations of Ninth Army, normally following in the wake of the panzers, were able to keep up with the armoured attack.

Panzergruppe IV, to the south of Reinhardt's troops, made considerably less progress and was not able to advance past its first objective, Istra, by the time the Russian weather made any further forward movement impossible. Panzergruppe II (Second Panzer Army) had at first made a fairly rapid advance, capturing Stalinogorsk and reaching the main railway line south from the capital by 25 November. However, on the same day a thrust for Kashira was repulsed. Two days later Guderian called off his offensive. Likewise the advance of Panzergruppe III and the Ninth Army came to a halt on 29 November.

The German armies were completely exhausted by their efforts and with men and equipment losses in many cases running at over 80 percent they were in no condition to resume

their offensive, even if the weather conditions had allowed them to do so.

The severity of the Russian winter put the final nail in the coffin of the offensive on Moscow. German troops, without winter clothing (Hitler had forbidden its issue due to the lowering of morale it might bring about), suffered terribly in the blizzards and freezing conditions now prevalent on the battlefield. By late November frostbite cases were more numerous than wounds in German field hospitals.

The weather got so cold that engine oil froze and fires had to be lit underneath tanks to thaw their sumps, enabling them to be started. Moving parts on vehicles froze solid, marooning them in the snowy waste that Russia had become.

On the other hand, the onset of winter was a valuable boon to the defending Red Army. It provided a screen behind which reinforcements could be assembled and ultimately provided a cover under which they were to launch their successful winter counter-offensive.

Whilst Operation Typhoon had been taking place Army Group South had been pushing further into the Russian interior in an attempt to capture the vital industrial area of the Donets basin. By capturing crossings over the Donets, Mius and Don rivers the army group would outflank the

Three smiling German infantrymen pose for the camera after their successful assault on Kharkov, 24 October 1941. (IWM.HU.5059)

southern end of the Soviet defence line. On the northern flank of this advance the German Sixth and Seventeenth Armies had pushed on rapidly despite their lack of armoured support and by 24 October, after several days' hard fighting, had managed to capture Kharkov, the main industrial centre of the region.

Timoshenko, arriving to take over command of the Soviet forces in the area the day before, could do little to prevent the city's fall but did organise an orderly retreat to a new defence line with what remained of the Red Army in the region. The German formations pushed on as best they could but with the weather growing worse by the day, and in the absence of any mechanised forces to undertake a deep penetrative attack, the Russians were able to conduct an effective fighting retreat to the line of the Donets river. Even though some German units did manage to establish footholds on the far bank, the impetus they once had was lost. Exhausted, the troops dug in for the winter.

Nevertheless, although no major encirclement of Soviet formations had taken place, the capture of Kharkov was a major blow to the Russians. The industrial area of the Donets basin provided much of Russia's raw materials; coal, iron and steel and without them her war effort was seriously hampered.

Further south von Kleist's Panzergruppe I had advanced from the Dniepr towards Mariupol on the Sea of Azov and Rostov on the river Don. The German Eleventh Army meanwhile continued with its offensive along the Black Sea coast and into the Crimea.

On 6 October the SS Motorised Division 'Leibstandarte Adolf Hitler', peeling off south from the right flank of the panzergruppe advance, reached the sea at Brdanysk, west of Mariupol, trapping much of the Soviet Eighteenth and Nineteenth Armies in a pocket between the panzergruppe and the Eleventh Army. After the pocket had been cleared 100,000 Russian prisoners were in German hands. Two days later the port of Mariupol was occupied. At the same time the Eleventh Army attempted to force an entrance to the Crimea through the peninsula's narrow neck. By 17 October they had managed to penetrate the Soviet defensive line. Two weeks later all of the Crimea except the port of Sevastopol was in German hands. The siege of this fortified naval base was to last a further eight months.

Meanwhile Panzergruppe I (minus the 9th Panzer Division and two mo-

A Sturmgeschutz (StuG) III assault gun and accompanying German infantry push up a street in Kharkov, 24 October 1941. (IWM.HU.5079)

An exhausted Sturmartillerie crew rest next to their StuG III after reaching the Black Sea near Nikolayev, 17 August 1941.

torised infantry divisions which had been transferred to Guderian for Operation Typhoon) continued to advance rapidly to the south-east, seizing crossings over the Mius on 20 October. Thereafter, with the deterioration in the weather, the advance slowed dramatically but by 20 November troops of the SS Motorised Division 'Leibstandarte Adolf Hitler' had managed to gain bridgeheads over the Don at the eastern end of the Sea of Azov. Three days later the strategically important city of Rostov-on-Don was in German hands. Von Rundstedt had completed the task set for him by Hitler on 10 November but by doing so had left himself dangerously over-extended. The panzergruppe, suffering from a lack of troops due both to the transfer of assets to Guderian's Panzer Army and severe losses from months of campaigning on the steppe, was unable to hold off a strong Russian counter-attack mounted four days later. By the end of November Army Group South had retreated back across the Mius, where it dug in for the winter.

On 8 December Hitler issued Führer Directive No.39 which decreed a defensive posture on the Eastern Front. Nine days later Goebbels announced to the German people that the front might have to be shortened in places, a tacit admission that the Wehrmacht had been forced to retreat. The German bid to conquer Russia had failed.

The German Army had taken 800,000 casualties and lost 2,300 tanks

Oberstgruppenführer Josef 'Sepp' Dietrich, commander of the SS Motorised Division 'Leibstandarte Adolf Hitler' (in sheepskin coat), congratulates one of his junior commanders, Brigadeführer Fritz Witt, after the successful elimination of the Mariupol pocket, October 1941.

during Operation Barbarossa. These losses, although nowhere near as many as those sustained by the Red Army, were enough to bring to a halt the offensive into Russia.

Many commentators have blamed the continual interference of Adolf Hitler for this failure. They have argued that by delaying the initial attack and invading the Balkans the Wehrmacht lost five crucial weeks of campaign time. Then, in the midst of the offensive, Hitler once again interfered, ordering the removal of troops from Army Group Centre as it stood poised to take Moscow. Then he once more reallocated Germany's panzer forces for the commencement of Operation Typhoon.

These continual organisational changes point not to the operational and tactical inability of the Führer (after all, two of these three changes of plan resulted in major victories), but to a lack of resources, particularly a paucity of mechanised formations. With one or two more panzergruppen the offensive towards Moscow could

have been undertaken much earlier, with more panzer assets. Operation Barbarossa might then not have been a costly defeat but a brilliant victory.

In the nine major pockets created by the advancing Wehrmacht a total of some 2,250,000 Russian prisoners were taken, along with 9,327 tanks and 16,179 guns. In thirteen smaller envelopments a further 736,000 men, 4,960 tanks and 9,033 guns fell into German hands. By the end of 1941 the Wehrmacht had captured nearly four times as many tanks as it had started the campaign with, three times as many guns and nearly as many infantrymen. And still the Red Army fought on.

As a result of the Führer's massive miscalculation of Russia's war-fighting capability most of the top-ranking officers involved in Operation Barbarossa lost their commands. Adolf Hitler was infallible, therefore the failings of the campaign had to be shouldered by the military leaders. Von Brauchitsch, Commander in Chief of the Army, was summarily dismissed, his position being taken by the Führer himself. Von

Rundstedt and von Leeb both resigned before they were sacked and von Bock went on indefinite sick leave. The panzergruppe commanders Guderian and Hoepner were also relieved of their commands for daring to speak frankly about the defeat before Moscow.

The failure to conquer Russia did not come about through any tactical or operational shortcomings. Blitzkrieg theory once again proved its validity on the field of battle, with the German Army winning victory after victory, even when massively outnumbered and outgunned. Operation Barbarossa did not succeed because of a gross miscalculation of the capability of the Red Army to withstand punishment and a lack of mechanised resources given to the forces in the field from the beginning of the campaign. These failures stemmed from the very highest level of the Nazi government, Adolf Hitler himself.

Soviet infantry advance through the streets of Rostov-on-Don during their successful counterattack of 27 November 1941. (IWM.RUS.1179)

Index